LEADER COMMUNITIES

MIKAEL HOLMQVIST

LEADER
COMMUNITIES

The Consecration of Elites in Djursholm

Columbia University Press / New York

Columbia University Press
Publishers Since 1893
New York   Chichester, West Sussex
cup.columbia.edu

Library of Congress Cataloging-in-Publication Data

Names: Holmqvist, Mikael, 1970– author.
Title: Leader communities : the consecration of elites / Mikael Holmqvist.
Other titles: Djursholm. English
Description: New York : Columbia University Press, [2017] | Includes
   bibliographical references.
Identifiers: LCCN 2017006008 (print) | LCCN 2017029210 (ebook) | ISBN
   9780231545396 (ebook) | ISBN 9780231184267 (cloth : alk. paper)
Subjects: LCSH: Djursholm (Sweden)—Social conditions. | Djursholm
   (Sweden)—Intellectual life. | Leadership—Sweden—Djursholm. | Elite
   (Social sciences)—Sweden—Djursholm. | Communities—Sweden—Djursholm.
Classification: LCC HN580.D58 (ebook) | LCC HN580.D58 H6513 2017 (print) |
   DDC 306.09487/3—dc23
LC record available at https://lccn.loc.gov/2017006008

Columbia University Press books are printed on permanent and durable
acid-free paper.

Printed in the United States of America

Cover design: Milenda Nan Ok Lee
Cover image: Photo © Bengt Nyman

To Dr. Konstantin Lampou, Uppsala University

A good friend and a discerning critic.

We're the cream of the elite, aren't we?

(Fifteen-Year-Old Boy)

This is a high-performance place for high-performance people.

(Man in His Fifties)

My parents always told me, "As long as you do your best that's okay."
But what does "your best" really mean? Working twenty-four hours per
day? Being good at tennis, golf, sailing, and having five children?

(Man, Thirty-Five Years Old)

I have worked with the richest children in the country. They are very nice,
they give me hugs, and they always say hello. But they are very lonely.

(Youth Instructor)

We're up to our necks with diagnosed students. "Why not a grade A?"
Instead of just saying it the way it is, that the student is not good enough
or doesn't work hard enough, they produce a diagnosis for him. Once you
have a diagnosis, you also have an explanation for a relatively poor
level of performance.

(Teacher)

When you give a student the wrong school report, as the student sees it,
you first have the student's hissy fit, and then the parent's.

(Teacher)

Imagine when they find out that I'm a faker—I don't know anything!
But, you know, everyone worries about that here.

(Woman in Her Seventies)

CONTENTS

CONTENTS

PREFACE

C LOSE TO where my family and I have lived for the past twenty years, there is a community named Djursholm; a place of beauty, calm, security—and impressive economic wealth. In this pastoral idyll of some nine thousand people located close to Sweden's capital Stockholm, there are large houses with extensive grounds; charming, winding lanes, surrounded by a varied and beautiful landscape; and a small commercial center with high-class shops, restaurants, and other services. There are few signs of poverty; people invariably look healthy and beautiful. In addition to the salubrious areas of greenery, the community offers its inhabitants scenic paths for walking along the sea, well-kept tennis courts, a golf club, sailing and nautical facilities, and a plethora of associations providing stimulating leisure activities. The schools are ranked among the best in the country with exacting entrance requirements and unsurpassed grades on graduation. In fact, the inhabitants of this community constitute an economic and social elite, whose position in society enables them to exert great influence over Sweden's economic, political, and social development. Possessed of a higher educational level than anywhere else in the nation, the residents work primarily as executives and decision makers in the corporate and financial sectors; but there are also famous artists and academics living there. A number of the country's "superrich" who figure on Forbes's "The World Billionaire's" list also live (or have lived) there. Income levels are at the top of official national league tables. Property prices are the highest in the country. The alert visitor will note such phenomena as athletic housewives and active nannies, well-behaved and healthy children, as well as expensive and exclusive cars and boats—all of which add to the community's aesthetic appeal. In the words of French sociologists Michel Pincon and Monique Pincon-Charlot, the place is an ideal example of a *beaux quartier*, where nice-looking people lead good lives in spacious and well-maintained houses or apartments on the strength of high incomes and large fortunes; greet one another by kissing cheeks; and where foreign languages are often heard, thus making it especially popular with expats, diplomats, or other successful global groups looking for a temporary base while staying in the country.[1]

Like many other exclusive suburbs in both Europe and the United States, this neighborhood was established at the end of the 1800s (more specifically in 1889). The four founders, all of whom were wealthy Swedish businessmen with social prestige ambitions, wanted to create a dwelling place for the country's economic and social elite, who no longer wanted to live in the noise and disorder of urban environments, preferring instead the peace and fresh air of the countryside. Prior to that, the area had just consisted of pasture and fields and an old castle. The founders were inspired by America, and its utopian ideals set the stage for the project. As soon as the purchase of the estate had been completed, the establishment of the new neighborhood began: large plots of land were sold off with the purpose of building private homes there, but in some instances houses were also built and sold by the four founders' jointly owned company. These, as a rule, were substantial and architecturally advanced. One of the first electrified railways in the world was constructed, connecting the area with the nearby city, and all other necessary infrastructure was swiftly provided, including electric power lines, water, and sewerage. At an early stage the founders also had a chapel (funded by American Quakers) and a private school built, the latter an imposing building in which children moving into the area would receive their education. The sizable plots of land (in the region of four thousand square meters per household) meant that only wealthy people could move there. In other words, the community was the subject of a good deal of social planning. The first prospectus was very much focused on the well heeled. "Domestic servants and workers only ended up living there as a consequence of their jobs: the community was not intended for them," one writer commented in an article on the place in the early 1900s.[2] In an article from 1940, another commentator suggested that the community "has always specialised in the needs of the bourgeoisie, and, to a very significant degree, it consists of academics and other holders of official positions, as well as those who are self-employed."

The founders, back in the late 1800s, were well aware that the natural beauty of the area, the new, magnificent houses, the modern railway, the fine school building, and so on, were not in their own right enough to attract the elite to move into the area. For this reason they set about persuading a number of well-known Swedish artists and writers to come to this world—as their presence would bring social legitimacy and cultural capital, in Pierre Bourdieu's sense of the word, to the young community.[3] Such "fine and honorable personages," wrote one of the founders, became an important spiritual foundation of the new settlement. The community's early history was to a great extent about creating an aura around itself by elevating its fundamental institutions and pointing to recent arrivals as leadership figures. The community did not want to associate itself primarily with financial wealth, rather with its cultural and intellectual equivalent— and this was a wholly decisive idea in its early social promotion.

And yet Djursholm has become a symbol of the unfair distribution of wealth and unequal opportunities in the nation. One newspaper article from 2008 explains that the expression "the sun always shines over Djursholm" was a classic line first heard in a TV documentary by a young local student bathing on one of the community's beaches, tanked up on sparkling wine, full of optimism for the future, and brimming with youthful arrogance. The documentary filmmaker "wanted to show the ease and affluence of the students, their upper class attitudes, and the good intentions of their parents." The newspaper also comments on how, as one takes a walk in the area, one cannot fail to notice the heavy scent of lilac and honeysuckle in the air and the immaculately maintained houses sticking out of the greenery like decorative objects. The inhabitants are described as "high-concept families and youths with slicked back hair." The milieu being pictured is attractive, while it also underlines the institutionalized image of the community as a very exclusive place. Another newspaper concludes in 2010: "This is the best possible place to live—for those who can afford it." In still another newspaper article, the school premises are likened to "modern offices." The youngsters are described as well dressed and making a polite impression, causing the reporter to muse on how the entire school is "embedded in a compacted atmosphere of civility." They are also pictured as privileged: "Fathers with their own companies, mothers who mostly stayed at home while the children were growing up. Supportive and encouraging parents. What lay ahead of these young people? Mainly overseas travel and academic studies." The subtext in this media reporting is quite clear: the neighborhood is a place for the privileged, a bright and attractive environment where the economically successful and the mighty choose to live. The concept of the place being special and remarkable seems also central to the social and mental boundaries that surround the area, the latter being quite essential to the creation and maintenance of a self-contained culture and spirit of the place. In a journal article from 1989, one resident writes that the area "has been formed by a conceptual and cultural inheritance which is both fascinating and, also, an obligation." Furthermore, it is clarified that the community is "not a mere suburb with detached houses, like all the others," but something utterly unique. In another report on the community, one resident claimed that, "Those of us who live here are a different kind, a class of our own. This means that we stick together."

For many years I remained curious about Djursholm and the people that lived there. Now and then I visited the area with my family for Sunday walks and sightseeing. During such excursions I devoted a good deal of thought to how this community could be understood and described. These reflections were engendered not only by my background as a social scientist but also by my childhood. I was raised in a well-ordered, idyllic small town, which, in some ways, resembled this world. Like many children and adolescents there, I also lived in a secure place, clearly separated from the socially more "discordant" and "untidy" society outside. My upper-secondary education as a day student at one of the country's most prestigious boarding schools brought me into contact with young people from wealthy environments. In addition to the academic side of things, I took part in ceremonies and rituals that were about manifesting the prestige and status of the school as an elite institution. My father's career in the Swedish cultural sphere also meant that during a period while I was young, it was not uncommon for me to meet people of the national and international cultural and social elite, at official events and so on. In other words, from an early time in life I was acquainted with people who in a variety of ways exerted power and influence over the surrounding world. My years as an undergraduate were spent in part in elitist surroundings and included studies at a prestigious Parisian *grande école*. Later my career as an academic included periods of guest research fellowships at similar institutions in the United States. In other words, I was carrying a particular sort of baggage as a result of experiences and impressions of certain social settings. It seemed to me that I had a personal style and mode of self-expression that at least to some degree had been formed by such environments.

Although my experiences from Djursholm date back to the late 1990s, my formal research study of the area started in 2010 and ended in 2015, and it included a large number of interviews and conversations with people living, working, or in some other way having a relationship to the community. It also involved many hours of participation in various activities, such as school lessons, reunions, parties and social activities, café and restaurant outings, religious services; repeated informal visits for activities such as walks, cycling, and jogging, days on the beach, treks in the forest; and, further, numerous questionnaires for children or young people and their families, detailed statistical research, and extensive studies of archival material and literature of relevance to the workings of this place (see appendix A).

My argument in this book is that Djursholm and similar places all around the world can be seen as "leader communities," by which I mean two things: first, places where leaders choose to live and exert their dominion, socialize with other leaders, and, most important, form families and raise their children into future leaders. And, second, leader communities aspire to be model communities, i.e., norm-setting environments that have the moral right and legitimacy to prescribe a certain lifestyle for people at large. By studying these environments, we may learn something about how leaders live; we may also learn about how societies at large are being led in a certain direction.[4] The term *leader communities* is thus broadly understood as defining specific groups of people living together in distinct places, and it stresses ideas of activity, entrepreneurship, and performance as social norms that contrast with any complacent and conservative upper-class behavior,[5] or what Thorstein Veblen called "non-productive consumption of time."[6]

Hence, leader communities, compared with, for example, scientific communities or rural communities, are places where groups of people share or resist a certain ideology centered on leadership—in other words, the ability to lead an exemplary life in accordance with a moral index of some form. Indeed, leadership is about what Chester Barnard famously described as "the creation of moral codes for others,"[7] and members of leader communities are defined by their ability to act as social role models. Michèle Lamont described them in the following way: "Members of this class have what most people desire and are what most people aspire to be."[8] To this extent, leaders are often considered "a power elite" in C. Wright Mills's sense, that is, a group of people who are able to exert considerable influence.[9] Admittedly there is no need to rise to the level of a Nelson Mandela, Mahatma Gandhi, or Mother Teresa in order to be seen as a leader, but what distinguishes a person of this order is the ability to present an elevated moral code that can inspire others to consider notions such as holiness and worship. Leaders are more or less expected to be spiritual role models—one can almost refer to them as angelic forms, capable of higher forms of moral excellence.[10]

As earlier research and descriptions and analyses have emphasized, people are often quite effectively molded into leaders by means of socialization in formally organized environments such as particular schools and universities, networks, and the professional contexts that they are a part of.[11] Sociological research has also largely focused on the formation of elite character in accordance with ideas on socialization and the creation of identity. My analysis is not principally devoted to socialization, rather it addresses itself to *consecration*, a concept that so far has escaped much systematic attention in studies on leaders and elite reproduction.[12] Leader communities involve socialization but they are also consecrating in a way that has not yet been sufficiently highlighted. As I argue in this book, consecration is decisive for the ability of humans to exert influence on others, and for how people in general are elevated to a higher social level on the basis of lifestyle.[13]

In all essential respects, *consecration* is about elevating a human being, imbuing him or her with certain higher moral and spiritual qualities. By the terms of my interpretation, a location does not become a *leader community* simply because, in comparison with other communities, there are more people there who are regarded as leaders, or perceive themselves as such on the basis of their profession or education. A leader community is actually such because, in a systematic, ambitious, and committed way, it *consecrates its inhabitants into leaders*, or, to put it differently, it contributes to sanctifying people from the ordinary and changes their status: they become objects of authority, power and influence, with the result that others learn that "they are not just anyone," but "elite." This occurs by means of the culture, history, traditions, ceremonies, rituals, and institutions of the place, which are possessed of a certain aura continually re-created through the actions of the population. Indeed, a leader community is defined by such intense accumulation of what Bourdieu would call symbolic capital that it becomes sacred, and the people moving into such a place are transformed from an "ordinary" or profane life into a sacred dimension—that is, if they toe the line. The prerequisite of consecration is social separation and differentiation on physical, mental, and cultural levels. As I try to show in this book, Djursholm offers its residents not only certain basic functional possibilities but also an environment conferring a value of an almost aesthetic kind, more than anything reminiscent of a work of art. The peculiar aura of a leader community provides an aesthetic conversion for its inhabitants and is an important precondition for their social consecration. To this extent, the value of living in Djursholm cannot be reduced to its economic dimension only.

As already suggested, leader communities are not only the abodes of leaders—they are also the places where their ideals, criteria, and norms are put to the test, and then turned into regulatory and formative frameworks for many other people. Leader communities are crucial for us to understand because they are expected to be exemplary in a moral sense, functioning as navigational markers, and often also to act accordingly. They dominate the surrounding world on the basis of an understanding of morality. Leaders are formed in them, and, in turn, they exert a formative influence on others. The lifestyle, norms, and values in leader communities thereby also become important in the broader operation of society as well as in its basic direction in a moral and ethical sense.

To this extent, they can be described as *shining cities on hills*, based on the idea that the lifestyle of those that live there is superior to the rest in a purely moral and social sense.[14] This becomes a social norm, in relation to which its inhabitants and the world outside are expected to orient themselves. To function as leader communities, they have to have aura, or a sort of symbolic added value, in much the same vein as in the book of Matthew 5:14: "Ye are the light of the world. A city that is set on a hill cannot be hid. Neither do men light a candle, and put it under a bushel, but on a candlestick; and it giveth light unto all that are in the house. Let your light so shine before men, that they may see your good works." Leader communities can be seen as sanctuary places, holy and consecrated environments. *Sanctuary* means a sacred space, a shrine, but also an asylum, a protected place, a refuge. In a sociological sense a leader community can be described as a temple of society, but also as a haven for leaders.

For an Anglo-Saxon reader, the choice of a wealthy and seemingly elitist community in a country that is known for its egalitarian ideals and ambitions may seem counterintuitive. On the one hand, a study of an elite environment in Sweden may contribute to a more nuanced picture of Sweden than that held by some outside Sweden or Scandinavia. That is not, however, my main intention. Sweden is, of course, not an isolated island; Djursholm is presented as an illustration of the global phenomenon of "leader communities." Of course, there will be significant variations, depending on each country's political, cultural, and social history, its security situation, levels of education, GDP, distribution of wealth and incomes, geopolitical factors, and so forth. Europe, for instance, is in many ways different from the United States, Scandinavia is different from the United Kingdom, and so forth. There are also differences between urban communities of this kind, such as certain neighborhoods in downtown London, Paris, Madrid, and New York, and these cities' suburban counterparts. And yet, in terms of the lifestyles pursued in these places, there are good reasons to claim there are substantial similarities. There is often widespread interest in sport and recreation and the importance of leading an active life in general; a concern with eating healthy food; the importance of aesthetic excellence in terms of people's bodies, clothes, and ways of talking and moving; as well as a high architectural quality of buildings, gardens, and public spaces. Also there is generally intense attention devoted to educating and raising children and adolescents, which is manifested by the presence of well-functioning and even excellent kindergartens and schools.[15]

To this extent, it should not come as a surprise that the anecdotal stories and reports by American journalist Wednesday Martin on the way people lead their lives in an economically wealthy part of Manhattan in New York City bear much resemblance to two Danish journalists' book on the life in Copenhagen's wealthiest suburb.[16] Nor should it come as a surprise that news reports on high suicide rates among teenagers in Silicon Valley, California can be attributed to a similar lifestyle that characterizes wealthy Neuilly outside Paris.[17] In fact, many of these places seem to share a "darker side of life" in terms of children growing up with a constant pressure to succeed, where stress, drug abuse, excessive drinking, and even suicide are relatively common. There are also feelings of emptiness as a result of distant relationships to their hardworking (and highly successful) parents.[18] Most important, however, in most cases leader communities are geographically and socially isolated worlds in which a certain culture and lifestyle can be maintained—co-option into these communities is not easy, particularly for economic reasons—and its inhabitants are typically strident about defending their community borders.[19] As Pincon and Pincon-Charlot concluded: "In all countries, the wealthy live in separate areas,

LEADER COMMUNITIES

protected from any undesirable social contact."[20] Sometimes there are walls surrounding them; but most often their borders and gates are of a cultural and cognitive character.

My general ambition with the term *leader communities* is thus to further develop some fundamental observations and descriptions of leaders and elite environments in existing sources, and go on to present a more profound and nuanced picture of the unique sociology of such communities and their significance within society as a whole. I am interested in a closer understanding of the social, cultural, and political characteristics and qualities that influence the inhabitants of a leader community. A central problem in this context is the means by which such people are formed into leaders through the particular practices, ceremonies, and rituals of consecration; and how these inhabitants, in turn, through their unique actions and behaviors, strive to re-create the norms and values that are unique to the community in which they live. This pivotal question is especially relevant for children and young people growing up in a leader community. Consecration, as embodied by social elevation, is what the lifestyle of such a world offers, and this both depends on and focuses on young people above all.

Mikael Holmqvist
Stockholm

LEADER COMMUNITIES

1

A SHINING CITY

The Emphasis on Aesthetics

JUDGING BY the high property prices in Djursholm, especially those commanded by detached houses, one would have to conclude that this is an extremely popular community, very much in demand, and that it offers a quality of life that appeals to large numbers of people. One of the implications of these high prices is that Djursholm is tangibly beyond the reach of the majority, this being a prerequisite for its way of segregating itself and drawing up boundaries against the outside world—these boundaries, in turn, are fundamental to what could be described as a consecration effected through social, aesthetic, and moral self-elevation. Whatever variety of reasons one may have for wanting to move to Djursholm, the community offers the same, unchanging response, namely, that it is separate from the rest of the country and will continue to be so. One estate agent, who had worked in Djursholm for a long time, explained: "The reason why so many people want to move to Djursholm is that they are looking for an area that hasn't been overly exploited, with a certain exclusivity about it. There's a lot of space between the houses here, obviously with the added benefit of having the sea right on your doorstep." With its generously proportioned houses and large gardens, its meadows, fields, woods, lakes, and golf course, Djursholm seems an increasingly unique fixture within the surrounding urban sprawl. Another estate agent suggested it was "really quite amazing that a community where there are almost no southwest-facing properties should be so sought after. Certainly there's the odd property by the sea with a wonderful position, but there aren't many of these. If you took away the name and mythology from Djursholm, the prices would come tumbling down."

Djursholm's financial value can never be reduced to an "objective quantity," as manifested by its houses, sculptures, books, and furniture—even the inherent qualities of its residents. One would also have to take stock of its aura, which holds great significance. As has already been suggested, Djursholm has a history of appealing to a mainly wealthy population— made up of individuals that put energy into social climbing, meaning they were not necessarily always so very wealthy. Today it is more expensive than ever to buy a house in Djursholm, yet the typical newcomer is far from financially independent and must as a rule work hard to afford a house there, while also shouldering the additional costs associated with a socially acceptable lifestyle: the clothes, vehicles, and other "socially essential equipment." One banker with many years of experience with mortgage applications in Djursholm and other places, made the following observation: "Of course it is high status to live in Djursholm, but people do borrow heavily. They pay a high premium for the address. Many who live there devote a significant proportion of their income to housing costs. Our upper lending limit is fixed at a multiple of six times the annual salary, and many applicants take it right up to that limit. After this, there really isn't a great deal left for anything else. Of course, we are not including the bonuses here. Most of them receive bonuses, and this keeps them in the clear." He concluded: "But of course, they do get so much in return." In fact, Djursholm cannot be properly understood using a purely technical perspective, like other suburbs, where, in a practical and well-organized way, prospective residents are offered a roof over their heads and a community in which to raise their children. Clearly Djursholm also offers these things, and yet, when compared with many other suburbs, Djursholm is hardly the most practical place in which to live. Its attraction is something else, something that goes far beyond mere residential or technical dimensions. Djursholm is more than anything a strong brand for private individuals and company owners—despite the stigmatization reported by some of its inhabitants. "A home address in Djursholm is quite clearly useful in your professional life," suggested one individual.

From the perspective of Djursholm, it is important to be seen as an attractive location but not for just anyone. The community is dependent on a constant inflow of wealthy people prepared to invest in their roles as local residents, defined by a sort of custodianship of established traditions. It offers aesthetic heightening in all significant senses, with the precondition that residents have to actually aspire to this aesthetic excellence. In much the same way, companies and organizations that wish to be associated with Djursholm must contribute in a positive manner, by adding aura and status, in order to reap the full rewards. Quite simply, their activities have to have elements of consecration, without ever gravitating toward the opposite end of the scale, namely, desecration.

As has already been suggested, there are plenty of examples of how living in Djursholm can also be seen an investment in financial capital. Having purchased a house, there is a tendency to be highly aware of the value of the community in purely economic terms. A vicar who presided over many ceremonies in the Djursholm's chapel spoke of how "for many, it is not enough just to have a zip code in Djursholm; it is essential to have the right zip code. Much care is taken over this; a great deal of money can ride on it." Another man, who had been living in Djursholm for twenty years, explained this further: "There are examples of families living in Djursholm who have made careers in the property business here, in which they have made a decent profit out of every sale." One of the estate agents that was quoted earlier put this into context by suggesting, "One of the reasons some people move here is that it's a good investment. If you can afford to pay a lot for a house, it could soon be worth even more."

However, most people who move to Djursholm today, especially families with children, hardly view it as primarily a financial investment that will yield returns in the near future. The investment is on another level. Residence in the area offers the possibility of potentially valuable contacts. The opportunity to rise socially, and being able to take part in the symbolic capital that the community offers, is important. One man stated, "The network you can have here, it's the beginning and end of the whole thing. It's an amazing environment for that." Another person explained, "For me, given that I work in organizational development at a high level in companies and other organizations, it feels absolutely given that I should be living here in Djursholm. I like it here, and many of the people who live here could easily be my clients." Yet another individual, who regarded the contacts as important in his career, explained that the golf club was a social and networking hub. Another believed that the possibilities of developing social contacts among businesspeople had always been an underlying reason for establishing oneself in Djursholm.

Contacts are one thing, but the social elevation offered by the community is something quite distinct. Djursholm offers many social arenas, which is pivotal, through activities such as golf, sailing, tennis, and so on. There are many associations, and the community offers a number of mansions in which grand social events can be staged. One mother explained, "Buying a house here is very expensive, but on the other hand you get a lot for your money. Your children have an amazing school, and they get to know all sorts of people they can make use of later in their lives. More demands are put on you here, which probably makes you put in more effort at work to achieve success." One grandfather, who had himself grown up in Djursholm, commented on his grandchildren's schooling: "I am impressed by how they are coached to get into the upper-secondary school in Djursholm, so they can complete their whole secondary education here. The competition is really fierce. The focus is on the children staying here, and getting the same foundation as the others, in the form of networks and contacts." If one happens to be a person with high-status ambitions, whether conscious or not, then a move to Djursholm could certainly be a crucial step on the way to achieving this.

Djursholm is hardly the sort of place in which one just ends up. For instance, refugees or recipients of social security will not be assigned a place to live there by the authorities, nor will people go there because it is cheaper than other places. The boundaries, as we have already noted, remain sharply defined on account of the high property prices. The target group is also distinct: financial wealth is the decisive factor for entry, and financial wealth is regarded as the measure of both a person's ability and respectability. In today's society, it is often assumed that a person who has made a lot of money is not only a *talented* person but also a *good* person in a moral sense—and these are precisely the sorts of qualities that Djursholm requires. What the recent arrivals may lack in the form of a certain tone and definition, in their movements, their mode of dress, and so on, Djursholm is able to supply to them, which is also part of the purpose of living there. This complicated issue, touching upon the relationship between so-called new and old residents, is something that I will come back to. Admittedly there are a few examples of social security claimants and refugees having been assigned accommodation in the community. But the small number of refugee flats in the locality are all at the very edge of town—one would hardly ever make spontaneous visits to central Djursholm.

There are people who have publicly expressed their reluctance to move to Djursholm, as they cannot see themselves fitting in. The neighborhood seems to have the ability to send out signals to the surrounding world that only *certain kinds* of people will like living there. In the blog *My Wonderful Life as a Housewife*, one woman describes how her husband wanted to move to Djursholm, but she got him to change his mind: "We wouldn't fit in there. We are too normal and too smart to live there. We would be outsiders, and I wouldn't like living there. Nor do I want my children to grow up there. I want my children to become modest people, with 'normal' friends. I don't want to talk about superficialities with my neighbors and at the children's preschool. I want to be able to talk about life, and to strive for a world where everyone is worth just as much, whatever their background." According to this source, in other words, people who reject the idea of moving to Djursholm, even if they could afford it, tend to be those who want to remain "normal" and who do not want to distance themselves from other groups of people.

One of the estate agents cited earlier emphasized, "Djursholm is very popular among certain groups in society, who want to get into a certain social milieu. Then there are people with a lot of money who do not want to live there for the very same reasons. There's a feeling that Djursholm is snobby, and a worry that this would have certain repercussions." Obviously it is not everyone's dream to settle in Djursholm, despite the community's general power of attraction. In a humorous article from 1940, published in a book by Djursholm's historic society, the writer relates how social relations between the residents in Djursholm could benefit from a bit more cordiality; otherwise the residents could get a bad reputation. This was in response to a question he had put to one of his friends: "I asked him once if he had any intention of settling in Djursholm. He looked surprised and answered, 'Are you mad? I get enough abuse as it is.'" Even among those who do move to Djursholm, there is sometimes a slightly guarded attitude. One woman told me: "I grew up under fairly simple circumstances. It was my husband who wanted to move here. I felt fairly tense about how things would be when we first arrived, and it has taken me time to like living here." Another woman explained, "I married into a family from Djursholm but I'm not at all from this kind of environment. I was on the other side. My background is something else. And I didn't want to move here; it took years of persuasion from my husband."

But most of the arrivals seem not to regret their decision. One woman, who moved to Djursholm in the 1970s, told me: "I still remember the first time I was here. It was like a river of harmony flowing over me, a calm, a total feeling of being at home." In an article from 1978, also published by the local historic society, one man describes his impressions of first moving into the area. In a forthright manner he explains how the house "after a five-minute inspection" was purchased, to a very large extent because the owner "was a sterling fellow, and his fine antique furnishings were of impeccable taste." The purely "technical" aspects relating to the condition of the house were considered less interesting; instead the house's aesthetic qualities (and its owner) were regarded as attractive. The house had only one fault. Its position was some 250 meters from the sea. But, as the writer goes on to say, walks are good for the health: "Everything has a positive side. Exercise is good for you." There were also other advantages in moving to Djursholm: "Our status rose among our friends!" Residence in Djursholm is regarded as socially upwardly mobile, which is well recognized, and this is a consequence of the consecration that the community offers. Since its inception, Djursholm has been regarded as a *finer* and *better* community (and even described as such in early prospectuses), and this cultural foundation has remained one of the most enduring factors safeguarding its popularity.

In my interviews and conversations with several of the parents in Djursholm, they consistently expressed one of the most important reasons for moving to Djursholm: that their children should have a safe and stimulating environment. Children are also essential to the social relationships and interaction of the adults. The children of Djursholm and their behavior, to which I return later in the book, are fundamental to Djursholm's aura. One parent maintained, "If you don't have children, you have no reason to be here. It is through one's children that one meets others. People who divorce move away; this is no place for singles. Here, families socialize with other families." Another parent suggested, "As a recent arrival in Djursholm without children it must be incredibly difficult to establish social relationships. Children are the entry gates to this community. I don't think it could work without them." The parents in Djursholm are extremely aware of their children's social environment. A mother of two girls, to whom I spoke during one of my school visits, felt that "parents often have a lot of views about their children's social connections, and this can lead to a great deal of intolerance. There's an attempt to control who the children see, and who they should not see, based on one's own wishes." Children must tap into the "right" part of Djursholm by means of appropriate relationships and institutions. Another parent explained, "There's exceptionally tough competition here for youth activities. As a parent you ask yourself what you should be focusing on, and doing, so your adolescents get good friends and social interaction." One father tersely commented, "You build up your network here through your children"; another father felt that his family's move was motivated a great deal by the consideration of the children's future social networks. He made the following assertion:

> For me, the international part is very important. It's important that
> our children shouldn't have to grow up in the same sort of ordinary

community that I did. Here they get to meet interesting and important people from all over the world. Djursholm is a really exciting environment, very dynamic, and it is very good for my children to have that as they grow up. . . . Where I grew up there wasn't very much to do and people were pretty much the same. Here there are lots of leisure activities; our children can try such an incredible variety of things. Riding, tennis, sailing, music, drama. Everything is on offer here or nearby. And they meet such interesting families—it's not exactly run-of-the-mill.

A woman of about sixty, who had been living in Djursholm for thirty years or so, said that she had never planned her children's lives as far as their social contacts, their education, or their careers were concerned. "But here one often has a very much more staked-out career, or at least fixed ideas about the children's schooling and education. Moving to Djursholm is only the first step in staking out the children's development. The assumption is that they'll gain a certain kind of knowledge that they couldn't get anywhere else. One wants the children to become something important." One young man of eighteen, whom I interviewed during a visit to the youth center in Djursholm, told me, "Sure, you learn a lot here that will probably come in handy in the future. And maybe you get some contacts. At least that's what my parents say. 'We can help you meet people,' and maybe that's how it is. You meet a lot of people here."

Following are opinions that emerged in interviews with preschool and school staff members that provide a picture of the community for new arrivals:

There's a spirit of strategic thinking and planning out here. Nothing is left to chance. For example, some parents have strong views on what classes the children should be in. There's a desire for the children to be in a class where they can have the "right" friends, usually the same class as where the parents' friends send their own children.

(Principal)

People here look for schools for their children well in advance. There is a real awareness about the importance of education. Many people moving into the area have been attracted by the schools, so of course they are very particular about this. At one meeting I attended, someone said, "All schools in Djursholm are good, there's no need to worry." And maybe that is how it is. If your child attends a school in this area, things will probably go fine. The same thing goes for preschools. Sometimes the parents come to visit with newborns. That's how early they begin to plan; they make their decisions consciously and years in advance.

(Preschool Head)

There is a clear pattern of socializing here between parents. It is not unusual to choose a preschool where you know other parents that you like, so the children can get to know each other and become friends.

(Preschool Assistant)

Parents here think in a highly strategic manner about their children and their school. It is not only about the educational excellence of a school. The social aspects are just as important. There are often a great deal of opinions about the classes in which one's child is placed; there is a desire for one's children to meet the "right" people. I remember when we had the children of a well-known entrepreneurial family here. At that time there were many parents who wanted their children in the same class. . . . The foundations for networking are put down very early here. Moving to Djursholm is a social investment for many; there's a hope that you can get something out of it professionally, and not least something also for your children. . . . One time we had to have a meeting with parents who weren't satisfied with their children's class allocations, because there were children from outside Djursholm in the classes. "What's the problem—the children seem perfectly happy?" asked the principal, only to be told that, "It's not about the children. We moved to Djursholm so our children could go to school with other children from Djursholm."

(Teacher)

Common questions from the parents are about which of the other children their own children are playing with. There are few questions about our pedagogy; rather it is the social games between the children that give rise to concern and interest. There are also questions about the formation of classes, that their children should have the right sort of friends, and so on.

(Principal)

Among the inhabitants that I met, the preschools and schools are considered an important reason for having chosen to move to Djursholm. This is not only about the perception of high quality and good pedagogic practice, which become vital social denominators, but also the fact that schools are pivotal arenas for social interaction between adults. I will develop this further at a later stage, but for now I simply propose that the schools of Djursholm have a vital consecratory function in the community as a whole. One mother explained it as follows: "Social life centering on the children is important. Sometimes there's a wine-tasting evening for the mothers in the class. I usually never go to those functions, but I know it is very popular. The children are what makes the social interaction flow, and that is why the children are so important for the ability of the grown-ups to make friends and acquaintances."

A father explained to me that it is not unusual for the parents to organize their own parents' evenings, off school premises. "We meet in each other's homes, or in town in some restaurant. At times it can be something purely social, a way of getting to know new people, and it's usually very appreciated by all." One preschool head explained that some parents who do not live near the preschool nonetheless choose to send their children there, because of the recommendations from other parents. The parents wanted to get into a social context, and in the preschool they saw social opportunities. She went on: "In some preschools they have Friday evening events, where the parents and children can socialize. I suppose the idea is to make acquaintances. This is one important reason for opting for one particular preschool rather than another. Sometimes I am asked if we arrange social events for parents, after school hours. Often the parents expect more of the preschool than just a place where they send their children; they seem to want to have social events connected to it as well."

In this sense, schools and preschools, like other institutions in the community, are vital arenas for the social training and elevation that Djursholm makes possible. The many different activities for children, which I turn to later, relate, therefore, to some extent to the social ambitions of the parents—the more activities, the more frequent the points of contact, with, as a result, better-established social networks. A child having classes at Djursholm's tennis club is not necessarily about the child learning to play tennis above all else; it may also be about personal development defined by the social relationships and the environment provided by the tennis club for its members.

It is considered crucial that one's children should have friends, become "popular," and conduct themselves pleasantly and with "social competence"—this can also have knock-on effects on the parents' opportunities to broaden their social contacts. One mother explained, "Our son is a bit all over the place; there are often issues with other children. We love him, of course, but we have occasionally chosen not to let him go to friends' houses to play—we know how things sometimes turn out. You don't want to come across as a bad family and have to be ashamed about it." One instructor at a leisure center said that parents "want their children to do a lot here. There are a lot of ambitions, expectations, hopes. Often, that is the meaning of the move to Djursholm. If the children don't behave themselves or have other problems, it can cause a lot of social pressure for the parents."

The behavior of children and young people is of general significance for the presentation of Djursholm as a well-functioning, pleasant, and successful community—but also a mark of its ability to maintain its status in terms of strategic relationships and similar expressions of social and cultural capital. As has already been suggested, the environment of preschools and schools is central to the creation of contact networks. One long-standing member of the golf club told me that "many of the juniors take part in winter training, but few of them play golf in the summer. There's a requirement for them to get into the club, but this does not necessarily extend to them actually playing golf." Another member of the golf club, who had been active in its development, claimed that "we are immensely attractive to the community. Many people want to become members, and the number of new members has also grown a great deal in recent years. The interesting thing is that wear and tear on the fairways is almost unchanged. I mean, even though we have more members than before, the number of players has not changed. . . . There's a general desire to show that you're a member; there are many people who pay the fees for full membership with unlimited access to the course, and yet they never play." In an article, the chairman of the golf club explains that it is "an important reference point if you live in Djursholm or the surrounding area." The club was unaffected by the financial crisis in Sweden of the 1990s that had such a strong effect in society as a whole—the waiting list was as long as ever. The rationale for this was that the club offers a strong social network in Djursholm.

Maybe what defines Djursholm more than anything else are the stately houses in the area, which make such a defined contribution to the overall character of the community—large, architect-drawn houses situated along winding lanes. Their grounds are extensive, so that the houses are well spaced out. With the exception of a couple of peripheral areas, where the architecture is of a simpler kind than in the more central parts, as a rule the buildings are large, technically advanced, and varied. The community overridingly consists of period houses, which testifies to a rather slow pace of development in recent decades. They are usually in very good condition, often with decorous patios, fine gravel paths, clean facades, and well-kept wood and metal-covered sections. The gardens tend to be lush, some of them almost like parks. There is a preponderance of hedges, bushes, and trees, while shrubs bearing gooseberries, redcurrants, blackberries, and raspberries are less common. Vegetable patches, with their associated soil, mud, and sprouting vegetation, are almost unknown. This creates an impression of a community in which the garden is a significant part of a general, aesthetic outlook—a place for social activities and relaxation rather than heavy, dirty physical labor.

As a result of conducting a number of interviews in the homes of local residents, I gained certain insights into their tastes and preferences. A useful way of deepening these impressions was to regularly peruse the house descriptions of various estate agents, as well as looking at the residents' own descriptions of their houses—of some importance here was a series of articles published by the local history association, in which residents wrote about their homes' furnishings, decoration, and style. In one of these pieces from 1981, "A Home in Djursholm," the author gives an account of his family's years in the community. The home is intricately described, and there are several photographs of various rooms:

> The house, constructed by a building contractor in order to be sold, was spacious and homely. A large hall on both floors with built-in benches and a staircase ascending two walls. Three reception rooms in line, as was customary at that time. The dining room was large and adjoined a built-in veranda with windows on runner, so that they could slide open and make the veranda entirely open. . . . From the veranda one emerged onto a sizeable terrace or for coffee after eating. The drawing room was also substantial and had beams across the ceiling and an open fireplace for many crackling fires. . . . The rooms were light, with generously proportioned south-facing windows.

I also interviewed staff members in boutiques that sell furnishings, mainly to local people. One shop owner suggested that the style in Djursholm "is overridingly classic—not provocative." Another salesperson in a different boutique explained, "We don't sell minimalistic items, white or black furniture or design items. Instead we focus on a lot of color, large sofas and lamps, many fabrics, rugs, and curtains. The pared-down house doesn't work here. The houses are big and classic; modern style doesn't look good here."

Based on my observations and other sources, it still seems popular to have crystal chandeliers, also designer furniture of various kinds, which adds to an impression of a community with prestige, character, and status.

The absence of IKEA furniture in the "official" parts of the homes is notable. As far as I have been able to ascertain, one of the most popular styles is Scandinavian, as well as a certain amount of rococo and baroque furniture; among families with children there are more expansive sofas and multicolored arrangements of cushions. Dark oak is in common use in furnishings and decorations. It is popular to have the walls decorated in a variety of colors, but wallpaper seems less common (with the exception of children's nurseries). Curtains are often light and discreet. Sofas and armchairs tend to be large. Often they are distributed throughout the house, to enable a cozy, familial interaction or the possibility of relaxing in more private surroundings. Many homes feature beautiful radiator screens made of wood, which tend to blend in very well with the style of the rooms. Persian rugs are often seen. In the larger homes there is space for several seating areas, also formal dining rooms in addition to dining areas in spacious kitchens. Occasionally I have seen a grand piano with an open music book on display, which adds a certain cultural aspect to the dwelling.

In estate agent descriptions, there is a preference for the term *country kitchen* as a way of describing the often lavishly equipped kitchens—many of them with open fireplaces. Unlike tables in other rooms, which tend to have a more traditional dining room finish, the kitchen tables are often rough-hewn and rustic. Classic, oaken drop-leaf tables in country style with matching chairs are not unusual, with a wooden floor of a more massive kind than in the rest of the house. Mirrors seem popular, and are frequently dotted about in the house. The art on display is varied, featuring everything from light, airy watercolors to heavy oil paintings. What the paintings have in common, however, is that they are seldom in any way provocative; the motifs and styles are calm, harmonious, and fairly vacuous. I have seen several examples of households where there is a marked preference for a naive style, or an appreciation of horses and animals associated with hunting, or a liking for framed maps. With a few exceptions, there is rarely much art on display. Sculptures are sometimes found scattered about—they are often colorful and of large dimensions. Bathrooms are invariably pristine—fully tiled and with exclusive fittings. From time to time at least one of the bathrooms has double sinks. The least costly rooms are usually the bedrooms, where the furnishings tend to consist of little more than a modest bed and a pair of bedside tables. If there is an armchair or some other item of furniture in bedrooms, it is often of a less exclusive kind than in the public rooms. It is rare to find exclusive or beautiful art in the bedrooms, and all in all there is no marked tendency to sleep in beds with costly bed frames. On the other hand, social consecration is not enacted in the bedroom. To sum up, Djursholm idealizes the home as a place of beauty and aesthetic awareness, and, in a sense, this lends further weight to the presentation of the community's character.

Historically, there has always been a good deal of spit and polish applied to Djursholm; for instance, there are plenty of stories from the early 1900s of impoverished women making their way to the community in the summers to work in people's gardens, or faithful domestics and scullery maids taking care of most of the work inside the house. Whenever I went to the houses to conduct my interviews, I was generally met by a clean and tidy environment, even in the case of families with children. Many told me that they had cleaners. Companies also take care of jobs such as hedge trimming, snow shoveling, and similar chores—which, on the whole, has a positive effect on the presentation of the community. One woman who grew up in Djursholm explained this more fully:

> Djursholm has always been a place where one had a great deal of help in the home, with cleaning, child minding, and gardening. This seems to be something people are not prepared to do without, even though many of them can hardly afford it. There is an unwillingness to stand there painting one's own house, or raking one's own leaves, or lying in the drive doing one's own weeding. But of course, it costs a lot to have people in to do all the work. I don't think it's just a question of not having the time to do it oneself. It's a part of the general package. . . . People in Djursholm are very concerned about appearances.

Private dwellings, as I have described, are well kept—both interiors and the grounds. Official buildings such as schools, libraries, and health-care clinics are also in good order. There are few old, rusty, or dirty cars; the vast majority of them are new and well maintained. Many are exclusive brands, such as BMW, Mercedes, Audi, and Lexus. Several residents I interviewed criticized Djursholm, as it is today, as a place defined by "showing off." An elderly man insisted, "Here it's about *esse non vivere*. A desire not to be seen. We are keeping our fourteen-year-old Volvo. Why should we change it when it works so well? We are not on exhibit." Nonetheless, it seems important to the residents, on the whole, that their community is clean and well kept and aesthetically pleasing.

To give an example, several letters in the members' magazine of the tennis club are about the physical environment both inside and outside the tennis halls, with criticisms that the premises are not sufficiently presentable. One member feels that "the gentlemen's changing rooms are starting to look a bit jaded"; another feels that the parking area "looks like a muddy field" whenever it rains; a third member feels that the sports hall seems "abnormally dirty" after weekends. Another individual points out that the courts are "full of fluff" and then goes on to ask how often this is cleaned—and so on. Nor are there are any messy recycling stations in Djursholm, a common sight in most other communities.[1] An article in the local newspaper brings up the complaints of two young female students, recent arrivals to Djursholm. They were renting a small flat and thought there ought to be a recycling station. The women describe how they searched for one: "We went around Djursholm asking people," without success. The article goes on to detail how neighbors have consistently challenged planning applications for a recycling station. A spokesman at the municipal authority explains: "It's difficult to find a site that is not challenged." The municipality had earlier found a suitable spot in Djursholm, but they had to change their plans: "The protests were so strong. We had to withdraw the planning permission." In other words, the residents do not seem excessively enamored with the idea of discarding rubbish in various containers (at least not in Djursholm), with all the associated headaches such as sticky, dirty hands and clothes and the noise of breaking glass. A recycling station is just not reconcilable with a place of consecration. Reasonably enough, when horseback riders from the riding school make use of public roads, they see to it that "any offending manure is gotten rid of," as a woman from the stables told me. She went on, "Horses are generally viewed without any negativity in Djursholm. Quite the opposite, many people like seeing us out there on rides, or when the horses go free in the fields, they say, 'Oh, how lovely.'" On the other end, one thing that is left along public footpaths is dog feces—according to my observations, few locals even bring poo bags on their walks. The dirty work of picking up one's dog's excrement is not the sort of thing one ought to be dealing with as a worthy resident. Djursholm's collective aura is based on the concept that these sorts of tasks are passed on to others, that is, to the community's "service staff."

There is hardly any graffiti, and I did not see any smashed-up bus shelters or anything similar. During my many visits to the town center, I never saw anyone sitting on a bench getting drunk, or peeing into a bush, or any such behavior one would otherwise consider to be a more or less normal occurrence in most other communities. The risk of bumping into a social security claimant with unkempt clothes, making his way to the municipal social security office, is as close to nonexistent as possible, given that this institution is located outside town. This also ensures that any potential visits there by residents can take place discreetly. Only executive functions have been retained at the town hall, as well as central consecrational activities in the municipality such as the department of schools, education, and culture, which in all significant respects contribute to the community's character. Rarely did I see any youths hanging about or smoking. In fact, smoking is extremely unusual in public places. For instance, I only very occasionally saw anyone standing outside a restaurant smoking a cigarette, and even when there are outside tables it is uncommon to see anyone lighting up. Smoking is generally not an activity that can be associated with the self-aware aestheticism of Djursholm. Nor have I bumped into people with dirty or bad-smelling clothes. Homeless people do not seem to exist.

When the residents figure in photographs in magazines, books, school photographs, or similar, they mostly look in good health. They are well dressed, their hair coiffured, with pleased, happy, or even jolly expressions.

This goes for both the young and the old. Judging by the popularity of low-calorie meals that can be purchased at the local pharmacy, people are accustomed to taking care of themselves and minding their appearance. "Many people here are slim, even the elderly. People are not keen on putting on a few pounds," one pharmacy employee told me. This attention to one's personal appearance, the employee went on to explain, could also be recognized in the sales of dental products (toothpaste, toothbrushes, mouthwash) and a variety of creams, particularly the more exclusive brands. Another employee pointed out that both men and women consume products of this kind, although "makeup and hair-care products are obviously mostly purchased by women." There is hardly an abundance of dirty, unshaven individuals in evidence, or women without makeup, and similar attention is paid to one's physique—irrespective of how one feels or the state of one's finances. This also holds true for the youngest members of the community. A teacher of a lower-secondary class told me, "When the children give talks at school, possibly about some assignment they have been working on, as a rule they arrive very well prepared, with an extremely professional PowerPoint slide presentation. Half of the boys here have their own suit or blazer, and people dress for these occasions."

One young woman, however, explained, "It was really hard while Mum's drinking was at its worst. I didn't have the energy to use makeup or bother about how I was looking. It felt unbearable to even have to think about that on top of all else." It can be particularly problematic for the elderly to maintain an attractive outer appearance. One employee in geriatric care in Djursholm related the following: "A lot of it is about keeping up an attractive exterior. When you get old you can't stay as active as you used to be. I've heard examples of people bringing their spouses for dinner although they are suffering from dementia, and things have not gone well. People want to hold on to their old lives. Women feel ashamed of their husbands, if their table manners aren't up to scratch or they don't quite behave as they're expected to." Nonetheless, added her colleague, who worked at a rest home in Djursholm, "When everything else has gone, what remains in these senile old gentlemen that I have met are their manners. They still remember to pull out the chairs for the ladies; they can stand up and hold a speech. They're quite capable of bursting out, 'Let's raise our glasses!' And that's charming, isn't it?" Another employee working in geriatric care explained that as a rule it is not difficult helping the elderly patients with showering and maintenance of bodily hygiene. "Even the elderly see the importance of being clean and tidy—they really do."

A man in his midsixties backed this up during an interview at his house: "There is a certain status here in having a good physique; you mustn't look disheveled or untrained. It's about how you come across to your surroundings. If you are well trained and well dressed, well, then people are prepared to listen to you and take you seriously." Possibly this is a contributory factor to the scarcity of Zimmer frames in Djursholm. I have not even met anyone in a wheelchair, or children or adults with any obvious conditions such as Down syndrome or something similar, which are not unusual in most other communities. Physical disability is not something one notices in Djursholm. The closest thing to it that I found was a group of children attending a special-needs school in Djursholm (at the time of my visit, however, none of the children in attendance lived in Djursholm). That the locals have been well brought up, claims one of the employees at that school, can be seen in the reactions these children have when "we take them into Djursholm to shop for food, for instance. We don't attract any particular attention. In other places where I have worked with physically lesser-abled children, people sometimes react, turn around, point, but that's not how it is here. I think it's the way people are raised. . . . People are very friendly and polite. They say hello to us when we go past, and it's very positive for the children; it gives them a bit of social recognition."

That the disabled children are not treated as different—that they are not, so to speak, stigmatized by staring or other reactions—is obviously something positive, but it also relates to a desire on the part of the locals not to attribute any particular importance to this particular group of children. The abnormal behavior of the children must not become *a part* of the community. It is therefore nothing that should be given any special attention. Once, when I was in Djursholm on an autumn day, an elderly man came walking along, wearing a hat, a tweed jacket, and a tie—but he was naked from the waist down. I remember that what I reacted to at the time was not that he seemed quite unaware of being naked as he strolled across the main square, but rather that most people in the square did not turn around, laugh, or point at him, which one might have expected. The scene was really very much like something out of "The Emperor's New Clothes," except that there was no child to call out, "But you're naked!"

There are plenty of service locations such as gyms, hairdressers, and beauticians, all helping men and women with the presentation of their bodies, and in this way contributing to the perfect exterior of the community. During my visits, both on weekends and on weekdays, I had the impression that these services were very much in demand. There are also other services available in health-care and various kinds of interventions. One dentist I interviewed explained: "There's a lot of bleaching of teeth going on here. People take care of themselves and their appearance. It's not unusual to change fillings that have turned slightly brown, even if they are still working perfectly well. You won't see any black teeth out here. Only pirates in films have black teeth or missing teeth! So cosmetic dentistry is important for us."

A prerequisite for an attractive exterior is a beautiful, appealing body, but there is also the matter of a "balanced" psychological outlook. The interest of the residents for exercise in various forms, as well as yoga, massage, and similar activities, is an expression of this—not least among the community's housewives. Another aspect of this tendency is an awareness of the importance of food. A precondition for one's body having the capacity to maintain a healthy lifestyle with walks, an active professional life, tennis, golf, travel, and so on, is quite simply that one does not get fat. One woman explained it to me: "I try to hold off on eating to stay trim." When I leaf through a school catalogue of one of Djursholm's schools, I can confirm that hardly any of the children in the photographs are so much as a kilo overweight. In my interviews with nursing staff working in the schools, my perception was confirmed: the pupils really do mostly have an absolutely normal body mass index (BMI). A man put it as follows: "In Djursholm you are not only supposed to be good at school; you have to be beautiful and rich as well. The children are so slim here; there must also be a socioeconomic dimension to that. But I think there may also be a genetic reason for it. Successful men choose slim women." The local minimarket has a well-stocked fruit and vegetable section, with a small variety of soft drinks, sweets, chips, and similar—according to the sales assistants I spoke to when I inspected the place. The most popular restaurants in the area do not offer much bulk—the servings are modest. Nor does it seem especially popular among residents to partake of fine patisseries or anything of that kind when they go to cafés, where they are on public display. One woman, who married a man from Djursholm, described her experiences of Christmas celebrations with his family: "When I invite people for Christmas dinner I make sure there's plenty of food. I want people to be satisfied! But with his relatives you only have these tiny, tiny helpings. Everything is very fine and tasty, but I have to eat before I show up." Another person explained that he came from the sort of place where "you eat plenty of food and I mean food of a reasonably substantial kind. The food culture here is something else. You get small portions of light food such as fish, rice, and so on. There's a self-control here which is about not eating too much, and there are guilt feelings attached to it." In general, physical appearance is connected to morality and lifestyle. Djursholm encourages its inhabitants to create well-trained bodies. This may be greatly significant for the impression they wish to convey to the world around them.

In all aspects, Djursholm strives to be "a shining city upon a hill," a "center of excellence" in terms of aesthetics. And it is not only the buildings and public spaces that are impeccable; the people generally look good, dress well, wear fragrance. You do not see many people with unsightly scars on their faces, or moving around with difficulty as a result of injuries; there is no poverty, homelessness, criminality, indications of unemployment, and so on. Djursholm presents a gleaming environment on all levels; you are expected to strive to shine yourself in order to be perceived as a "normal" and "attractive" resident. And, most important of all, these behavioral norms mean that you are contributing to the maintenance of the community's unique aura.

2

A PRIVILEGED WORLD

Economic Power and Wealth

THE PRIVILEGED STATUS often enjoyed and displayed by the inhabitants of Djursholm is central to their self-image as dwellers in a high-status community—and this primarily relates to good finances, with a life in Djursholm as the emblem of their economic potency. Phenomena such as nannies, housewives, exclusive cars, fine restaurants and cafés, large motor yachts, and so on, are further illustrations of this reality. One nanny remarked, "You have to have your nanny; you have to have your cleaner. That's what it's all about. I notice the way they mention their nannies. If you don't have a nanny, it makes you look poor, or as if your job isn't demanding and doesn't take up all your time." A nanny can also give one's children obvious advantages, beyond the associated added status—as explained by a preschool teacher in Djursholm: "Many of our parents have nannies because they work so much. They are usually the ones to bring the children in or pick them up. Some of the nannies are foreigners and in this way the parents are probably hoping that their children will pick up another language. And, of course, this is a fantastic opportunity. If one opts to have a nanny, well, why not choose a foreign one rather than a native-born girl?" Letting a nanny teach one's child a foreign language can turn out to be an important social statement, in addition to a purely intellectual development. In a community like Djursholm it is reasonable and relevant for small children to learn foreign languages at an early stage of their development. Not only does this enhance their ability to navigate in socially interesting situations in the future; it also contributes to the aura of the community as one of cultivation and cosmopolitan refinement.

The fact that Djursholm can graft a sense of grandiosity and nobility onto its inhabitants is dependent on various expressions of the community's status and prestige, which are intimately connected to financial potency. This makes it easier to act like a proper leader—very much in line with generally held ideas about entrepreneurs and how they operate. As an example, I might mention a newspaper article about a previous CEO of a large Swedish bank, who decided at the age of about fifty to sail around the world and not continue pursuing his successful career in the world of banking. His position was summarized as follows: "As a top-flight director and board room professional, he has earned millions over the years." He is also quoted in the same article: "I am aware that I am in a highly privileged situation. When I resigned from my board positions I felt for the first time that I could do anything I wanted. It was a euphoric feeling." Obviously it is not a generally granted freedom for all people to give up their jobs once they reach the age of fifty in order to devote themselves to their leisure interests. And obviously there was no question of renting out the family's home while the former CEO was away—instead it was considered an excellent opportunity for refurbishments. When he and his wife got back to Djursholm, he writes in a book on the journey, the house had been renovated and improved: "On the 10th of November we touched down after a year and a half away from Sweden. It felt exciting to come home to our house. Some building work had been completed during our absence. The library had been rebuilt, the pool had been re-tiled, the place had been thoroughly redecorated, and we had new TV screens in the library and in our bedroom. The house looked lovely, and we spontaneously felt very happy to be home."

Another example of the wealth and privileged status of Djursholm is evident when one looks at the many donations to worthy causes and associations, which significantly contribute to the community's well-being and ability to present itself to the world outside as a spectacularly functional place. For instance, associations and banks provide funding for annual grants and prizes for young people attending schools in the area. The local history and folkloric association has, for several decades, been able to run a fairly lively program thanks to substantial donations. A local foundation has donated money for various projects, not least in schools and health-care institutions in the town, for many years. On one of the school's websites, there was at one stage a link to something called "crowdfunding." When I clicked this link at the end of May 2013, I found information about twenty-one students at the school, who were working on a project that included a research trip from Sweden to Hawaii, which had to be financed by private means. A table showed that almost all the required money had already been raised by donations, very likely by the parents of the children. A member of Djursholm's tennis club, with inside knowledge of the club's activities, informed me of the following: "The main hall burned down fifteen years ago. A large part of the financing for the building of the new tennis hall came from private sources. One individual here who was the CEO of a large company, saw to it that the company went in with a major donation. Another family offered more funds. And yet another family helped us come up with the sum we still needed. When it's required, people here step up to the mark. In Djursholm there are a number of families who really have loyalty to the community. You can't rely on the municipality for things like this." A member of another sports association offered the following opinion: "Well, there are a number of 'donor families' that we can always rely on. We usually always turn to them if some special need arises." In a newspaper article, I read that the low level of public money that goes to associations in the municipality "does not affect three of the most active sports clubs in Djursholm: the golf, tennis, and curling club. They finance rebuilding works with private capital." This private capital, which has such a defining presence, plays an important role in the aesthetically pleasing character of the community and its general beauty ideal, but also impacts on the range of relevant activities on offer, which could be seen as important networking forums and as training schemes to promote the sort of social approach needed in the professional roles typically held by the residents.

When I met young people in Djursholm, a number of them usually referred to rich and varied experiences of travel to all corners of the globe. They give off hints of affluence in other ways as well. The lives of children and young people seem to be, above all, defined by possibility. Many of the families I met described their children as being engaged in a host of activities, many of them costly, such as private tuition in foreign languages and music. One mother put it as follows: "Of course, it's not exactly cheap to go horseback riding, so it tends to be a special sort of group that does it. Here in Djursholm I'd say that most families can afford to let their children ride." Even adults are active, and one person claimed, "In this place people can afford to go riding several times per week, and it's hardly like that in many other places." The tennis courts are, in principle, always fully booked. As one man explained, "I play four times per week, and in the daytime it is full of women and pensioners here."

A general impression from the preschools that I visited is that a lot of left-behind clothes and items end up as lost property, which no one seems to come back for. One principal showed me a room where such things were kept for a month before being donated to charity: "There's quite a special view here when it comes to valuables. We get masses of telephones, computers, and clothes, which no one seems to want to recover." Just as people are unwilling to sort their rubbish in public at a recycling station and possibly end up getting their hands dirty, or devalue themselves socially, parents are unwilling to spend their time in lost-property rooms looking for their children's socks, hats, or whatever else is missing. Djursholm's consecration of people into leaders is very much about implementing the sort of actions that are socially edifying and aesthetically elevating—none of which would seem to apply to the act of rummaging about for lost property. In addition, not seeking to recover one's children's possessions is another way of underlining that it is a place of privilege and exclusivity.

At another school, the caretaker commented on a similar phenomenon: "You're hardly taught to economize in Djursholm; there's a lot of chucking out going on. There's pretty much nowhere here to buy secondhand children's clothes." One teacher told me, "It's a very tough environment at school in terms of money and material things. If you don't have the latest iPhone, you more or less have to explain yourself." In another school, one of the headmasters explained, "The children are well-to-do; there's no issue about material things. People don't worry about losing their back-pack; they scatter their things all over the place." To view one's possessions as trivial is a reasonable outlook in Djursholm, and it even becomes a way of confirming one's higher social position. It is not the end of the world if one loses one's mobile phone or school bag, nonetheless there is an expec-tation that these things have to be top-notch.

Sound finances are a prerequisite of life in Djursholm, which is, as al-ready said, also evident in the inhabitants' approach to health care and personal grooming. When on one occasion I visited the pharmacy and spoke to two of the assistants working there, they stated that the custom-ers are basically not concerned about prices. To maintain one's social status it is vital that the objects with which one surrounds oneself, such as furni-ture, clothes, and so on, should all contribute to this status. This also applies to health-care products and medicines. An exclusive cream is not only significant in order to affirm an already well-established high social position, it also actively contributes to the elevation. The very act of apply-ing a well-known and exclusive cream to one's face is a physical enactment of one's social position as a resident of Djursholm.

Elderly people can choose to live at Djursholm's rest home, either paying for this privately or, in rarer cases, with the help of public subsidies. Several of those who live there do pay substantial sums of money for superlative levels of service. The residential section is located in a magnifi-cent building, which also offers beautiful sitting rooms, a library, and a dining room very much like a restaurant, with an alcohol license, table ser-vice, and white tablecloths. The complex includes a gym, an indoor swim-ming pool, a sauna, a woodworking shop, a weaving workshop, a painting studio, a *boules* court, a chiropodist, a hairdresser, and a general store. The property adjoins Djursholm's golf club. A residents' support organ-ization puts together excursions, a choir, film screenings, gymnastics, and celebrations during festive periods. The home is popular, and people have told me that they could not possibly imagine living anywhere else when they grow older. One resident made the following statement during my visit: "There's a calm, friendly atmosphere here. Normal people live here; it's nothing special. We have a lot of communal activities. There's something every day: bridge, board games, talks, films of operas. The various houses also arrange activities. In the summers it's mostly very quiet, many people go away, of course. I don't think there are communal Christmases; at least I've never experienced one. But between Christmas and summer it's full steam ahead!" It is all a far cry from the common perception of a municipally run old people's home, with hospital-like corridors. The medical care, general care, and attention given to the residents is probably no better in Djursholm than in other places, but the social aspects make it an institution of unsurpassed excellence.

There is no need for residents to be elderly in order to gain access to the excellent health care that is the very trademark of economic and social exclusivity. Djursholm has a way of socially distancing itself from the world outside and the "normal folk" that live there. This affects the outlook and self-perception of the locals, who see themselves as somehow different from and, in a moral sense, more advanced than others. In a newspaper article it was said that "a group of friends from Djursholm noticed how badly the public pediatric care was working according to their standards and requirements—and they realized that there was a chance to make money here." The article relates how one particular individual invested large sums of money in setting up a private children's hospital: "I have no interest at all in spending seven hours with my daughter on a Friday evening in the accident and emergency ward. And nor do my friends." One employee in the Swedish national health-care system, responsible for public health in the municipality, explained to me that "in Djursholm people have their own resources to a very large degree; they don't have to come to us, to the public health system, as the first port of call. They take care of their own problems. Only after they have tried a lot of other things, they may possibly come to us." Another local employee in the public health system explained: "Certainly we are talking here about a privileged group of people, people who are on a different level. If you have resources when you end up in difficult situations, you can do more than others. The national health system is limited, after all. People here go private. They have coaching and therapy, which we can't provide. And then on the whole they're prepared to speak out and be insistent, and everyone knows this pays off in the health system. Sometimes you really have to be willing to argue your case."

Another employee in the health system claimed that medicine was more easily obtainable for residents in Djursholm. "You don't always have to go down the health center. Many people here know the doctors, who write out prescriptions as a favor, and then people don't have to go and wait in line at the health center." I also interviewed a dentist, who told me that the standard of dental care in the municipality was high. "People go for regular checkups and take care of their teeth. Extractions are rare; there are few acute cases, and few root canal treatments. All this is a sign of an affluent, well-educated community. Nor do we need to concern ourselves with any sort of credit system. People pay cash for their dental work, even for the more expensive interventions." Having access to privileged care is important for the self-perception of the residents, and it also contributes in a practical sense to their good health—obviously not an unimportant attribute in terms of their ability to enact their social roles according to prescribed conventions and norms. That they have quick access to health care is also a factor in the community's ambition to display social prestige. Quite simply, one does not need to "see" illness as one does in other communities. And, in order for Djursholm to continue giving off its customary shine, it needs a healthy population.

Residents not only get to avoid the ever-present lines associated with public health care in Sweden, with all the significance this has for the consecration of individuals in the community. Lines are also short in the shops, in banks, and in other commercial outlets. Financial power brings its own stringent demands for better service, and this high level of service is also, as we have already seen, a defining characteristic of Djursholm. As one shop owner put it, "Customers here often know exactly what they want. They demand a high level of service and expect good quality." One of the employees at a restaurant explained that catering was generally popular, but that they also delivered food every day to elderly people in the area. Not preparing one's own food, even when one gets old and has plenty of time to do so, is a behavior that fits perfectly with the social norms. Or, as another employee at one of the restaurants put it: "Here, there's no shame attached to not cooking your own food, quite the opposite." The reaction of others to the phenomenon of catering seems relevant, in the sense that it reinforces the "self-evident" privileged position of the community.

When I spoke to one housing officer, he explained to me that the municipality sometimes chooses to be "flexible" on the requirements for obtaining various financial housing benefits in Djursholm, when there have been changing circumstances in families, such as divorces: "It can be a massive challenge for people to seek help from us, when they are used to a very different sort of life. According to the established rules you have to register as a job seeker. It's a whole new ball game for them. They are quite capable of putting up resistance to it. And often they are unwilling to move out of their large houses, which they can no longer afford, and take a flat instead. You have to be prepared to move anywhere in the county. We give them a bit of slack there. The municipal office will hardly force some housewife to go and live in some rented flat in any old place. One argument we often hear is that 'the children can absolutely not move out of the house, or change school.'" A banking employee testified to a similar positive discrimination in his workplace: "If you are working at a bank you can't just say yes all the time; sometimes you have to say no. We try to be supportive. For instance, we might say, 'You have a couple of nonpayments here and there, but if you try this approach instead we might be able to . . .' We try to find solutions and other ways of doing things. Sure, we may be inclined to run it by the manager one extra time because the customer lives in Djursholm." The special treatment shown to local residents is a recognition of their social status, and it is also significant in terms of corroborating their sense of being honorable in an actual moral sense. That the people around them are willing to show them respect and treat them differently enhances their perception of themselves as dominant people—as leaders— which in turn is based on the concept of the inhabitant of Djursholm as someone *worthy* of respect and being listened to. In other words, it is the actual community that gives influence and power to the people who identify themselves as inhabitants.

If the police ever intervenes against residents, it usually concerns young people who in one way or another have broken the law. Usually it is a case of lesser misdemeanors, such as breaking the speed limit on a moped, riding a moped without a helmet, or having committed some sort of act of vandalism while under the influence of alcohol. One police officer told me that, in his view, the tendency of young people in Djursholm to immediately admit to what they had done was indicative of good moral values—although it was also a way of minimizing any ensuing social damage. After all, the alternative would be to deny all charges, with legal proceedings as the demeaning consequence. The police officer went on: "When I call them in for questioning, most of the adolescents come in with their parents. They're incredibly polite, and I think we usually manage to achieve a constructive dialogue. We all want to sort things out in the best possible way. The vast majority of parents are grateful and helpful. We often have incredibly positive exchanges." A colleague of his had a similar experience, although, in his contact with the parents, he chose not to refer to anything such as "interrogation" or "questioning" but rather to "meetings," which he claimed had a positive effect on their interaction. There is generally no feeling of the police going in hard. Even when crimes have taken place, residents of Djursholm can expect an approach based on an image of Djursholm as a socially well-functioning place, which, in an otherwise dysfunctional and grimy world, stands out as an ideal place, indeed a shining city!

All in all, the future seems bright for Djursholm's children and adolescents. One writer, who grew up in Djursholm, explained in a book on his childhood, "[While] we were growing up here we were always incredibly aware of being privileged. To belong here was a measure of status and self-confidence. Although my family was middle class I felt things would go well for me in life, I felt I could succeed." This feeling is an important social characteristic—it takes the form of "good self-confidence." Furthermore, he made the following claim: "To live in Djursholm is an expression of social capital and self-assurance. Young people there believe things are going to go well for them, even if they are getting bad grades at school. What I've noticed while I'm giving readings from my book, is that this self-confidence allows me to be curious and own up to my weaknesses." If young people seem to be going off the rails, "the parents send them to other schools or overseas. A change of scene is usually enough to get them back on the 'right track.'" The author feels that Djursholm is characterized by a high level of self-confidence, and, as a result, it does not need to involve itself in the social one-upmanship that he believes is so prevalent in the rest of today's society: "People being aware of their worth can be highly provocative and unbearably annoying in certain situations. But at the same time it's a relief when people no longer want to compete with one another, given that they are already in the elite division in so far as status goes." The status to which he refers here is intimately connected with Djursholm, and this is what makes one a winner, which would not be the case if one lived in another type of community.

One person explained to me: "I'm sort of full-steam-ahead and not very restrained about work things, although I'm only twenty-five and fairly new to it all. The whole thing of 'knowing your place' doesn't really work for me. . . . Having grown up with parents who were executives and who socialized with other executives makes it easy for me to associate with those people. It doesn't worry me in the least to go for some dinner where the CEO of our company is also present." A man in his forties told me that his father was a well-known person in corporate and political circles. "Because we had many social functions at home, I got to meet a lot of high-up people, and you quickly lose your fear of them. They're just normal people; some are great and some are not so great, like any others. You learn to have a relaxed approach to people with power; you learn to socialize with powerful people." Another interviewee took a similar position: "To come into contact with success and successful people, and maybe even get to know them, does you a lot of good. You don't get overwhelmed by reverence for them. For myself, I can't stand authority." And a person who had been living there for forty years, explained: "Growing up in Djursholm, well, you know, it must be as close as you can get to a guaranteed good job and good life. If you don't get yourself a decent job you can compensate for it in other ways. Growing up here gives you possibilities like nowhere else." One woman who had lived there for a similar length of time felt that "when you grow up here it gives you the security of knowing how to behave yourself. The parents also help their children a great deal. A lot of resources are put into tutoring and other things that cost money." One mother, to whom I was talking about how she was raising her children, explained to me that children in her area were better set up for life than children in other places. "The other night I did a Myer-Briggs test on my daughter, and last week I was discussing various career options for working in China with my son, who's studying Chinese. I'm sure this sort of thing doesn't happen everywhere."

One of the teachers I interviewed clarified that children in the community are no smarter than any other children. "They don't have a higher IQ. But they often grow up in academic homes, where people are accustomed to studying, and this gives them an edge. Often they get professional support, such as private tuition, which maybe parents in other places wouldn't be able to afford. The environment here gives the children a lift." This "lift," as I explain later in more detail, is not primarily intellectual, but first and foremost social. Children learn, by the economic resources placed at their disposal, that they are privileged and because of this also better, which, in turn, helps continuously fine-tune the aura of the community. Another teacher made the assertion that "children here don't think about the objective possibilities for success at school, or indeed their parents' successes. This is a community that gives children huge opportunities in life. People prefer not to think about this, which one can well understand. Instead they entertain the notion that they're smarter, have a greater capacity for work, and are generally just 'better' than other people. But this is really a way of ignoring the social milieu and its possibilities and limitations." One successful entrepreneur, a man in his midthirties that was born and bred in Djursholm, told me that he left school after completing his upper-secondary education. Formal knowledge and academic qualifications had not played a part in his professional success and his position as a leader. Yet there was something else that had been extremely important: "I have built something up, I've created the opportunity to buy a house here in Djursholm, and I've made a lot of money. Obviously I can't ignore the importance of growing up in Djursholm and how this has affected my success. All my relatives live here as well; I'm not an *underdog* in any way. I'm not an *outsider*." In other words, the mere fact of growing up in Djursholm implies significant social possibilities, thanks to the value conferred by economic, social, and cultural capital.

As has already been implied, the exclusivity of Djursholm is ultimately maintained by the comparatively high living costs. These become the basic social markers. Good finances are a prerequisite for being able to purchase a house in Djursholm and to live there without deviating too much in one's general behavior. Money is an ever-present part of social life in Djursholm, and it has been so for many years. For instance, in one newspaper article, there was a description of a resident's grandiose seventieth birthday party, which was held in Shanghai. Another of his parties had taken place in Boston, where he had six hundred guests taken in chartered planes. Entertainment was provided by, among others, Elton John and Stevie Wonder. At the same individual's housewarming party in Djursholm, there was a performance by Diana Ross.

But the idea that Djursholm is a community that has always been awash with money "is a truth open to interpretation," as one woman put it. She went on: "Property taxes forced a lot of people out, not least the elderly who had bought their houses a long time ago and now only had their pensions to live on. Their wealth was locked up in their houses; they didn't have money tucked under their mattresses." One woman in her midthirties who grew up in Djursholm made the following comment on her childhood: "While we were growing up we weren't always in the black, especially not when the property tax had to be paid. My parents had quite a tough time balancing the books. We had no financial possibilities for going away in the summers or anything like that. We stayed at home. . . . Today Djursholm is to a very high degree about showing your affluence and success. You buy yourself an address. You totally refurbish the house, both inside and out. You gut the place." And one mother of three in Djursholm stated: "The children here go abroad all the time. It's difficult for our children; we can't afford it. Our children haven't been to Dubai or Thailand. If we had lived anywhere else we would have been in the high-income bracket, but here our salaries are absolutely mediocre." Another person that I interviewed at one of Djursholm's schools told me that during the financial crisis at the end of the 1990s things were pretty tough here for some families. "That was the first time I heard the children talking about money as if it was a problem. I realized that things at home were difficult financially. That was a new experience for the children. Many children living in other areas experience this every day, all the time. But here there's usually no question about money—it's just something you have."

But in the final analysis it is not financial capital that has built up Djursholm's aura, but rather the community's ability to create an almost spiritual differentiation from the world around it, through the capacity of the residents to portray themselves as responsible, socially restrained, stoic, and so on—which gives them the sparkle of social and moral elevation. Money is necessary to maintain this status, but only up to a certain point. Too much money can rather create the opposite effect. There seems to be a general impression that the community's economic exclusivity is growing a little too much. One man felt that "very many people in Djursholm today are so impressed by money." In an interview with another man, I was told that "people now seem to show off about how well they're doing in a way that didn't happen before. And the house prices are enough in their own right to be giving out those signals." One estate agent, with years of experience of selling property in Djursholm, confirmed that "before the 1990s you didn't have these extreme valuations. Houses now are going for astronomical sums. Having said that, living here has always been more expensive than anywhere else in the country." Djursholm is often described by its residents as a place that was founded by liberal freethinkers who were not at all interested in money, and not even wealthy in their own right (which was probably only true of a very small minority of them), but that the generation of founders was quickly displaced by incoming wholesalers and other economically powerful groups. One man explained it as follows: "First came the liberals, the philosophically inclined people, and then came the bank directors who built the really big palaces. And now the financial people are taking over. . . . Things really started changing in the mid-1980s; that was when the money took over"—and this was generally regarded as a threat to the status of the community. In other words, Djursholm's privileged character is not automatically associated with money, at least not in the eyes of the inhabitants themselves. Their consecrated lifestyle is built on other values and ideals. An elderly resident commented: "Today it must be mainly company directors living here, but no so many intellectuals or artists. The top people in corporate life are attracted to each other, I suppose." Certainly it is true that the financial wealth of Djursholm is vital to the self-perception of the residents as living in an exclusive, privileged community. And yet, paradoxically, the affluence of Djursholm poses a challenge to its aura and character as a place of cultivation and refinement.

Nor could one say that it is generally the case that the residents are busy "showing off" with their material wealth. As already implied—I met a number of locals who expressed concern and anxiety about the materialism and excesses that are putting their mark on today's Djursholm. One woman said: "I want to protect my children from this focus on the material side of life. Material consumption is just empty. I think many people here are just trying to fill their empty lives with consumption." One well-known corporate figure asserted to me that he did not at all feel that money was an expression of status in Djursholm. "Money has no value here. The people coming in and buying up the houses with their financial wealth don't impress people at all. If they also manifest their wealth in other ways it actually irritates people. My sense of it is that I have been given a place in Djursholm not because of my money, but because of my way of living, and my position in the financial world." Another resident commented similarly: "No one here cares if you drive an old beaten-up car; in fact, it's viewed as something positive. There's more anxiety about that in normal housing estates. Here, the assumption is that everyone has money." One man explained, "When Djursholm was first built, there were mainly liberals moving into the area, at the beginning of the 1900s. Now you have to be very rich. At the start it was a liberal heartland. Nowadays, everything has to be top-notch. Before it wasn't money above all, the important thing was culture in the sense of genuine values and traditions. But I feel this culture is still there; it's what sets us apart and makes us feel that we're living in a unique place."

Nonetheless, Djursholm's privileged status is based on financial worth—and always has been. With economic wealth comes social partitioning focusing on elevation. The consecration of people into leaders, as the example of Djursholm suggests, is quite simply a very costly business.

3

SIGNIFICANT PEOPLE AND WINNERS

THE MANY IMPOSING and impeccably maintained houses, the often stately ambassadorial residences, the expensive and exclusive cars, the impressive castle located in the middle of the community, the internationally recognized mathematical research institute housed in an eye-catching house set in parklike grounds, the many wealthy people who live in the community and who often feature in the media, the sky-high property prices, the regular and sometimes spectacular burglaries, and the frequent celebrity parties and weddings are just some of the examples of how Djursholm can be seen as an "important" community where a lot of influential people live. In my interviews and conversations with the residents, it was also often pointed out that "highly respected and significant individuals"—which is the phrase often used—have been living in Djursholm ever since the community was first founded. As a visitor it is also fairly easy to arrive at the same conclusion, and not only because of the houses, the cars, and so on. On a number of occasions I came into contact with or interviewed famous Swedish personalities—not only from the corporate world but also other spheres—who live in Djursholm. When, for instance, I took part in an evening meeting of children and young people in the local scouts' club, a famous businesswoman calmly strolled past with her dog on their evening walk, and on another occasion I met a well-known academic.

One of the people I interviewed offered, once we had finished our conversation, to take me for a spin around town in his car, which turned into a regular "Who's Who of Swedish Business in Djursholm." The entire trip was punctuated by comments such as, "Here lives the financier X," and "There's Y's house," and "This was where Z lived before she . . . ," and so on and so forth, all of which gave the impression that Djursholm in its entirety was populated by significant personages—which is the same as saying that the community is significant. And when I paid a visit to a person living in a housing association in Djursholm, he told me of a number of, as he would have it, famous personalities who either had lived there or still did live there today. As a resident, if one is able to see, socialize with, and read in the newspapers about one's neighbors, friends, and acquaintances, fully aware of their positions in society, or their pursuit of socially upstanding lives, the latter will tend to become role models for how one should live. These people spread their renown and polish over the community, and they contribute to the manifestation of it as a "community for leaders"—in the process they become icons of the social elevation offered by Djursholm to its dwellers.

A run-through of the articles published by the local history association since 1925 brings to light a number of pieces on the various notables who, for longer or shorter periods of time, resided in Djursholm. Especially in the early days of the community, as already mentioned, it was vital to attract so-called significant people. Their presence began to construct the local status; even today, in spite of a many-faceted capital consisting of prestige, status, and aura, Djursholm has need of a constant inflow of notables. These are not in a majority, quite the opposite. But their role is to consecrate the community, so that value can be conferred on the other inhabitants. In a book from 2008 about Djursholm, the author, a journalist who grew up there, depicts a conversation he had with a friend who lives there, in which the friend expresses the view that other people seem to believe that Djursholm is populated by people who are "in some way important." A life in Djursholm, the author goes on, symbolizes the very crème de la crème. Among the many people I met in Djursholm, I noted the concept that they consider themselves important in some way, irrespective of whether they hold any formal positions in society that correlate to this sense of importance. This self-image, then, is not based primarily on formal qualifications, knowledge, or skills, but rather just that one sees oneself as someone who lives in Djursholm. In all significant respects, this self-image is a collective one and quintessentially just means that one considers oneself to be a leader. Following are some examples from my interviews and conversations that are illustrative of this dynamic:

We're the cream of the elite, aren't we?

(Fifteen-Year-Old Pupil at a School in Djursholm)

God in Djursholm is the demanding God, not the merciful God. I think many people think that "God is on my side" in this kind of environment.

(Preacher at Djursholm Chapel)

This is a high-performance place for high-performance people.

(Man in His Fifties Working in Djursholm)

The Events Committee is discussing suitable names for the presentations [at the association's meetings]. Several members in our association have contacts, and they have only to pick up the telephone to get highly interesting people to come. There is no question of any remuneration.

(Man, Member of Association)

When I was new in the parents' association I realized that there's something quite special about Djursholm. Most of the mothers and fathers there were working in stock exchange–listed companies, and many of them had experience of board room procedure, so it was all very professional and formal. I don't think things work like this is many other places.

(Mother of Pupil at a Secondary School in Djursholm)

Djursholm is where successful people live, people who want to get somewhere and who want to make something of their lives.

(Woman in Her Forties Living in Djursholm)

When I run a search for "Djursholm" in a Swedish database of newspaper articles, I get a certain number of hits for residents who are being congratulated in the newspapers' family sections (usually these are people with leading positions in corporate life), and then I get several hits for people in corporate life who live in Djursholm. What they have in common is an apparently superior level of ability and capacity, which is not primarily related to intellectual ability but rather to lifestyle. For instance, in one piece on a well-known businessman on the occasion of his birthday, it emerges that alongside a hectic and successful professional life and authorship of an internationally best-selling book on leadership, he is also the father of five children. There's a similar description of a world-famous artist, who, as well as enjoying remarkable achievements in his working life, also has four children. And so on. Some of the birthday greetings are not about famous people living in Djursholm but actually focus on "normal folk." Yet even in this instance, these normal folk are presented as dynamic people with forward motion and responsible, important jobs, which are viewed as an expression of moral excellence and a hardworking outlook. One example of this is a woman who is celebrating her sixty-fifth birthday. She is presented as a highly active person in her professional life, a person who in her own words is "better at working than taking holidays." When she does manage to take holidays, they have to be active: "Lying still on a sandy beach is not for me," she explains. Her professional background, the article goes on, is as a horseback riding teacher, TV journalist, writer of children's books, chief physician, and medical counselor for the county council. Furthermore, she has academic qualifications in psychology, pedagogy, and as a medical doctor. The underlying message here is that Djursholm is populated by extraordinary people who are capable of *more* than others.

Hence, the inhabitants have an idea of themselves as significant not primarily on account of their professions, their formal qualifications, or their knowledge, but rather as a result of their choice of lifestyle. This was also underlined when I ran a search in a database for obituaries of residents who had passed away in the last decade. In these it is emphasized throughout that the deceased lived exemplary lives. One woman is described in the following glowing terms: "Despite only having being educated at an elementary girls' school, [person's name] managed through a combination of enthusiasm, an inquiring mind, and a progressive outlook, to quickly establish a brilliant career." A number of people, admittedly, are referenced by their professional status, such as "managing director," "medical doctor," "architect," "school principal," "lawyer," "professor," "psychologist," and so on. This is particularly true of men, whose various positions as leaders, managers, and the like are accounted for in an almost chronological manner. Above all, however, the supposedly active and dynamic aspects of the deceased are highlighted. They are described as "groundbreaking," "pioneering," "talented," "of unbreakable will and powerfully ambitious," "entrepreneurial," and "creative," to name just a few of the attributes on offer. One woman is described as "a very hardworking professional woman. She was unconventional, strong, and always full of new ideas. If she wanted to bring something to fruition, nothing could stop her." One man is said to have been "active unto the last." The general, strongly felt view is that each person in question was extraordinary. One of the obituaries is rounded off with a simple statement: "She was an unusual and unique personality . . . 'We shall not look upon her like again.'" In another we hear that the person "moved with the same assurance at embassy receptions as she did at courses for pensioner, and she felt that what she wrote was important." The obituary finishes with the statement: "She was really Somebody."

And yet it is nowhere near as evident that Djursholm has fostered quite so many outstanding individuals over the decades than when I walk through the beautifully positioned and well-tended cemetery in Djursholm. There is even a book in Swedish that designates Djursholm's cemetery as a resting place for an extraordinary number of dead Swedish famous persons. Certainly only a small number of the graves testify to the social position of the person buried there—instead, small and almost insignificant graves dominate, creating more than anything an impression of a community populated by fairly insignificant people. Possibly this can still be explained by the spirit of elevated equality that defines life in Djursholm, and not by any sense of the community viewing itself as socially modest. The inhabitants of previous generations have made a contribution to the way present-day residents see themselves. This is not some place full of vandals and troublemakers; this is a world where people of substance have walked and lived and exerted themselves. As a resident of Djursholm you can have an "ordinary" job, or even no job at all, as in the case of the housewives, yet one can still *be someone* merely on the strength of being a person who lives in this community.

The idea that exists in Djursholm of being important irrespective of any formal position of power in society seems well established and, as I have explained, is based on the notion of Djursholm as a socially elevated community. It can be backed up by statistics that those who live there are better educated than most others, earn more money, are unemployed to a lesser extent, are less likely to claim social security, and so on—which, as a whole, illustrates social respectability not only through one's profession and education but also through one's lifestyle and moral outlook.[1] One of the employees in a local association in Djursholm showed me an e-mail from a parent who had been involved with a sports event. The message, which had been sent from the parent's workplace, where she clearly held a high position, went as follows:

Hello! While I was standing there making sandwiches for 3 hours between 8–11 on a Sunday morning with my 15-year-old daughter, while my husband was coaching our son's football team, I reflected on whether it's really reasonable to ask parents to put in this kind of effort . . . and came to the conclusion that it isn't. If anyone had asked anything of that kind for my parents (which sports clubs didn't do in those days) they would definitely have been turned down.

The activities were clearly seen as socially degrading by the person in question, simply as dirty work, not the sort of thing she and other residents should have to get involved with.

If one has a self-image of leadership, which can be established or further developed by means of a life in Djursholm, it may not be so curious that one should not be averse to communicating with other social elites and feel a sense of community with them. In an example taken from a newspaper article, a woman describes how she first came to realize that her husband had a serious drinking problem and needed help. Her first impulse was not to call the municipal health service or some addiction clinic. Instead she simply put in a call to the best-known theater in the country, where director Ingmar Bergman used to set up plays. "I asked them: who helps your famous actors if they have alcohol problems?" Another story, which appeared in a different newspaper, outlines how a group of men with high positions in the world of finance and property had set up a burglary ring to steal for fun from the rich and famous; they struck against one of the most well-known businessmen in Djursholm. Fine wines and desirable art were taken. The owner wanted his things back, but he did not do what most people would have done under the circumstances, namely, contact the police. Instead he tracked down a debt collector and hitman, who found out the identity of the thieves and arranged the return delivery of the items to the businessman. Once again, he choose not to go to the authorities for help. There was no perceived difficulty about hiring criminals to solve a crime of this kind, the reporter states in the article. "According to the hitman, a well known profile in the underworld for the last 20 years, there is a well established phenomenon of collaboration between criminals and the financial elite. He has himself been instrumental in helping about ten financial heavyweights buy back property of theirs that has been stolen."

Even those who are not famous are raised to positions of prominence by sheer dint of living in Djursholm, as we have already seen—most visibly in obituaries or birthday greetings published in newspapers. The importance of the inhabitants is reflected by the responsible jobs they are offered in society. The community is proud of its famous men and women. During my interviews, the names of well-known individuals were mentioned several times, both living and dead. Some of these people are particularly emphasized in writings about Djursholm; some are even distinguished by streets, schools, and squares that bear their names—also by statues and paintings in public areas. One very famous resident who is, however, never mentioned, is the master spy Stig Wennerström, a Swedish colonel who worked for the Soviet Union between 1948 and 1963. By all standards, he was a well-known and respected resident in the area and well integrated. However, his home was the place where he communicated by radio with the Russians, and where he was eventually caught by the Swedish police after a tip-off by his housekeeper. When he died in 2006, it created news stories all around the world. But in Djursholm, people kept silent.

The idea of Djursholm as a leader community, then, is constantly reinforced by the mere fact of one's neighbors, friends, and acquaintances having national, and sometimes even international, importance and reputations. Residence there is often synonymous with personal celebrity, and it is no surprise that many of the inhabitants appear in the national and international media, which, in contemporary society, can create a feeling of significance and mastery. But the position of the inhabitants is also solidified by the ability of "normal" residents to feature in the national media. All in all, this creates an impression of a community worth listening to, not just locally but at a national level—a world of people who, in one way or another, can be leading figures in societal evolution, people with something of substance to convey. Whenever one reads in newspapers about people from Djursholm, it is easy to get the impression they all have extraordinary qualities. Few or none of the articles describe residents as mediocre or even just "bog standard." That powerful and famous outsiders are willing to come to Djursholm to give talks at association meetings or to preach at the chapel are other tangible examples of the community's standing. One association member summed it up as follows: "Quite simply, what we have here in Djursholm are opinion makers. That is why people come here to lecture or to sign books. They know this is a place where you can make rings spread on the water." The writer August Strindberg, who lived in Djursholm in the late 1800s with the purpose of trying to raise money among the wealthy inhabitants to finance his new theater, understood this very well. He did not much like the place, however, and he did not stay for very long. An individual who used to be a preacher at the chapel, put it as follows: "When you come to Djursholm, you are really entering the 'the right circles,' so to speak. As a preacher I was fulfilling an important social function." The many lectures and talks given by influential people at the numerous associations—prominent authors in the public eye and other players from the power elite—are important for the ability of Djursholm's residents to portray themselves as knowledgeable, competent, and weighty. The lectures do not only have a significant role to play from a simple information perspective; they also contribute to a general feeling among the locals of being included in a broader fraternity of worthies debating important social questions—which, of course, adds a bit of sparkle.

A central idea among the residents, much like the feeling of their own importance and how this is a prerequisite for the consecration of the community, is a conviction that their community is and has always been a home for cultivated and highly educated people. This conception, with its roots in the early years of Djursholm, has enormous relevance for the prestige and status by which the community defines itself, and it is highly influential in the creation of the inhabitants' self-image. One parent explained this to me as follows: "Children who grow up here benefit from a far richer cultural and intellectual climate than in many other places. I come from a simple home, and obviously I never had the opportunities while I was growing up that my children enjoy." Another inhabitant developed this further:

One may think Djursholm is formed by its entrepreneurial spirit. True enough, there are many entrepreneurs here, and there's an appreciation for new thinking, a curiosity. But there's also a cultural legacy that people want to live up to, and this reins in their curiosity and willingness to take risks, which true entrepreneurial activity involves. There's a cultural inheritance here and a world conservatism that points the finger at anyone who departs too much from the norm.

In another of my interviews, a resident expressed the view that in addition to family life it was the intellectual environment that defined Djursholm:

"You could say that Djursholm, historically, has offered an intellectual family life, where the children were brought up in an academic spirit of broad horizons and an interest in education and further study." Another woman, a friend of the interviewee who was taking part in the conversation, concurred. "There has always been a very broad church in Djursholm, people are accepting of different opinions. In the 1970s, the so-called champagne socialists were causing quite a commotion. Even so they were accepted here in Djursholm." In an article, a municipal politician toes the line of established ideas and explains that Djursholm attracted not only bourgeois wholesalers when the community was first set up: "Also professors and young intellectuals came here in the early days, which made this rich garden city a magic kingdom for humanists." The picture of Djursholm as a world of cultivation, primarily populated by artists and an intellectual elite, is also reproduced in many contemporary newspaper and magazine articles about the community. One man in his eighties explained to me that when Djursholm had just been founded "the very rich did not come here, only the educated and moderately wealthy. A cultivated elite came here, and it's their legacy we're trying to preserve." Another elderly gentleman clarified that "when Djursholm was formed it was mainly doctors and professors who came here."

Some of the inhabitants I spoke to maintained that Djursholm *used to be* an intellectual place, but that this is no longer the case. One woman, after listening to a presentation of my research project at a school, in advance of interviewing some of the staff there, wrote me an e-mail afterward: "I was talking to a few good friends there, and I more or less told them, 'That's what I've been saying, someone should do some research on what happens when the CULTURAL COMMUNITY turns into the NOUVEAU RICHE COMMUNITY.'" Another woman, in an interview, claimed, "Djursholm has changed from cultural elite to corporate elite." And a man in his sixties explained, "Djursholm has changed from a liberal, cultivated community that valued knowledge and culture very highly, to a community that above all values money. We moved to Djursholm in the late 1960s but moved away a few years later. I think it was a good thing that the children didn't grow up in Djursholm, the way it turned out." He went on to point out that it was once a cultural community where all roles were accepted by people. "In the new Djursholm there is no respect for education and competence, now it is other things that are highly rated, such as financial shrewdness, the ability to get on, or just the superficialities, and status." Yet another person expressed the view in our conversation that Djursholm "has a fairly constricted idea of education," and that a career as a librarian or a teacher "is hardly held in very high regard around here." One woman told me that she felt "this is definitely not an intellectual environment, even though the level of education is very high. People don't like 'academic discussions' that don't go anywhere. They want things to happen. These people are all about getting things done, and if that's what you want you can't spend too much time thinking." Another resident in Djursholm took the view that "in Djursholm one meets a lot of very pleasant and on-the-ball people but they tend to be very uncultivated. . . . I have a soft spot for education that has no particular financial value, but that's not the sort of thing that is appreciated in Djursholm." When I interviewed a successful man working in the Swedish financial world, who was living in Djursholm, he made the following statement:

Djursholm is extremely important to me; it's a sort of utopian form of a better world, a world protected from all forms of stressful materialism and modernity. But unfortunately it is about to collapse. The original idea of Djursholm as a place of liberalism and freethinking, is incredibly attractive. . . . When we moved there I still believed it was an intellectual place with a sense of social justice, meaning a place where people had the will and power to influence the community, and have opinions about things. Many of these people are still here, but most of them are now elderly. Our own generation, on the other hand, are so busy with themselves, and have so much money. They're not interested in society per se, only themselves and the little world they live in.

Another man of a similar age, who grew up in Djursholm but moved away, explained that it is not an especially intellectual or academic community. "Certainly a lot of people have completed university educations, but they are not academics. We missed that among our neighbors." According to him, there is usually no interest at all in "deep or reflective discussions that look at problems."

So the question is whether Djursholm, irrespective of the wealth of its inhabitants, is or ever has been an intellectual or cultural heartland. It goes without saying that the idea of the place as the home of highly educated people with a hunger for cultural enrichment is an attribute of the community's capacity for consecration and leadership, based on a socially exemplary lifestyle. The question, in other words, is whether the reality has ever reflected the narrative. One person told me: "Djursholm has never been an academic community like Oxford or Cambridge. The academics who live or have lived here are those that have succeeded financially and materialistically. Of course there are exceptions, but this is the general rule." An elderly resident clarified, "While my father was an academic, he was also very entrepreneurial, and he set a lot of things up. I don't think you'll find a lot of classic academics here, immersed in research, sitting at home reading. The people that are attracted to this place tend to be doers." One elderly resident summed up his views rather matter-of-factly: "The citizens we have seen in Djursholm over the decades have not been cultural emissaries. In the old university town of Uppsala you see an emaciated middle class: teachers, librarians, lecturers. You can tell just by looking at them that things have not always been so easy. But they give off a certain intellectual approach that is entirely lacking in the people of Djursholm."

It may be the case that it was once a cultural, intellectual place, but this is not to say that today's Djursholm can be labeled as such. Despite its fine, well-ordered public library, its captivating literary readings in the evenings at the local bookstore, its ambitious culture biennial, and art and books on display in the homes, there are other values at work here, and other ideals that rule the day. Art and the world of academia have always played central consecrating roles, and they add value to the lifestyle of Djursholm, and yet there is no evidence of a scramble to get young people to become academics and artists in their hearts and souls, with all that this involves, such as deep reflection, intellectual analysis, temperamental tendencies, and social introspection. One woman commented in a similar vein: "If you bear in mind the cultural personalities that have lived here, well, you'd have to say Djursholm is a cultural community. But it's hardly anything very challenging; it's very mainstream, nothing unapproachable."

One idea in general currency among the inhabitants that I interviewed, young and old, women and men alike, is that there is an "expectation that you'll make a success of your life and be someone," as one person put it, which could obviously be construed as a very logical sort of expectation in a community striving to create an aura around itself as a place of success and leadership:

There is an expectation here, a motor, a will to succeed.

(Man, Eighty-Five)

To be and become more and more successful here is a norm, and it's impossible to see things in any other way.

(Man, Forties)

There's a sort of success theology going on here.

(Woman, Forties)

Growing up in Djursholm is about the expectation of doing well for yourself. There's nothing bad about pushing and shoving. Everybody studies hard, you have to be good at a lot of stuff, I mean sport, languages, music, general knowledge. Those who can't live up to it sometimes feel bad. In other schools it's not quite okay to be the best and to be smart, but here it is okay.

(Girl, Seventeen)

The children have to do as well as they can, they have to do their best. The specifics don't matter. One can deliver in a variety of ways, but one has to deliver. If one has the capacity to become the best librarian in the country, that's what one should do. People have to do what they are good at, they have to develop their talents.

(Teacher at One of Djursholm's Schools)

There's an unspoken general rule here, which states that you have to succeed.

(Woman, Thirty-Five)

As an elderly resident put it, "The measure of success in Djursholm was never money in the olden days, even if people were wealthy. But certainly even then it was about making one's way in society and becoming a person of influence. Both among new and old residents, and young and old, everything is about being dynamic and active and strong." One company executive stated bluntly: "I am a *high achiever*. My son is not. That is obviously a disappointment to me." And, continuing with this theme, a teacher at one of the schools in Djursholm felt that "some of the parents here have enormous expectations of their children, and by this I don't mean that they want them to become something ordinary. Here, people like to think that their child could become an acclaimed lawyer, a successful head of a company, or some sort of power broker at the international level. People feel they can see these kinds of qualities in their children, and they expect them. And then they put everything they have into getting their children to attain these high ambitions." A colleague of hers went on to elucidate, "Here, you're not supposed to be an electrician or a carpenter. I suppose you might be accepted by your peers if you succeed as a self-employed person in something like heating and ventilation, but then it would have to be based on your being an employer, and not doing any of the manual work yourself. Formal educational qualifications are a must, they're the beginning and end of it." One young man in his midtwenties clarified this to me as follows: "I think my parents would be pleased if I ended up in a successful profession. I mean I wouldn't be so happy myself if I had a kid who got a job at the supermarket in town."

One man explained his economic success by having lived according to the device that "nothing is impossible." This, according to him, meant that one did not limit oneself, but always looked ahead in a positive spirit and believed that "things can be accomplished," and in this way quite simply relied on an entrepreneurial attitude to live. Another individual put it slightly differently, and clarified that living as a self-employed person was basically "about freedom and doing what you like." He went on: "I think 'onward and upward' and throw myself from one project into another. And that's the general spirit here; people don't see the obstacles, and if there are some obstacles, you just break them down." Also another person I met felt that "Djursholm is all about 'anything can be solved.' You know what channels to go through, what people you should be talking to, and what to say." In other words, a successful Djursholm life is about progressing and succeeding, which has to be based on a self-image of being someone of substance. This idea is absolutely crucial for the aura of the community and the consecration of mere people into leaders. Every obstacle on the way becomes a source of frustration and disappointment—there is simply a strong expectation of success.

This even affects the residents' attitudes to rules and regulations, whether significant or trivial, a tendency recognizable in the following selection of quotes:

You can't say, "No, it's impossible" around here. Everyone's well used to working their way past a no. That's a part of the entrepreneurial culture here. People don't recognize any limits to their ambitions and ideas. These are people who rarely say no themselves; they might make themselves unavailable or delay answering and in this way make it clear to you what your prospects are. But they won't just say no to your face. . . . Legislation is not the sort of thing that impresses this group of people, even though they're highly educated. The law is fine as long as it backs up your own interests. But if it blocks you from what you consider to be right and proper, then there's no hesitation about breaking the rules. This could be a case of speeding, parking, cutting down trees on public land, some underhand financial dealings, and so on.

(Municipal Civil Servant)

Some of the financial people couldn't give a damn about the rules, traffic regulations, and things of that kind. I suppose that's how things are at work, and that must be why they've earned so much money. Anything goes so long as it isn't illegal. But then even certain illegal things are also okay. There's an attitude of not really going along with collective rules. "No one decides over my head." But what happens to children that grow up with that sort of attitude?

(Man, Sixty)

There's this idea here about Djursholm as a world in its own right, with its own rules and regulations. One man was pulled over by the police, he was over eighty and he was driving a car that hadn't even passed its service. "But I'm only driving in Djursholm," was his answer. Djursholm is viewed as a sort of oasis that is above the rule of law.

(Police Officer)

When the students get an assignment they want to do it in their own way and not just *go by the book*. They want to test things out, avoid the usual maneuvers, they want a free hand. This does point to good self-confidence and a willingness to try things, check new methods, without any enthusiasm for the rules or keeping slavishly to convention.

(Teacher)

People aren't so particular about going through regular channels here; they just contact the person they believe will get things done. It might be a case of a principal at a school, or some counsellor in a high position at the municipality. As a civil servant I really have little power to change things, but they contact me anyway. They think in hierarchies, because I am in charge here they think I can press certain buttons.

(Municipal Civil Servant)

There's a general attitude here of "I'm first" among the parents. For example, when the children are dropped off in the mornings. It often gets chaotic, people beeping each other, getting irritated. Someone leaves the car with the engine idling while they take their child inside, blocking the way for everyone behind. You ask yourself whether the way the adults treat each other affects the children?

(Woman, Thirty-Five)

All in all people are unwilling to be prevented if they have ideas about rebuilding their houses and grounds and apply for planning permission. "I've voted for your party all these years, and you answer by turning down my application!" That's the sort of attitude you sometimes get here. And there's plenty of illegal building going on, people expect us to approve the work afterward. Or there's planning permission for five hundred square meters and you can bet your life that in the end the building plot will cover five hundred and ten square meters. And so on. . . . As a rule people don't like it if their neighbors build extensions. Then they put in complaints at the Planning Department. They don't like being prevented themselves, but they're quite happy to prevent others.

(Local Government Politician)

And yet there is also an emphasis in Djursholm on everyone being "equal before the law." For instance, Djursholm's boating association takes care of allocating berths for the residents' boats. On the association's website, the FAQ tag, in all essential respects, is about this queuing system. It is emphasized that only the harbormaster is in charge of allocating berths—as he or she "applies a strict code of first come, first served" there is "no point in contacting individual board members on the subject of berths." In theory, then, it should not be possible to avoid the queue. Yet other associations are more flexible, and one top official in one of them made the following statement: "As a rule there's a queue. But there are short cuts. If you get involved in the association as a parent your child will be moved to the front of the queue. . . . One girl aged nine came up to me the other day and said, 'They moved me to the front of the queue when my mum became the head.'" On one occasion there was a message on the scouts' home page that one of the groups was fully subscribed—"but there are ways around it," the message went on, these being that the association would "make occasional exceptions for children whose parents are actively involved in supporting the scout movement." This information can be interpreted in two ways: first, that "nothing is impossible"—lines can be bypassed as long as one has something to offer; second, that parental involvement is the condition, in this case the condition of cutting in line. Obviously what is being encouraged here is activity, or, to put it another way, certain steps that have to be taken if one wishes to avoid the line. Similar norms and cultural values are also central in forming people's perceptions of themselves as leadership figures. In a community where one is almost expected to "assert oneself" in an entrepreneurial manner, this will ultimately become a norm, and it will certainly be viewed as socially acceptable behavior.

There is an awareness that behavioral norms and values that apply in Djursholm, which might be seen as expressions of a successful and entrepreneurial community, are not applicable in the broader society outside the community boundaries. The social acceptance of these norms in Djursholm is explained by the idea that leaders are above the law, and that Djursholm is a community occupying a higher position than others. However, if these norms are "exposed," Djursholm risks damaging its aura as a morally advanced community. One example of this came about when a minister in Sweden's government was forced to resign from her post under humiliating circumstances after it emerged that she had been using a cleaner in her home in Djursholm, paying her cash without declaring the transaction, and in this way depriving the state of tax revenue. In a newspaper article it was reported that "the minister looked quite crushed as she met with reporters last night, emerging into the garden of her house in fashionable Djursholm with a cup of tea in her hand." A few days later another newspaper reported that "the disgraced minister, exposed as a tax-dodger and also reported to the police for non-payment of her TV license fee" was now leaving the country and "panic-selling" her large 323-square-meter house with extensive grounds of 2,400 square meters in Djursholm. The newspaper went on to report that several estate agents had declined the opportunity of handling the sale. "We don't wish to sell it, because we don't want to be associated with the activities with which she has been involved," one estate agent commented. But quite clearly it is not only the surrounding world that can occasionally put a dent in the residents' enthusiastic theology of success. Also within the community there are strong norms and values of what one can, and cannot, do. One famous case, well known in Djursholm, concerns that of a well-known financier in the process of building a house in the town. According to one newspaper, he took it upon himself to have a tree stump removed outside his property. The neighbors were furious, and the municipality charged him with putting the damage right by putting in another tree stump. Having an image of oneself as an important person may not, in other words, give one carte blanche in every possible social context.

Despite all this, the typical resident in Djursholm is a self-confident individual who moves forward with power and self-assurance. One woman of about twenty, who grew up in Djursholm and was studying at the university at the time I spoke to her, said: "I have always been allowed to decide for myself and be responsible; I was never made to feel any limitations. It was a shock when I started working and I realized that others would be making the decisions for me. I wasn't prepared for that. In other environments I think children would learn to 'know their place.'" The norm of success in the community urges its inhabitants to do great deeds, where sometimes the end justifies the means. The consecration of people in Djursholm into leaders is precisely about this: they are expected to act in a socially entrepreneurial manner and manifest an enviable lifestyle. Their behavior as it has been outlined here can be best understood as an expression of a general conviction that their moral outlook is superior, based on critical norms in relation to which all the members of this community must try to navigate with varying levels of success. Their activities, to this end, confirm the norms and cultural definition of this community as an environment of progress, commitment, and willpower—a place where the inhabitants receive a course of practical training in how to organize themselves in the art of efficient, well-ordered lives.

4

SPORTY TEENAGERS, WINSOME PENSIONERS

THE BRIEFEST of walks through Djursholm offers up many impressions of the dynamism of this community. There is no sense at all of a place becalmed or resigned, or the merest hint of a community struggling with unemployment or social exclusion; quite the opposite, a typical morning gives ample signs of optimism and confidence. At the very heart of town, in the central square, cars drive back and forth in a steady stream, and there is keen competition for the parking spots. While this may not seem so unique, the cars are nevertheless often driven too fast, and the drivers are not hesitant about sounding their horns if something gets in their way. On one occasion I observed a woman, with three children in the back of the car, attempt to make a three-point turn in her top-of-the-range BMW SUV, on the main thoroughfare that cuts through the town center. Because of the size of the vehicle, this was not an altogether simple matter. As a consequence the traffic was blocked for a moment in both directions, which evidently caused a frisson of irritation among waiting drivers. When they finally pulled away, their feelings were vented in the form of wheel spins, and several of the men shook their heads in disbelief, evidently upset about having been impeded. Another time I witnessed how a woman pulled over and left her car at the bus stop so she could run an errand in a shop. The bus, which arrived right behind her, was unable to stop in the turnout, and the driver started sounding his horn and shouting at her to move her car. When the woman failed to respond to this, the driver chose to get out, follow her into the shop, and literally usher her back into the street. That the driver was annoyed goes without saying, but the unexpected part was that the woman was also extremely upset. In front of him and the ten or so people waiting at the bus stop, she justified herself by exclaiming: "I'm also in a hurry, you know, and I don't have time to look for parking!"

As a general rule one could say that the speed of the traffic is analogous to the residents' perception of themselves as busy, important people. One woman I spoke to felt that the flow of traffic in Djursholm was too hectic. "When you're driving here, it's often quite stressful. 'Out of the way—here I come!' That's the feeling it gives you." One shop owner told me, with a crooked smile, "There's quite a lot of damage to cars here when people are parking. Sometimes we watch when stressed-out parents with small children in the back try to get their SUVs into parking spots." An article in the local newspaper raises the topic of large numbers of motorists being pulled over for speeding outside one of the schools. A photograph of a boy standing by the side of the road is used as an illustration of the problem: "The cars pass the school at considerably higher speeds than 30 km/hour. It is difficult for [child's name] to get across." According to official statistics, traffic violations (such as speeding) are the most common misdemeanor for which Djursholm's inhabitants are booked (whether there or elsewhere); they account for 76 percent of the total number of court cases. And yet some of the inhabitants seem to feel that excessive speeds on the road are not much of a problem. In a letter to the local newspaper, one resident expressed the opinion that recently reduced speed limits in Djursholm from fifty to forty or thirty kilometers per hour "had extremely detrimental socioeconomic consequences." He calculated that speed reductions in Djursholm were costing the country millions per year. Therefore he proposed that speed limits should be raised by between ten and twenty kilometers per hour.

Meanwhile, as the world speeds by, the many clean and graffiti-free park benches in the town square and along the seafront are rarely used, apart from the odd elderly person taking a breather. To sit down and peruse the surroundings, or take a moment for small talk, is not a normal feature of life there—with the exception of days at the seaside in the summer. There is little of what one might refer to as small-town tranquility. The town square, the main communal exterior space, is not a place where people meet or talk. It seems little more than an arena in which individuals display their high-octane lives by rapidly passing through on their way to somewhere else. Leaders are usually characterized by their dynamism and energy, not by their capacity for sitting down, immersed in solitary reflection. As a behavioral norm this can be easily surmised from a quick inspection of Djursholm. The only people I see waiting in the central square are the few individuals who rely on the bus. Apart from the odd adolescent and pensioner, those who use public transport do not bear much physical resemblance to the other people crossing the square: they are rarely white and they tend to speak with a heavy foreign accent. The typical resident does not use public transport and seems unwilling to be seen standing here *waiting* for a bus. On a couple of occasions I ran into a busker of foreign extraction, playing outside a shop. But I never saw anyone sleeping on a park bench or on the pavement.

On the other hand, while one rarely sees Djursholm's residents sitting still, an important detraction from the rule can be noted in the community's restaurants and cafés, all of which are frequented mainly by locals. In such places I often observed how people took their time, ate calmly, or enjoyed the weather if they chose to sit outside. Of course, sitting in a restaurant or café is not quite the same thing as waiting on a park bench or hanging about on a street corner—it is a peculiar social activity, the expression of a choice, and a social demarcation both in terms of time and space. By frequenting restaurants and cafés, one also benefits from an additional training in how to become a proper resident. Here one can learn by imitation the codes and norms of successful behavior, such as eating or drinking in particular ways, or the practice of kissing on the cheek rather than the usual prosaic embrace. This is especially true of children and young people: going to restaurants and cafés for them is less about eating than learning the correct mannerisms.

Many of the inhabitants also act as internal and external role models for an appropriate, successful lifestyle, in which socially approved behavioral patterns are put on a pedestal and made into a general ideal. For instance, I found one newspaper article about the private and professional life of a well-known performer living in Djursholm, who was described as highly ambitious in her work, which involved very long hours. And yet, the article went on, when she was at home she did not exactly spend her time slouching in the sofa. She busied herself with picking dandelions, redesigning a bathroom, ironing clothes, baking buns, or mowing the lawn. The article is presented alongside a photograph of the attractive, smiling woman standing in a lush meadow full of flowers. In fact, most of the residents of Djursholm live similarly active lives, often with challenging and stimulating jobs that involve long days at work and constant trips all over the world. They seem to enjoy a stimulating variety in their leisure: they travel, some have one or more holiday homes, and many own boats.

During school holidays the population of Djursholm seems to reduce materially. Particularly in the summers, the community more or less empties, which is also evidenced by the closure of a number of local service providers, and a less intense program of events at the chapel. Taking it easy and staying at home is not the sort of thing a typical resident could ever be at ease with. Or, as one woman put it in our conversation: "I suppose it's not really viewed as okay to stay at home over Easter. You're supposed to have traveled somewhere." On this same theme, one elderly man assured me that "the norm in this community is not to be at home during holidays—this is when you're supposed to go skiing, or lie on a beach somewhere. Nowadays people travel all the time, whereas before they might just go to their summer homes." The locals tend to be in dynamic professions, with a high turnover of jobs at the executive level. One of the estate agents that I interviewed, who had sold many properties in Djursholm over the past twenty years, explained the phenomenon: "There's a fair amount of movement. Obviously there are families here that stay on from one generation to the next, but it's no longer typical. People move. These are people who have opportunities, and they take their opportunities. They don't want to stay on in the same old jobs, they're always switching things around, and sometimes they also relocate."

Having a lot to get on with and doing as much of it as you possibly can is viewed as something quite normal and desirable. It reinforces the idea of Djursholm as a socially and therefore also morally elevated place. Many of the activities in question demand a great deal of people in a cognitive sense, but they also add to the image of Djursholm as a place always and forever focused on future possibility. As one man in his forties put it: "My wife was working sixty hours per week, and I was working just as much. A house project in Djursholm was a good collaborative venture for us. It forced us to do things together; it was really good for our relationship." A teacher in Djursholm said: "Most of the parents run their children in with their cars; only the odd one cycles. It has to be quick; you have to squeeze in as much as you can into the day, and get the maximum out of it." Obviously not every single individual in Djursholm is constantly busy, and several of those that I spoke to reflected on the norm of "constantly being on the go" in life. However, it is a standard mode of behavior, and residents have to take a position on it if they wish to live there. One company executive put it as follows: "My wife has a kind of *default Djursholm mind-set*. I'll give you an example. One time when our children had been out all day, I said to my wife that I thought it would be okay for them to slouch a bit and watch some TV. My wife didn't like that at all. You have to be *doing something* nonstop." He went on: "In Djursholm you can't just sit at home writing poems. Maybe as a hobby it's all right, but not in the sense of something you might have a vocation to do, or feel passionate about. If my son told us he didn't want to go out with his friends or play football, he just wanted to stay at home and paint, I think he'd get very lonely in this place. And we'd worry about him."

Many of the parents I met with were keen on their children enjoying a rich and varied leisure, with many different kinds of activities on offer. One mother asserted: "I want my children to experience a lot, so I want my daughter to try the scouts, or play some kind of instrument, or tennis and golf, or whatever the case may be." The fact that certain activities are rather costly, whether for children or adults, does not constitute a hurdle as it might for people living in other areas—Djursholm has a level of private finance that allows for an active life in the form of experiences (travel, sport, courses, etc.).

One term that kept resurfacing in my interviews with the inhabitants was *multitaskers*, by which they mean active lives devoted simultaneously to a number of different occupations. The multitasker is, by definition, not an expert who concentrates on a particular activity and in so doing continually refines his or her knowledge of it. Experts can be active and involved, but the multitasker is even more so, because of the many different activities into which time and energy are devoted. One person described herself as "an artistic and creative person, with many interests and a drive to get involved in them all." Multitasking also expresses an idea in Djursholm that can readily be recognized among its young people, who tend not to go for any kind of elite commitment whether in sporting terms or anything else. As a future (business) leader there is no need to know about anything in exhaustive detail, yet what is absolutely essential is your ability to organize your life in a social sense.

Multitasking tests this ability and could be interpreted as a training method in a crucial leadership quality, namely, the ability to be organized in your life. The diverse activities are consecrating because they demand and elicit an ability to organize oneself in an exemplary manner, and also because they create social creatures with a capacity for handling a great variety of situations. One girl of about sixteen, whom I met at an event organized by one of Djursholm's associations, told me that playing the piano was one of the things she did, and actually did quite well. Yet her piano playing was just one of many other leisure activities. "No, I'm not going for music. There's far too much competition; the demands are way too high to reach the top. I wouldn't have the energy for it." This may not be a unique expression for a society such as Djursholm, but it illustrates a critical ability in leader societies: being able to master many social contexts and having the flexibility of the generalist rather than the specialist. Indeed, multitasking is often referred to in Djursholm's residents' obituaries. With women, it is often pointed out that they were not only good mothers and highly competent in their professions—on top of this they were active in associations, liked to paint, and enjoyed spending time and exercising in nature. In cases where women have not had professional roles, other "professional-sounding" activities are mentioned.

The appreciation and value locals attach to activity and change can also be seen in the ever-changing commercial activity in the community. Certainly there are a number of stable service providers. But these apart, there are frequent changes in ownership, which seems to signify that inhabitants quickly get tired of things and prefer to live in a community in a state of flux. One person employed in geriatric care in Djursholm reported that many of her clients liked seeing "new faces" among the staff, for the simple reason that they enjoyed "something new coming into their lives." All in all, this is a community that appreciates change and variation and that asks of its citizens to embrace these ideas. These factors are instrumental to Djursholm's character of dynamism and self-confidence, as well as providing social training to encourage the formation of leaders.

As a part of this study I accessed statistics from the Swedish National Board of Health and Welfare for twelve of the most commonly prescribed pharmaceuticals for people living in Djursholm in 2011, subdivided into age groups and gender, with a comparative look at the rest of the country. The products most in use among the residents are those that promote the pursuit of an active and engaged lifestyle, both on a private and professional level. For instance, there seems to be a lower tolerance among Djursholm's parents for keeping their children at home in bed when they are ill—there is a higher demand for penicillin, the assumption being that it aids a quicker recovery in cases of, for instance, ear inflammations. Another example would be the consumption of pharmaceutical products known as *urological medications* (mainly to treat erectile dysfunction) among men aged forty to fifty-nine, which is considerably higher than in the rest of the country: 5.74 percent as compared with 3.66 percent. This anomaly also persists in the older age group of sixty to sixty-nine, where the proportion of men in Djursholm using these kinds of medications is 13.03 percent against 9.56 percent for the rest of the country. In the seventy to seventy-nine age group, the proportion of men in Djursholm using urological medications rises to 19.21 percent, while for the rest of the country the figure is no more than 10.41 percent. Hence, middle-aged and elderly male residents seem to be more sexually active than their counterparts in the rest of the country. As has already been mentioned, illness (also aging, which I discuss in more detail below) is problematic in Djursholm, because of its tendency to limit the usual activities and experiences that contribute to the aura and status of the community. If there are medications available to minimize the symptoms, there is certainly a readiness to use them.

As one employee in geriatric care in Djursholm put it: "Someone who has been a driving, forceful person in their life and then just ends up lying in a bed, totally helpless—well, it must be horrific." One doctor working in and around the area made a similar suggestion: "Of course no one wants to get ill, but around here it's particularly awful when you can't keep up any longer, both for your own sake and those in your surroundings. People don't even want to go on sick leave. They want to go to work. This even applies to the children, which isn't very good, actually. People prefer them to go to school or preschool even when they should really stay at home." One employee in school health care added: "There is an early warning system here among parents. At the first sign of a problem they contact us, because they think we can nip it in the bud. But that is not so easy. Sometimes a bit of a sore throat can be a sign of a heavy cold or flu, but it could also turn out to be nothing. People aren't prepared to wait here until the child actually gets ill." Being healthy is an expression of a *better* lifestyle, in contrast to an apparently passive way of living. It is almost a precondition of a community with sparkle that it has to be full of sparkly, active people and not types that stand about, mope, or in any other way seem to be slow, unhealthy, or disengaged. The active, engaged resident is nothing less than a normal person there, a person making a contribution to the general definition of the leader community. Being ill or in any other way incapacitated puts this in jeopardy.

The apparently high level of activity among the inhabitants seems especially to relate to children and young people. One woman in her midthirties, who grew up in Djursholm, made the following assertion: "You always have to be engaged with something extra, such as tennis or horseback riding. Apart from school you're busy with a lot else. I hardly ever relaxed; it was full steam ahead. It was often fun, but sometimes it all got too much." One mother expressed the view that "excursions to the woods, to museums, libraries, the theater and similar things are extremely important. Nature groups, scouts, and this sort of thing are crucial. The children's leisure time has to be 'meaningful.'" When I spoke directly to children and young people in a variety of contexts, for example, during visits to the youth center, schools, or family homes, I had an impression that people were basically in favor of an active lifestyle. One thirteen-year-old boy made the claim that "it's fun when there's a lot going on," and a sixteen-year-old girl told me that, in addition to schoolwork, she was involved with a charity organization, learning to dance, and practicing a musical instrument. The father of a family I was visiting similarly emphasized, "As a teenager in Djursholm, you don't just hang about, or stand around in the town square, like young people do in so many other communities. Here, you learn to make full use of your time. You study, you have a part-time job, you run a company, you play a sport, you join associations, travel, and, in short, you make the best possible use of your time." One mother told me: "In our family the children have a lot of activities. My boy has tennis twice a week and football three times, and then he also plays an instrument and has extra English tutoring." Being active, in motion, and constantly occupied is viewed as normal life—passivity therefore becomes something odd, maybe even something to be looked down on. Or, as one mother told me:

> My husband and I work hard, and we put in long hours. We try to go running twice a week and go to the gym to keep in shape. The children have two activities each week, usually sports. But we don't want them to take it to elite level, because the most important thing is their schoolwork. Quite often we put pressure on them to study on Sundays. They are free on Friday afternoons and Saturdays. But on Sundays they have to prepare themselves for the week ahead. That's a good system—I mean, that's what you do when you become an adult. We are preparing them for interesting professional lives.

The activities in which the children and young people take part do not only have a formative aspect, in the sense of learning to organize themselves and take the initiative, but also contribute to their image of themselves as highly developed individuals in a social sense. This often takes a purely lifestyle-based expression, and bases itself on aesthetics and morality: as an active young person you learn to see yourself as a highly functional individual, cutting an attractive, admirable figure to the outside world. A youth worker at one of the schools told me, "Homeless people and the unemployed are probably the two groups in society that are held in general disdain by some of the children here. The feeling is that it's their own fault; they haven't put in enough effort. I think this reflects the attitudes of their parents." By definition, the unemployed become antithetical to the idea of leadership, in the sense that they are deficient in their levels of social activity and lifestyle—and so, by definition, there must be something wrong with their character.

How the unemployed live their lives in Djursholm, doing without the basic daily activities that are a norm for most people in the community, is very difficult to know for the simple reason that there is such a small number of people in this category. As a result of my conversations and interviews, I managed to find three unemployed men, or at least unemployed according to a standard definition (there are plenty of unemployed women in the form of housewives, but they belong to a different social category and their home-based lives are a personal choice). None of them referred, however, to themselves as "unemployed," opting instead for the term *between jobs*, which is an expression denoting movement and change rather than passivity.

Being active is what counts in Djursholm, and this includes those who obviously do not have positions of formal employment, such as housewives and pensioners. Even these groups, in some instances, devote themselves to income-generating activities. Several of the housewives I interviewed had small companies, which they were running on the side. Several retired men were also fully engaged in working life by means of "senior positions" in boardrooms, or similar. And a number of the people I met presented me with business cards—which one would usually only expect in a professional context—although these cards only offered basic information such as their names and telephone numbers. According to already reported official statistics, the level of unemployment is very low in Djursholm, yet the number of people of working age in gainful employment is lower there than in the rest of the country, which could have something to do with the relatively higher number of housewives. Being a housewife there could in a certain light seem like a form of unemployment, even if a somewhat gold-tinted version of it, and in this sense it might risk being viewed as passivity. However, in my interviews with housewives and my subsequent observations of their lives, it does seem that the typical housewife in Djursholm is extremely dynamic and keeps the agenda filled with any number of appointments and events, which, even if apparently superficial, do point to an amazing appetite for activity as an end in itself. One housewife wrote as follows in her blog, dated 2012:

Ooooh, this week I have a lot of nice stuff on my agenda! Lunch today at WaterFront, meeting with Johanna on Tuesday, lunch at Mocco, cocktails tomorrow evening, swimming school end of term party, press opening at the new shopping center, lunch at B.A.R., coffee with girlfriends @ my residence, manicure, and also something very Spring-like, I mean taking the car in to have the summer tires fitted. This is always a highly appreciated sign of Spring being around the corner! Less noise, and nicer tire rims.

Housewives are not only an important part of the symbolic capital used in the consecration of Djursholm; they also play a practical role in the community's elevation of mere mortals into leaders. As one of them explained: "It's the women who organize family life and keep everyone on the ball. Many women here are also highly active in the community and charitable projects, so they have plenty to be getting on with." Another woman told me: "When the children had grown up, I didn't just want to hang about at home; that was not at all what I wanted. So I got involved in associations, went to courses, and so on." One of the preschool teachers at a Djursholm school described how "the women go to yoga and psychosynthesis, that is how you legitimize your existence. You absolutely can't just stay at home or go out for the odd walk. The housewives live their lives in the fast lane, and the days whizz past at a high rate of knots." One forty-year-old man told me in an interview: "You can't have some lazybones for a wife. That won't work in your social life." Because these women tend to be active, well trained, careful about their clothes and appearance, they add a certain aesthetic quality to the town. In turn, Djursholm elevates them: they are not unemployed in any sense; their lives have no such undertone.

As already suggested, few of the residents I interviewed, whether young or old, ever expressed any misgivings about their highly active lives. The general feeling is that activity is enriching in many ways—and it is seen as an expression of the Djursholm lifestyle. On the other hand, when I conducted interviews with staff at preschools and schools in Djursholm, and similarly with employees at the various associations and sports clubs in the community, the commonly held view that I encountered is that Djursholm's youngsters and children are expected to do far *too* much:

> The children live extremely hectic lives. There are many trips and parties and celebrations. They are very open when they are with us; they tell us everything. Parents here just drop them off and pick them up, and then on the weekends they are all stressed as they ferry them about between various activities. The other week one girl arrived in her ballet clothes, and a boy came directly from tennis training. One time when we were relaxing at an end-of-term barbecue, one father came huffing and puffing and dragged his son off to a party. Couldn't he just have given it a miss? I don't think his son even wanted to go. The agenda is always stuffed for the children, even at weekends.
>
> (Instructor at a Leisure Club)

> There are a lot of activities for the children, too many I'd say. They have tennis, riding, dance, and football. Things get very late; the children get to bed too late and they often seem tired, almost run-down. A lot happens in the afternoons and the evenings. They spend all day here,

sometimes it's quite demanding with a lot to do. And then it goes on late into the night. There's no peace among the parents, something is always going on. You absolutely can't be a layabout here.

(Preschool Head)

Many of the children are troubled by all the activities they have to participate in. They're not allowed just to exist. There's so much to get on with both after school and at the weekends. I once had a girl who crawled under her desk at the end of the day. She didn't want to play tennis or have extra language tutoring or whatever it was.

(Teacher)

Just staying at home during the holidays, relaxing, or making the odd little excursion, would be very unusual in my experience. After the holidays the children mostly talk about their trips. You get the impression that hardly any of them have even been at home.

(Teacher)

I have twenty-eight pupils. Seven of them need a lot of support, and have been diagnosed with conditions such as dyslexia, Asperger's, ADD, and ADHD. But then there are some that just have enormous concentration problems; they are always getting up and moving around. They have great difficulties just sitting still. . . . Sometimes we give them "stress balls" that they can sit with. This gives them a response, because sometimes it is just the lack of a response from their surroundings that makes them overactive. We also put in screens, so they can have a quiet space in the big room. . . . Two of the children have ADD rather than hyperactivity, so they don't get into gear at all. They're excessively passive. So we have to try hard to make them activate themselves. Obviously neither ADHD nor ADD are very good; a middling level of activity is best.

(Teacher)

That staff members in schools and preschools feel that the children and young people have too much to do is simply proof, as far as the residents are concerned, that *their* lifestyle is superior to that of others—after all, they do not as a rule feel that they have too much going on. It is only a question of efficiently organizing one's life and daily routines.

On several occasions I directly experienced the packed social program of even elderly residents in Djursholm. For instance, on one occasion when I was giving a presentation about my research project at a retirement home, only a handful of listeners showed up. "There is so much to choose between here as an elderly person," one person explained to me. "You have to weigh up your priorities the whole time." There are also so many role models for the elderly in Djursholm, exemplifying how one maintains an active, fully committed lifestyle and resists any notion of slumping into the passive, comfortable existence of the pensioner. Two of these role models are celebrated actors. In one of several newspaper articles written about them, it is described how they continue working hard and giving acclaimed performances in large theaters in Stockholm at a time when they are both more than eighty-five years old. One article is entitled "New Jobs in the Wings for the 85-Year-Olds." The journalist eulogizes as follows: "The wife receives me at the front door and I am quickly struck by the energy that emanates from her. . . . The same vitality is also seen in her husband—they have been married for 62 years—as he comes down the stairs." The subtext is similar in tone to a throw-away comment made by an employee at Djursholm's municipal office: "The age category among lenders at Djursholm's public library is high, but this would also be true of Djursholm in general. The pensioners here are very active." Or as one elderly resident put it:

> There's no problem keeping busy as a pensioner in Djursholm. For my own part, I am involved in several associations. Often you run into the same people, but in different contexts. . . . It's an enjoyable social contact. In the art club, for example, we have art trips, we visit cultural and historical places or maybe museums as a group. . . . My engagement with several of these associations probably has something to do with the pleasure I take in organizational questions, planning and preparing events, and getting people involved.

By maintaining an active involvement in several associations, as in the above statement, people retain a certain ability to be organized and focused. But it is just as important to stay socially effective: smooth, sympathetic, and outgoing. Social events are socially formative in all environments, but in a place like Djursholm with its manifold clubs and associations, the socially adapted and highly functional citizen is perfected to a much higher degree than communities where few activities, or no activities at all, are offered to the elderly. The retired inhabitant is not the typical loner in a country cottage, but rather an extroverted, "highly functional," and pleasant elderly person. Club events are mainly social events with dinners, lunches, and mingling as their dominant theme, but there is also the possibility of group excursions and trips. It is not just the social dimension that is consecrating—also the substance of the activities themselves performs the same function. Generally the associations have a long list of well-known and topical lecturers, whose presence lends a feeling of significance and potency to the events—quite distinct from the humdrum daily life one often associates with pensioners' lives.

If Djursholm, as I have concluded, is a community defined by its high level of activity, then the lion's share of this activity takes the form of physical activity. As one man explained to me: "The inhabitants are very good at being busy in their spare time; people jog here, they go skating, go for walks, or skiing in the winter. People really use their leisure time to the full." Or as another person informed me categorically, "Everyone here plays tennis and golf. People pursue sports and keep themselves moving." One elderly woman, talking to me about her childhood in Djursholm in the 1930s, said, "If any one thing has put its mark on Djursholm, it's the great outdoors. Both rich and poor always kept active. They went skating in the winter and sailing in the summer. Skiing was extremely popular. All in all it was an active life, lived in constant motion. There were no couch potatoes living in Djursholm back then, and I don't suppose there are any now either."

The community's palette of sporting activities is by no means only on offer for the adults. In fact it is to a very large degree focused on Djursholm's children and young people, which is obviously understandable, given that they are the actual precondition for, and also the object of, the consecration that is enacted. Schools in Djursholm offer the usual physical education during school hours. But even during lessons, some schools for younger children have "activities on the timetable to develop physical awareness," as one principal put it to me in an interview. In addition to normal school sporting activities, some of the schools offer extracurricular sports activities. A teacher at one of the schools told me that for a while they had tennis for the children, and they booked the tennis hall. "That was popular with the children." A physical education teacher explained: "There are a lot of sporting activities outside of school hours run by the school sports association. There's football, hockey, basket, indoor bandy, but also riding, golf, tennis, and downhill skiing. About 20–25 percent of the pupils in every year take part. That's a good turnout."

One man in his midtwenties, who had grown up in Djursholm, said: "When you grow up here it's important to have friends, to be good at a sport; you get pushed into doing various activities, to try lots of different things, there's a real push for that. People talk about all the football clubs, and which ones they are hoping for, even while the children are small. A lot of the children and young people are probably not involved in all these activities because they enjoy it, but because there's an expectation for them to be involved, active, meeting friends, and all that."

In spite of its many active sports clubs, however, Djursholm can hardly be described as a "sporting community." To see it in such terms would be a challenge to its unique status and aura. One parent offered the following opinion: "The football club here has always been marginal. This is not the sort of football community where everyone backs the local team. We have good teams in all the years, but we're fairly anonymous about it." Rather, the sporting associations emphasize that that they are "broad-based clubs"—to which all (residents in Djursholm) are welcome. Or, as the director of one of the clubs put it: "This club is not trying to be an elite club. We have broad vision. There are a lot of teams here, and every team has a really broad reach. We don't have an elite team where we put our best sporting talent, as other clubs do. . . . This is sport for everyone, and every-one should take part. The idea is for this to be a pleasant meeting place for all ages." At the golf club, one of the members made it clear to me that the club was not about elite performance but rather saw itself (in accordance with its tradition as a "family club") offering interesting social opportunities to local inhabitants. One man, a father of young children, told me at a sporting event that "sport is an interesting arena for parental ambition. Not so much because the parents are looking for the children to become sporting professionals, which is the sort of thing parents in many other places want, but because it lets them learn a certain mode of behavior in the form of activity, teamwork, performance, winning, and setting themselves high goals."

Djursholm, in other words, could be described as a community with a clear interest in sport, but not as a community that values sporting activity for its own sake. Children and young people should be sporty without seeking to become elite athletes. This emerged when I interviewed young people and parents, or when I read in newspaper articles about the choices made by the young people, from which it can generally be seen that studies always come before sporting activities, irrespective of how talented one may be. Certainly one would have to say that sporting activities are consecrating, but only if conducted with moderation, as described. When I interviewed one man who had lived in Djursholm for five years, he made this claim: "If you look at our young people, they seem more purposeful in their schoolwork than adolescents in other places. People here are brought up from an early age with the idea of having targets. School work is highly prioritized. Sporting activities can never be the main occupation or the principal goal. It's good to busy yourself with sports—it keeps you active and fit—but it has to play a subordinate role to studying."

The level of sporting activity in Djursholm, as already suggested, has many important social dimensions that promote a perception of oneself as a leader on purely moral grounds. One of these is about training oneself in being more organized and self-disciplined. But of even greater importance is the feeling of social superiority that comes from living a sporty and healthy life. Associated with this is the physique that is a by-product of it—a beautiful, slender body is generally considered more attractive than one that is limp and corpulent. As a fit and sporty man or woman one feels like a winner, and one can make a contribution to the presentation of Djursholm as a success story. If Djursholm were overwhelmingly populated by pale, overweight people, it would significantly damage its reputation as an abode of winners, also its reputation as a highly functional, morally superlative world, in terms of the generally accepted norms and values in the labor market and society. On the whole, being outdoors is considered important in Djursholm, which is further enabled by many residents owning houses with extensive grounds; so that children and young people have every possible opportunity of enjoying a physically active life.

A physically, socially active life, in which a great many different undertakings are considered more important than a single preoccupation, and a dynamic, forceful, and committed lifestyle, are certainly fundamental aspects of all forms of responsibility and the ability to self-organize and set targets for oneself. In this sense, Djursholm is not especially different from other places in terms of molding and socializing people into leaders. But the culture of activity plays itself out against the social and cultural status and aura from which the community has benefited over a long period of time. As I have already pointed out, the sporting activities and clubs, whose dominant forms are horseback riding, tennis, sailing, and golf, are linked to an elevated aesthetic outlook. Football may be popular, but only at the junior level. One is not likely to see blood, sweat, blows, and kicking when Djursholm gets into action mode; rather there will be a great deal of walking, riding, golf swings, and tennis playing. In a corresponding way, the various associations offer pensioners lectures and aesthetically edifying events. Even this becomes an arena for consecration. Whether the associations are about sport or something else, they do not make their members into experts in certain fields—in fact, more than anything, they are converted into aesthetic dittos.

5

FRAGRANT, SOCIABLE PERSONAGES

T HE PEOPLE who, historically and also in the present, populate Djursholm have often worked in professions that placed great stress on
their ability to control, discipline, organize, and guide their own
actions, whether as company executives, professors, military officers,
doctors, lawyers, civil servants, or similar. The same thing might be said of
a housewife. To a very great extent the capacity to project such qualities is
about transmitting a particular kind of social impression to others. These
virtues are highly valued in Djursholm, and one can see them fully expressed in obituaries of deceased residents, or in panegyrics published in
local newspapers, for instance, on the occasion of birthdays. One employee
in home-help service in Djursholm felt that "the elderly folk I meet are
usually very disciplined. They have their agendas in order; they have complete control over both the big and the small things. I'm far more bohemian and disorganized, so it has actually been good for me to work with
the elderly in Djursholm. They give me structure. I have learned that if one
organizes one's time, it is possible to get a lot more done. I mean, time is
life! By being so well organized they save time, after all." One man who
had grown up in Djursholm expressed himself as follows: "Many of the
people who live here are maintaining the fabric of society. They're executives, lawyers, medical doctors, and professors. These people can't detract

so very much from the system, because they are the system. In this sense they are stable and predictable people."

In Djursholm it is unusual for people to lose their composure. As already said, it is not a "socially discordant" or untidy environment. When I eat in a restaurant or café frequented by the locals, the atmosphere is rarely noisy or confused. People talk in muted tones, they do not laugh loudly, and as a rule they avoid coarse language. Although people may feel a certain disquiet or upset, they know that they have to restrain themselves emotionally: in this way, the aesthetic qualities of the community are retained. To a great extent, the self-discipline to which the residents collectively aspire is about conveying a certain personal and social tone, rather than displaying a sort of "technical rationality" in day-to-day life. Getting angry, irate, raising one's voice, getting worked up—this is not often seen in the public space. For my own part, I have not once come across people fiercely arguing in a public place or parents yelling at their children. One man clarified this to me: "You have to make an effort, and try to be nice. There's a payoff when you're nice; it's never worth creating hostilities. We're supposed to have a pleasant time, and we're supposed to be pleasant. I think we know how to do this out here. You can make a difference. And you do it by being pleasant."

The ability to control oneself, in Djursholm, is based on certain norms of social behavior, which emphasize the manner in which people interact with others. Eye contact, tone of voice, and body language are important in this respect. The word *pleasant* often comes up in conversation, for instance, when one runs into someone in town or when parting after a meeting. The clubs put great emphasis on the importance of events being "pleasant," as opposed to provocative, thought-provoking, or challenging as in certain other clubs. That political debate (to the extent it at all exists) in Djursholm is "civilized" also helps form the inhabitants into *pleasant* people, as opposed to affected, heated, or, even worse, cantankerous debaters. The pleasantness in Djursholm has an important aesthetic value: it contributes to the making of a community that appears so much *better* than places that are characterized by disunity and contention, dirt, noise, heated and hollering people lacking in poise. As a general rule, it is

considered ideal to be sympathetic, friendly, and congenial in one's relations with others—in short, to have a socially presentable and harmonious
manner. To remain socially "civilized," to act in a "civilized" manner, is
admittedly to a certain extent about "technical" factors, but it is far more
about behaving in a worthy, dignified, and stoic manner. This is at the core
of Djursholm's aura and its capacity for consecration: statesmanlike behavior implies a higher morality and a better mode of living. It is also at
the core of all effective leadership, by the setting of norms calibrated by
lifestyle factors, particularly against a background of the ideals that generally influence the cultural and conceptual framework of corporate life.

The fact that especially children and young people in a variety of ways
are trained in organizing themselves and learning to appear in a certain
light before others can be exemplified by the leisure activities with which
they are engaged. In the schools, to which I return in detail later, much
emphasis is placed on the ability of pupils to organize themselves. One
teacher explained it to me: "For me, responsibility and participation is
important for the students. You are not only supposed to be responsible for
yourself, but also for your surroundings. We actually form each other's
environment. One has to ask oneself, and others, to think about how one
is behaving." Also the children are trained to be socially responsible for
their lives at home, which in all significant respects is about the ability to
present oneself in a socially acceptable manner. When I spoke about this
to a student, she told me that every Sunday she and her mother made a
plan for the coming week. "Mum wants me to be involved, so I can take
care of all this myself later." Her mother elaborated further: "The important thing is to be able to organize one's days so one can get the maximum
out of them. Before, I was the one who pushed this, but now she takes the
initiative and wants these planning meetings." The shared activity between
mother and daughter was not only about organizing the coming week, it
was also a way for the mother to pass on some of her values in terms of how
one approached the challenges of life.

Life is not to be lived spontaneously, but in an organized manner. This
can be seen in the children's self-awareness in various social milieus;

through self-observation they control their (childish) behavior—at least in certain situations. One of the instructors at a youth activity center felt that "the children are not so creative or filled with a sense of initiative; usually the instructors have to push things along. The children are not used to trying things out." This was also the view taken by an organizer in another club: "The children and young people we meet here are not super-self-sustaining; they're not so dynamic. We have to organize and keep things chugging along. They're used to being spoon-fed or having someone else that calls the shots, but I also have a feeling that they worry about doing things differently from their friends." In a socially and aesthetically conscious environment, where great weight is placed on *how* one does things than what those things are, it is easy to make mistakes. Yet at the same time it is the ability to behave *in the right way* that gives the young people of Djursholm a social head start on others. They are brought up to organize their lives by being "subjected" to a legion of activities; this conditions them into a certain behavioral approach to the world.

The consecration of people into leaders in Djursholm, especially children and adolescents, is not about creating rebels but rather socially aware individuals. By definition it is all more about being determined and active than highly creative. The elevation offered by Djursholm forms people's social dispositions, which is about apparently occupying a high moral position on the basis of established norms and conventions. One company executive informed me, "If you can't perform and hit targets, it creates an insecurity in you. This is not a community that values experimentation and play." He went on: "Society, and this is very much relevant to Djursholm, is extremely focused on measurable results. Those who are good at these measurable attributes do well. So in Djursholm there's a focus on certain abilities in the children and adolescents. It's about tangible results. There's no interest in risk; there's a fear of being a social failure and making a fool of oneself. All the energy goes into attaining certain targets that have been set, and because of that there's an unwillingness to try out different, alternative routes." Another resident, also a company executive, told me, "The young people learn to be administrators, to handle things smoothly, and keep their heads down. They learn to be cautious and self-restrained. That's not leadership or the entrepreneurial spirit as far as I'm concerned. I'm sure many of these young people will find themselves good jobs, but they won't take the top spots. You don't win the Nobel Prize because of your contacts and by being polite and pleasant, or flexible and adaptable." Another resident felt that "people here are a bit too comfortable to become dogged entrepreneurs, who will mortgage their homes and sleep on camp beds because of some idea they burn for, an idea they're prepared to risk the approval of their friends and acquaintances for—or risk anything at all for."

That the children and young people, much like the adults, in fact, could be described as well brought up and showing a high degree of self-discipline, I was able to confirm for myself in a number of interviews and observations in the field. For instance, this might be seen in their way of dressing or expressing themselves, or, as one person explained: "We have a *code of conduct* here." During a visit to a sport club, one of the instructors called over an adolescent training there, a young woman who presented herself to us and more or less saluted before engaging in conversation. Once the instructor was satisfied with her answers, she was given leave to go away, which she did without delay. A teacher at one of the schools described the children as "socially well behaved; you have to be pleasant around here. They can be real blockheads sometimes, but they're taught to behave themselves." One mother who had recently moved into the area told me: "The children in Djursholm are so conforming; they don't learn to question things, or even discuss or criticize. They learn to walk on a leash, to be unobtrusive." One twenty-year-old who had recently moved out of Djursholm, felt similar: "Young people there are more appropriate and willing to fit in. They don't stick out; they're careful about what they say. You find the original types among the older people, with the odd exception."

There is a broad emphasis on children and adolescents being conscientious and pleasant. As I have already pointed out, they are pivotal to the aura of the community, and their behavior is instrumental in the process of consecration. As one father put it: "As a child, you are obviously expected to take care of your studies, you are expected to handle yourself appropriately." Many parents emphasized to me the importance of raising their children to have common sense and good manners. One father in his midthirties put it to me as follows: "If I have to mention one thing in day-to-life that I try to communicate to our children, is that they must say 'hello' and 'thank you.' Anyone who knows that, can go far. It brings a lot of positivity. One makes a good impression. My parents said, 'this is how you do it, no elbows on the table, a firm handshake.' If you want to be noticed, get yourself a job where you can run things with good manners and common sense as a cornerstone." And "common sense and good manners" are essential in child rearing, a central expression of the moral elevation that a life in Djursholm confers.

The possibility of exerting leadership through moralizing is based on a perception in others that one is a sensible person well worth listening to; in this, obviously, one's social behavior is absolutely essential. One elderly resident told me: "When I was a child we often had to help serve food when we had social events at home. These were big parties for friends and neighbors, three courses, and dancing. One learned a lot from that." The head of one of the sporting associations, who did not himself live in the area, felt that "the children from Djursholm have been taught how to behave themselves. They shake hands, they practically bow to you." One person in her eighties, who grew up in an orphanage in Djursholm, told me: "I had several friends who lived with their families, and several of them came to visit us. I think they enjoyed coming to us; there was so much going on. In their own homes it was very calm and controlled, more or less an adult environment. . . . But we'd all been taught manners, we said thanks and we curtsied, and we knew how to behave. In that way I don't think we stood out from the other children in Djursholm." Staff working at the schools and preschools gave similar opinions:

The children are very nice and polite. They never call one "bloody old cow" or similar.

(Teacher)

Our children talk in a very proper way; it's almost cultivated. There's no slang, no swearing. They know how to handle themselves at the table, their manners are perfect.

(Preschool Teacher)

The pupils here are very polite. On my first day here they shook my hand.

(Teacher)

Most of the children here are very well brought up, they're extremely polite and always say hello, they always have something to say for themselves.

(Teacher)

The children are well mannered; you can have conversations with them that are really pleasant, and illuminating. They're precocious, you might say.

(Teacher)

Most of the students know how to behave with adults. You are treated with respect and politeness. You would never find yourself being sworn or yelled at.

(Teacher)

Child rearing in Djursholm is largely about the ability of the children to make a certain impression on the surrounding world of themselves as socially functional, sympathetic, and pleasant mannered. One of teachers that I interviewed maintained that "the young people here are coached into giving the right answers, solidly and clearly, which creates an impression of a competent outlook." A youth worker made the following statement on the same theme: "There was a project a few years ago, where many of the young people from Djursholm where working with similarly aged people from a socially more mixed area. You noticed enormous differences. The adolescents from here were extroverted, worldly, and very grown-up in their manner. When they met adults they walked up to shake hands and knew how to have a conversation. The adolescents from the other area almost tiptoed along the walls and mainly looked as if they'd like to disappear into holes in the ground." The head of a preschool told me: "When our five-year-olds come to the end of their time with us and move up to the classes for six-year-olds, we're often told that they are very advanced socially, they can hold their own, and they're open, too. Basically they are quite social in their outlook; they've come far in their ability to function in groups and interact with other children and adults. I think it's to do with how we consciously train them from an early age to learn the social game, to have that ability to function socially." One woman in her midtwenties who grew up in the area felt that "already at the time of preschool we were drilled to behave a certain way. I learned to shake hands properly from the age of four, to hold out my hand and look the other person in the eye. And hold the cutlery correctly and say, 'Thank you for the food.' When you are having drinks you have to introduce yourself to everyone. You notice the people who never had that kind of training, they can come across as fairly handicapped." Her girlfriend added: "When you grow up in Djursholm you learn to be an extrovert, to be interested and open, and not let yourself be trodden on. You're expected to take the chance if it comes up. Those of us who grew up there are quite driven; we've all had parents who worked hard." Another interviewee, a man who had lived all his life in Djursholm and had both children and grandchildren living there, explained the following:

> There's a certain panache to this place. The children also have panache, they introduce themselves properly, and so on. The children are taught to shake hands properly; you don't get some limp hand like a dishrag. They squeeze your hand and look into your eyes when they talk to you. Eating properly is also very important, not slouching with your elbows on the table or talking with your mouth full. People generally don't have table manners anymore—so how will they get through life? When you get out there to look for work, well, it's not only your medical training, your legal education, or whatever, that is important. It is also your general

education in how to conduct yourself that counts, how to say hello to someone with a steady gaze, and eating in a pleasant way. The children have to be inculcated to have a sanguine, confident, and correct manner—this can only be in their favor. . . . Public speaking is also important. I think that children should be schooled in that from an early age. For instance, if they are with one of their friends and meeting the parents and maybe having dinner there, surely that is a good opportunity to hold a little speech to say thank you for the food and how "it's very nice to come here and play."

The demands and expectations concerning the good behavior of children and young people is a constantly recurring theme. As has already been argued, children are of central importance in the aura of the community as a well-functioning, well-organized, pleasant, and, in every possible way, attractive environment. The children are not only vital for the adults in creating networks; they are the foundation, as well as the target group, of consecration. For this reason child rearing has always been a matter of priority, and it is not the sort of thing that is left to chance. The main focus is on sociability. Some of the clubs and associations have prizes for schoolchildren, with the idea of promoting the social skills of young people. One of the prizes is called "Best Friend" and another club offers the so-called Friendliness Award, both of which recognize a certain kind of social behavior. The latter, according to the association's website, is about rewarding schoolchildren "who help create a sense of comradery at school" or "take practical steps to promote a spirit of community."

In a community like Djursholm the priority is very much about turning children into adults—and by this I mean responsible, active, highly committed individuals—which is also a guarantee of the community's elevated aesthetic values. This theme will be revisited later, as it is a central part of pedagogic approach in Djursholm and absolutely vital to its ability to function as a leader community. Children, wherever they are, tend to make things untidy and ruin the peace. There are varying levels of tolerance for this, depending on where one is. For instance, a number of letters to the members' magazine of the tennis club in Djursholm are focused on the question of the social milieu. One member wrote as follows: "When my group of male friends come to play in the middle of the day, it is almost not possible to get changed because of all the children's clothes in the changing rooms—children who don't hang up their clothes on the hooks, merely throw them on the benches or the floor. The children are also very noisy, and this ruins the setting for our visit to the tennis club." Indeed, Djursholm always seeks to be a well-ordered and aesthetically attractive environment.

On the web page for Djursholm's tennis club, one can find a document entitled "Rules of Behavior for Juniors." In it, the following desirable social attributes are stipulated for juniors playing matches, training, or simply visiting the tennis hall:

- Listen to and respect your playing partners and trainer.
- Always do your best.
- Be punctual.
- Be a good friend.
- Listen and be attentive to your trainer.
- Ensure you are appropriately dressed for tennis.
- "Pep yourself up" positively.
- Also "pep up" your friends.
- No uncalled-for comments are required.
- Always try to do your best and enjoy yourself on the court.
- Stick to sportsmanlike behavior.
- Be a "good" loser.
- Be a "good" winner.
- Maintain a positive body language.
- Be a fair judge (fair play).
- Go in and have fun on the court.
- Thank your opponent at the end of a match.
- Bear in mind that you represent this club.
- Contribute to a good atmosphere at the club.
- Strive to have team spirit and a sense of community.
- Treat others as you would like to be treated.

- Put your shoes in the shoe rack at the entrance, or use shoe protectors.
- Do not disrupt those whose games are in progress.
- Hang up your clothes neatly and tidily in the changing rooms.
- Use the bins provided for rubbish, etc.
- Be polite.

The list, quite clearly, is long—and demanding.

Adults are also expected to perform social heroics, as is tellingly described in a book by a professor in social anthropology who grew up in Djursholm. It suggests that the community is formed by a cultural code that "stands for a broad fabric of life covering etiquette, style, and tone of interaction. . . . The basic components of it are: family, tradition, modesty, loyalty, sport, and music. . . . An outward sense of modesty and an ability to conduct oneself in more or less any social situation, which might be anything from a quick encounter in the supermarket to a grand dinner with the royal family, without for that reason slavish adhering to the prevailing etiquette—these are some other traits that characterize the inhabitants." According to the author, this social code also contains certain taboos: "Above all this includes the wearing of any sort of synthetic material in clothes and accessories, as well as any sort of overly obvious consumption of luxury articles, the latter being a sign of insecurity typical of new money. The combination of several luxury articles is particularly negative. One is permitted to have a few, indeed, one must have a few—this is a necessary part of the whole."

As a visitor or observer in Djursholm one might be impressed by the locals and especially the children and young people's pleasant, civil, and all-in-all highly presentable style, and yet from time to time all this proves to be without substance. On the whole there is a wish and an active attempt to *appear* flawless, but the reality is rarely as simple as that. One business owner by the central square explained the following: "Many of the youngsters, especially the girls, smoke like chimneys. They come here to eat, and then they sit somewhere out of sight so they can have a smoke." A study conducted by an independent company in a school stated that the students were "pleasant, positive, polite, and calm"; also that the school itself was "a tranquil place, in an area of natural beauty"; further, "in the two days that we have been on the premises we have not seen a single instance of any rules being broken" and that "the school has an extremely pleasant atmosphere," where "there are rarely any instances of mobbing, bullying, or exclusion," and so on. The picture that emerges in the report is that of an exemplary school, which is conveyed by the behavior of the children—a paradigm for the whole country, one might say, with children that almost seem admirable. And yet, at the end of the report, an additional comment is made: "The pupils are careful to behave in an exemplary manner during our visit, and they know that they are effectively representing their school. In various conversations during meetings with staff and pupils, it emerges in their statements that some of the pupils have apparently acted in such a way as to 'keep up appearances.' They know how they must behave in day-to-day life and in school." When I interviewed one of the principals in Djursholm, he made the following claim: "There's a lot of 'looking good' going on. . . . They want to be seen and regarded as capable, smart, hardworking pupils. Pupils caught cheating are very upset, not about the cheating per se, but rather because the illusion has cracked, the illusion of being excellent students. They are all incredibly aware of the social codes." Children and young people are expected to behave in a socially impeccable way, with emphasis on being sympathetic, approachable, and thoroughly pleasant. This becomes a codex for a morally superior lifestyle. In this context, the ability to maintain this lifestyle is significant. And yet it can hardly be considered a startling fact that not everyone lives in accordance with their own teachings.

Whenever I was out and about in the public space (with the exception of the playgrounds), I was always struck by how rarely one sees children and young people making a commotion, so to speak, and spreading themselves around, especially in the town center. There are "zones" of play for children, primarily preschool and school playgrounds. Outside these zones there is little room for such exuberance. Public places do not seem to be intended for children to play in—with all the ensuing implications of not thinking about the consequences of such behavior. Children lacking self-discipline and ability to, so to speak, "handle themselves" in the community, is the subject of critical scrutiny (as the example from the tennis club suggests), and when the issue is analyzed in context, this may not be so very surprising. The aura of the community always hangs in the balance. Local newspapers contain letters from persons living in Djursholm who have views on the behavior of the youngsters. In one such letter, for instance, a woman criticizes the raucous atmosphere among students during celebrations at the end of the summer term. "Must one really drink, yell, and throw bottles?" she asks. "Parents and schools have to react. Not make light of it. When a student at one of the schools accepts a grant with his hat on and his hands in his pocket, is not this a sign of insecurity?" And then she sums it up: "Surely people of all ages benefit from a measure of order and style!"

The aura and prestige that confer value to the inhabitants presuppose a social environment that seems not only sympathetic and charming but also stable and socially harmonious. In this context, one has to be able to deal with setbacks and crisis in life without losing one's composure and thereby risk putting oneself in a light that might appear to be irrational, unforeseeable, illogical, emotional, and, quite simply, "uncivilized." One woman clarified this to me in an interview: "People handle things here. When I got divorced, none of our neighbors wanted to take a position either for or against my husband. And hardly anyone even wanted to refer to the fact that the family was splitting up. Anything emotional is sensitive ground; anything sensitive is sensitive ground. But people were probably not indifferent or neutral about it; there was probably a good deal of talk, even if I never got to hear it." Another woman put it as follows: "I feel absolutely like an outsider in Djursholm and I don't want to be like the other wives. I think I'm a happy, spontaneous person, not so guarded or self-restrained. I do what I feel like doing, express my feelings, cry, laugh a lot—laugh loudly. Quite simply I don't have the check on my impulses that is so important out here." A girlfriend of hers who took part in our conversation added: "In Djursholm you're not allowed to feel bad; you can't be feeling down, or look sad. The idea is that you should think ahead and never look back. You're not supposed to brood on things and walk around in a gloom; you're supposed to surge on ahead and not be dejected.

On the other hand, you're not to be too cheerful either, or worked up. Positive is good but not euphoric." The lifestyle and norm stipulate that you should seem an engaged, positive person. It is vital for problems and concerns to be portrayed as positive challenges rather than just as problems and concerns.

An employee at one of the preschools in Djursholm made the following assertion in an interview:

> The children don't know any other life than the one they have, with all the activities, so I find they are mostly in good spirits. But sometimes I have to say it's not so serious to be bored from time to time; children have the ability to keep themselves occupied and it's even good if they have to create things to do on their own, without the adults always organizing it for them. . . . I feel that one isn't allowed to have a "dull" time in Djursholm; it always has to be "fun and challenging," and the children are expected to be happy and positive. This is really a positive and active community. We see that in the parents, who are always so well turned out and cheerful and so on. They don't go around with sorry faces; at least we don't see any of that.

Great emphasis is put on what is sometimes colloquially referred to as "social competence," which more precisely means to be socially presentable and distinguished. On one occasion I spoke to a company executive, who told me: "My job has to a very great degree been about showing my face, being absolutely there in the companies where I was working. It has been an important factor to know how to carry myself and adapt to various situations." A highly developed capacity for self-control and self-discipline (or, in other words, moderation) could be seen as a typical requirement of the kinds of jobs that the residents have today, and have had in the past, and decent social skills have also always been crucial. One man said: "I don't have any difficulties when I come into new environments. I have social competence, I'm not a back-office guy. I love doing business; I mean, it's about meeting people and achieving good results." A woman asserted, "Being a lone wolf here doesn't work, at least not if you're a housewife like me. You're expected to be sociable, cheerful, and positive." And a young man of eighteen who had just finished his upper-secondary education felt that "in Djursholm you can't be a nerd; you have to be socially active and attractive." One woman in her midtwenties who grew up in the town felt that "social competence is an important attribute to succeed and be accepted; in the sense of having a sense of curiosity, of being able to adapt, and be smooth. To fit in and be a leader." An instructor in one of the youth associations pointed out, "Sure, you learn to be a dynamic person here who raises his head and doesn't just melt into the crowd. But you're not supposed to stick out too much either, or make yourself difficult. You have to be fluid and work well socially." One elderly resident felt, on this topic, that "you should be rounded and generous in your approach. You can't just be pushing your own agenda *no matter what*. The idea is not that you should kick people around; I mean, we have to live together out here." Social fluidity is taken for granted in Djursholm.

An important condition for this community's emphasis on social ability and training is the private homes. All in all it seems as if the houses have almost been built for the purpose of social events and so-called hospitality. Many of the people I interviewed mentioned their large circle of friends and acquaintances, and several also spoke of strong ties with family and relatives, this being an important arena for social training, especially for the children. That the process takes place in a milieu like Djursholm also affects the social behavior that is developed. One man put it as follows: "My wife and I socialize with in the region of one hundred people, and fifty of them are very close friends." When I met people in public places, such as cafés and restaurants, some of them were keen to accentuate, throughout the interview, the many people they had to greet. Quite simply there was a good deal of "hi, hi," especially among the men, almost as if they wished to manifest how many people they knew, the large number of people with whom they socialized, which also surfaced in the form of name-dropping. On the whole, such factors give expression to a person's social attributes. Living in large houses where a great number of people can come together and living in a community that places emphasis on one's social skills are both contributory factors in the formation of one's identity and self. It's something quite different from living in a cramped apartment or subsisting in a life of limited social interaction. Djursholm's social character is of a regal kind—one in which a "larger world" is expected—and on offer. This contributes to the formation of not only the social personality but also a grandiose social personality that is put together in such a way that it functions in important social contexts. Djursholm consecrates people into leaders through the norms by which its inhabitants more or less successfully orient themselves, which to all intents and purposes are about living a certain kind of life, in which active and sociable living is idealized. After all, this consecration takes place in the light of the community's social *esprit* and culture, the latter making Djursholm seem so much better and more functional than the surrounding world. Being trained into a social outlook is thus emphasized with children and young people in Djursholm, a great deal of activity being seen as something positive in one's definition among other people, but certain activities also being viewed as preferable to others. As one fifteen-year-old girl explained: "Horseback riding is an individual sport; you get better at it all the time. I take it in turns with football, so I also learn to work in a team."

As I have explained, the lifestyle is very much about presenting oneself as active and positive. It is important that problems and concerns are portrayed as stimulating challenges. One employee at Djursholm's municipal office stated:

> When it's a question of getting parents involved here, for example, to get them to come along to parenting workshops, you mustn't have a problem focus, because if you do, no one will come. Instead we have to put it another way and make it seem more positive by reference to certain phrases such as "coaching your teenager into not drinking" or "how to be stronger as a parent," and so on.

A teacher at one of the schools emphasized to me that "here in Djursholm there is a belief in the idea of everything will work out for the best. It's a good ideology in many ways. People don't give up so easily, and they don't get so discouraged by setbacks. If your child is weak when it comes to mathematics, well, then you do something about it, for instance, by organizing private classes. Or you emphasize the child's superior language skills. People don't let themselves be put off by problems. The whole approach obviously also transmits to the children."

Many parents spoke to me about the importance of their children's activities being "fun and engaging," irrespective of whether this related to school or sports or other club activities. One father went on to explain: "My children found it so dull in school; they were not inspired or involved."

There are also plenty of festive occasions in the form of special anniversaries or similar community institutions or clubs, all of which contribute to a social expectation of a certain mode of interaction between people. And on this basis one could go on to say that there is a norm in Djursholm that stipulates that one should be positive and always communicative, and look toward the future with confidence. Even when there are actual "tangible" reasons for sorrow and concern, such as poor health or divorce, there is a desire to describe oneself in a positive and "socially presentable" way. In one newspaper article, a well-known person living in Djursholm makes the following statement: "Hell, yeah, I feel quite good. A lot of people think a heck of a lot's happened in my life. But yeah, I feel good. It's a choice I make. I've faced up to what's happened in the past and I've built up my strength." She describes her philosophy on child rearing. It's about engendering a "can-do" feeling in the child. She goes on: "When I bought a TV weighing about 60 kilos, it said in the brochure there had to be three of you to assemble it. 'But Mum, there are three of us,' said the children. 'Yes, I've done it! They've got it!' I thought." The broken marriage, meanwhile, is handled by "making the best, not making a song and dance of it, and being a grown-up."

6

COMMUNITY AND SOCIAL PARTITION

D JURSHOLM IS A PLACE in which there has been a keenness for everything, since its inception, to be viewed as a part of a community, where a certain culture, spirit, and organization puts its stamp on the day-to-day life and creates a social homogeneity and solidarity among its inhabitants—quite simply, a sense of community among the residents. One man told me: "Djursholm is not a suburb; I have an issue with that word. Djursholm is a town; it's a community in its own right." The fundamental values create the boundary by which Djursholm is separated from the world at large, and they become a cultural and cognitive device for the inhabitants to interpret that world. One man expressed his opinion of those moving there as follows: "They thought they were just buying a house, but they found themselves in a community. The nouveau riche are schooled here into activism; people are expected to get involved once they are living in Djursholm." A rudimentary but illustrative expression for this is the prevailing culture of meeting and greeting in the community, which I noted on many occasions and which is based on a notion of the residents belonging to a certain social constellation. Not saying "hello" to one another when meeting on the street almost becomes a challenge to this idea, but also a confirmation of social outsider-hood. One man told me: "Djursholm today is attracting people whose values leave a lot to be desired. It's always been something quite natural here to say hello to people when you run into them in the street. Those who don't say hello are not from here. But the people moving into the area now are different; they actually don't say hello to you. The people coming in now lack basic values; they have totally lost their human values." The residents want to own something together, something that separates them from the surrounding world—a feeling that they have a collective sense of fundamental values.

One teacher, who worked in Djursholm but did not live there, felt that "when you come to Djursholm you get bothered by the level of social interaction," and a staff member for the home-help servicemen explained her view as follows: "What is the meaning of Djursholm? It just means sticking together." A recent arrival said, "All the parents know one another here; it sometimes feels a bit daunting. Many of them have been friends since they were children, and it's not easy entering into networks like that." Several of the residents or others that I interviewed explained in a variety of ways that Djursholm as a place is defined by a significant level of social cohesion. What follows are a series of illustrative citations on this theme:

The thing that really defined my growing up in Djursholm is the feeling of belonging to a fellowship, or a network, if you will. You are a part of the group. You know everyone; you know where everyone lives, or where they have lived.

(Man, Forties)

The scurrilous image of Djursholm is that it's a community where everyone serves his own interests, that we're all egotistical types. But when I grew up in Djursholm it was a community where there was a lot of closeness between people, and I think there still is today. There were holes in the fences between the gardens so the children could run from one house to another.

(Woman, Fifties)

Certainly there are a great many people who move to Djursholm and aren't concerned about their neighbors or the community as a whole. There is also a group of egotists here. But there are also lots of people who are very involved in their community, in the schools, in the life here. There is a great deal of fellowship. The egotists are not from here, and they don't want to, or can't cope with entering into the spirit of community here.

(Woman, Sixty-Five)

Maybe the foremost expression of the desire to manifest and tangibly maintain a sense of fellowship is the very active local history association, which counts many of the households in the area among its membership. The association publishes books about Djursholm, awards prizes to worthy local citizens, arranges cultural walks in the area, and in many other ways acts as a social institution for the dissemination of the community's unique cultural values. Other associations fill similar roles, for instance, the home owners' association, which offers residents a meeting place and a way of collectively responding to various questions, while at the same time trying to have an impact on the character and form of the community by handing out prizes for garden design and house refurbishment and extensions. Another example is the association of one of the local schools. According to the constitution of this association, it functions as "a joint venture between teachers, ex-teachers, and ex-students of Djursholm School." The purpose of the association is to "promote fellowship among the students and act for the good of the school and in support of the studies and outdoor activities of the student body." The various editions of the association's annual refer to a range of jubilees and commemorations, and there is always a reference to the annual meeting, which is like a party with a good deal of glamour. Most of the articles are richly illustrated, mainly with photos of students and ex-students. The men wear suits, dinner jackets, or tails, depending on the occasion. The women are attired with similar formality. As a general rule the many associations seem to indicate that the residents wish to get involved in their community, for instance, by means of charitable activities. In general, the associations make a contributory effort, especially the sporting associations, such as the tennis club, the golf club, the equestrian club, and the football club, where people can meet and socialize across the generational divide.

This becomes an important exercise in mutual learning in terms of what it means to be living in Djursholm while also marking out the clear boundary of social distinction from the rest of the world. One of the people I interviewed felt that "the sporting life plays an important social function in Djursholm, both for young and old." Another person explained: "We are members of various clubs and associations here." And another put this in context by saying, "Clubs and associations are how one socializes here." An elderly resident went on: "There is intense activity at club level here. As an elderly person you have no problems at all keeping yourself busy. People are active and involved. But the younger families seem to socialize more among themselves than older people." There are also plenty of events that reveal the extent to which Djursholm would like to see itself as a community with a high level of sociability. For instance, at the library there are repeated exhibitions about the community, as well as authors' readings. Every year there are markets in the main square, where the residents can meet in a spontaneous and unforced manner. Two institutions are of particular importance for the sense of belonging and togetherness of the community: the old Djursholm Castle and Djursholm Chapel. The former is popular as a venue for association meetings or private parties and offers a majestic environment, a fitting location for Djursholm's population. The chapel, frequently used for christenings, weddings, and funerals, is especially popular around Christmastime. One person who was involved with the running of the chapel explained that Christmas Eve is particularly intense, with services at nine o'clock in the morning for the youngest children, then at ten o'clock for the slightly older children. Christmas Mass is held at four o'clock in the afternoon and eleven thirty in the evening, followed by an earlier service the following morning. "Many residents come for two services, usually both for Christmas evensong and Mass." Indeed, the chapel holds symbolic importance for the residents. A previous vicar made the following statement: "The chapel remains an important institution here, a meeting place for the families." One of the elderly residents felt that the chapel, in its own right and through the various activities it organized, "has a strengthening effect on the sense of community and belonging here." However, the foremost social arena, as mentioned earlier, is the schools, and I come back to this later.

It certainly seems a quite reasonable supposition that Djursholm is a sociable area with plenty of meeting places for the residents, and that the community nurtures a shared identity and foundation of values. There is absolutely a strong collective identity, embodied in a particular kind of lifestyle. Yet the type of social togetherness that is desired, idealized, and in many cases also pursued, is nonetheless also in many respects remote, formalized, planned, and organized. Or, to use another term: the community is *individualistic*. What this means is that spontaneously instigated relationships with people in Djursholm are sociably hazardous for oneself—also for the prestige and aura of the community as a whole. Consecration is a delicate process and highly sensitive. Social relationships established by means of associations and other organizations, which often imply that one has been formally "accredited" as a member by a process of selection, are significantly more secure. Djursholm's aura, its status as an elevated community with an enviable lifestyle, is dependent on the behavior of the residents. The value that can be conferred by its culture is based on its continued position of being generally perceived as a high-status place by the surrounding world—quite simply, that it has an aura.

As has already been confirmed, children are viewed as a prerequisite for becoming a part of the unique fellowship of Djursholm. Yet the mere fact of having children is not enough to guarantee automatic integration. The children must first be viewed as socially attractive in terms of the norms and values. Some families are not very likely to pass muster. A local civil servant expressed the following:

> We have housed a number of refugee children at a certain address in Djursholm. I often ask myself, "Did we do the right thing to these families?" After all, they are already at such a huge social and economic disadvantage in relation to others in society. On the one hand, at least they won't come into contact with any gangs that could lead them into criminality, but, on the other hand, they are unlikely to integrate in any way. They will remain alone and isolated. How are they received? Do they get invited to parties? I hope so. At any rate they stick out here, and those that stick out are rarely popular. We actually get some complaints

from residents in the area, who say that "the children are disruptive." How could anyone object to having children playing in a yard? Or is it because they "stick out" too much?

But whether one has children or not, a number of the people I interviewed testified to the difficulty of being accepted into the larger fellowship of Djursholm, and that the relationships remained distant. This, as I argued earlier, relates to the social risk one takes as a resident in becoming intimate with another inhabitant. One man explained, "If you come to Djursholm as a neutral person not yet properly marketed, then you don't exist. I was a well-known person when I got here, and that has kept me going ever since. I was already on the residents' radar when I came here." He went on to make the following assertion:

One might think the atmosphere is a bit stiff in Djursholm, but if one says hello to people and acts in a friendly manner, people are much the same as anywhere else. If one is open and disarming, one is similarly met by openness. But the spontaneous mode of life here is not informal or open. I am a fairly sociable type, a likable sort of person, and that is how people know me. It has made it easy for me to make my way into this community, but I could hardly claim to know any of the people here very well. The old families keep to themselves, of course. They are playing on the other half of the pitch. But probably one has to go along with that, it is probably much the same as in many other communities.

Famous people are precisely that—famous—and for that very reason they are less risky from a social perspective. A recently arrived family without any prior connection to the community is received cordially, yet with a certain caution. It must show that it has the capacity to contribute to the development of the community in accordance with the existing norms and values. After all, a lot hangs in the balance for the Djursholm resident, both socially and financially. To become associated with the "wrong" person can become far more damaging than in other places. And so there is a feeling among the new arrivals that I spoke to, meaning those who had not grown up there, that the establishment of social contacts in the community as an adult is far from easy. One woman in her seventies, who had lived the greater part of her life in Djursholm, explained: "Some of the new people coming in say, 'Oh, it's so hard getting accepted in Djursholm.' Well by the time you get to our age your social group is full; we have a lot of acquaintances. If you're going to let anyone new in, well, there has to be something quite special about that person." One man told me that, in his view, it was a sealed-off world to which newly arrived families found it difficult gaining entry. "I think people ask themselves if they can really *trust* the new family." One mother told me in an interview: "I don't think I'm the only mother who has had the experience at every parents' evening at school of there being a group of mothers who stand and talk among themselves, and don't let anyone else into the group. No wonder their daughters turn out just the same!" Djursholm's aura, which is so central to the consecration of the residents, is based on a sense of social distance from the rest of the world. For this reason relationships must also retain this sense of distance.

One crucial categorization, which most of those who decide to move there must face up to, even if they are coming back after a period of absence, is that of the "new" or "old" resident. A teacher at one of the schools explained it to me as follows: "There is a strong sense of hierarchy here. You notice it when people meet. The new faces are on the bottom rung of the social ladder, but even those who have been living here for a fair length of time may be regarded as 'new' and, for this reason, less important." The designation *new resident* is commonly used in a critical or even derogatory sense, to describe shortcomings in the recent arrivals, in terms of a lack of tact and tone, custom, behavior, and habits, which are set against the alleged more morally advanced and socially elevated mode of living among *old residents*. The new group, of course, is expected to form impressions and adapt in accordance with the norms of the latter. The well-established residents are considered to be those that give Djursholm its character and soul. In the following section I present a number of quotations from my interviews, all of which illustrate the phenomenon of the *new residents*. Whether young or old, these are the opinions of individuals belonging to families that have lived in Djursholm for one or more generations, which is to say that they are the so-called *old Djursholm people*:

The wrong values are coming in.

The new IT and finance people moving into Djursholm don't have the right sort of style. They gut their houses and build everything new, none of the original fittings are left inside.

New people are coming in and demolishing houses. You just don't demolish a house in Djursholm. That is not acceptable. You have to know things in this place. You respect people who know things, not the types who come in and demolish just because they lack a proper cultivated outlook.

Many of the nouveau riche don't understand the sort of place they are moving into. They dynamite rocks, they build stone walls, and they tear out everything inside their houses. A lot of cultural value is being lost.

The finance people don't deserve their place here; they often lack the right feel, tact, and tone.

The new people have no style and no class; they lack dignity. They're show-offs. They drive too fast and they have over-the-top cars. A real old Djursholm person is mindful of proven and genuine things.

I socialize with the people I went to school with here. The new people coming in don't have any sense of style; they think they have to behave in a certain kind of way. But sure, this is a place that puts you under a certain obligation.

One man I spoke to emphasized that the so-called new residents had always presented a challenge to the well-established inhabitants. "Those who are old guard today were new yesterday. When Djursholm was young, it was the wholesalers and directors that irritated some of the founding families. Then came the military families, who brought their customs." Another man explained that "new families" and the "nouveau riche" have always been separated from "old families." He went on to explain that the new families had to continuously manifest their wealth and success, and strive for social acceptance. Old families, according to him, were more *low key* and "not so influenced by modern times—they hold on to their traditions and do not try to fit in all the time."

What this actually means is that the new families are consecrated by their well-established counterparts; they are permitted to share in the cultural capital of the latter, which is generated as a consequence of living in a particular way. If the newcomers fail to show a proper respect to the old guard, the aura of the community is directly challenged. Obviously it is a somewhat simplistic assertion that all recent arrivals should be regarded as morally and socially subordinated to the already established families; however, there is little doubt that the older families regard themselves as superior to other groups in the community. This was very well put by one of the old-timers, who had been a member of the golf club for many years: "Everything has to be so egalitarian today; these days anyone can become a member. Before, you had to be voted in, and then you had to have a guardian who made sure that you stayed in line. It was a very good system. Today we can't control who joins the club. But at least we have 'The Thursday Club,' which is like a club within the club. And there you get voted in by recommendation of an existing member."

In spite of this, Djursholm is hardly a community whose basic culture and values are being challenged by waves of new arrivals; quite the reverse, as there seems to exist a desire among the new residents to let themselves be integrated and to stay compliant with the cultural status quo. After all, this is viewed as the norm with which one is expected to orient oneself. There is a desire to become a part of the culture, which is perceived as an ideal, which could confer significant value to those who are receptive to its rules. In general, people do not move there with the intention of changing the society, nor are there any such tendencies among residents who have lived in the community for a few years. Quite the opposite. A move to

Djursholm is very much about becoming a part of its culture. Based on the high property prices, and general ideas about Djursholm in society as a whole, it is a feasible conclusion for new arrivals that they have reached the very best of places, and that it can only be to their own benefit now to let it make its mark on them, rather than the reverse. Besides, what can a single individual add to a world that seems perfect, at least from a distance?

Something that I observed at an early phase of my study was that relationships between people were characterized by a mode of social distance. This can be illustrated by something known as "the parental contract," which the parents' association at Djursholm's largest school has produced. One father explained the implications of this contract to me:

> The parental contract is an initiative of the parents' association, which aims to keep a better check on what the young people are up to. It speci-fies, for instance, that if Alice says she is staying the night with Emma, Alice's parents should call Emma's parents to hear if this is all right. Otherwise there is a chance that the young people will pull the wool over their parents' eyes, and they will end up staying somewhere else. Some of the parents think, "Oh no, you can't behave like that; you can't call people and bother them," but I don't see any problem with it. . . . There is too little spontaneous contact here between parents. People get to know each other at preschool, where they drop off and pick up their children, but after that people go their separate ways. People live in big houses here, with extensive grounds so you don't exactly have a chat by the fence. There's also a culture of discretion, and spontaneous meetings are not appreciated. When moving about in the community, people are usually in their cars. All this means that people don't have much insight into each other, and maybe it's even worse when it comes to their children.

In other words, the parental contract is a formalization of relationships between parents. It is about "shared guidelines between parents for the handling of our children's leisure," as one mother put it. In the absence of more informal social norms in relation to young people's interaction and, even more important, collective parental efforts to ensure their children's safety and proper behavior, there is a need for a formal agreement, which in this case is denoted as a "contract," a well-known term in corporate life. It enables a continued sense of distance in social relations. A teacher at one the schools made the following statement: "The sort of social control that one might expect in a little community like this one, simply does not exist. It works more like a large city here. No one seems to be concerned, or to react, to young people drifting about drunk at particular weekends. Possibly a call will be put in to the police, but hardly more than that. In general there is not really any intolerance toward heavy drinking. I mean, if you come here for the graduation parties, you'll see that the booze is absolutely flowing without any checks or bounds." One parent felt that when it came to this issue "parents are not especially concerned. They'll buy a service like riding classes. But there's no sense of involvement in the club. A nanny will drop off and pick up the child. Almost no parents are willing to put themselves forward as volunteer workers." One of the heads of a sports club explained that "it is often fairly halfhearted when parents need to get involved. If we ask the parents to come and help us sell raffle tickets to raise money for the club, there are some that just prefer to give us a cheque so they don't have to take part. To put it simply, they buy a big wad of raffle tickets. But they miss out on the sense of involvement with the children, of standing there together and selling the tickets." In general terms, a great many people that I have met seem to feel that in Djursholm you may know a lot of people, but few of these relationships have any intimacy. "There are a lot of lonely people here with many acquaintances," an elderly woman told me. And she continued: "You feel quite alone when bad things happen, even if you know lots of people. . . . I think the way some people think here, is more or less like, 'If you can't pay, you're not getting any help.'" She went on to suggest that much of the social cohesion was largely based on the ability to pay. "Many of the residents are lonely. But they go out to shop, they eat at the restaurants and they are recognized, and they have a chat here and there. But they have to pay for it. Even membership in the associations comes at a cost. Nothing is free in Djursholm."

The community prioritizes big social events over more intimate relationships, and this has something to do with the very nature of the dwellings.
As already suggested, the large houses seem to almost demand large-scale
social interaction. Using the property sections of newspapers where
Djursholm dwellings are up for sale, I have been able to corroborate that
many houses have expansive sitting rooms with several sofas, and dining
rooms with large tables and lots of chairs. One person informed me:
"These large houses are as if made for networking and mingling. It makes
you *want to* invite people back. You don't want to be on your own there; if
you are, you just feel lonely. Filling up the house with people from time to
time is a way of making the house serve its purpose." The emphasis on
mingling and large groups rather than more intimate, close time spent
with friends also indicates how in Djursholm there is an admiration for a
certain kind of social ability—and coaching in how to excel at it. As one
person put it to me: "People are open and interested, but at the same time
not very interested." In all essential respects it is about scanning one's social surroundings rather than deepening any particular relationships. A
nanny who worked for one year in Djursholm had the following statement
to make on this theme: "Something that I was struck by was how they
asked things but did not listen to what you said. I noticed how I would tell
people several times about my family, but they didn't seem especially concerned. They kept asking the same questions."

This alleged lack of deeper, closer relationships is also expressive of a
tendency to want to report other people to the authorities. Djursholm is
hardly the sort of place where one runs the risk of being beaten up, robbed,
or in some other way assaulted. This fondness for reporting one another
could rather be explained by an unwillingness to personally confront those
who are bothering one or causing a sense of unease. A policeman in the
district told me that, from time to time, the police receive tip-offs about
young people driving about in the town center on their mopeds on weekend evenings, with the clear suggestion that the police ought to give them
a warning. The mere idea of going down to the square to have a word with
the youths, themselves, is out of the question, even though the risk of verbal abuse or at worst physical assault is likely to be more or less nonexis-

tent. Another police officer I interviewed claimed that "one of the quirks of this place is a tendency of neighbors to report each other to the police. When these kinds of reports come in, often for the sake of some triviality, as a rule we ask, 'Have you spoken to your neighbor about this?' and usually they haven't. People want *us* to sort out *their* concerns." He also described how residents would often call in to complain about traffic jams outside preschools and schools. "But we can't stand there controlling the traffic flow. The problem in Djursholm is that most people drop off and pick up their children by car, and often they are in a fair hurry. People don't seem to talk to one another."

A local politician, and also a resident, told me, "Neighbors here make no bones about making official complaints about each other, for instance, if a hedge is encroaching on a pavement; and then there are lots of complaints in relation to planning applications. People are used to getting their own way, and they are also used to keeping their neighbors at arm's length. In which case it is even less serious if they don't get along with those neighbors." A previous employee of one of the sports clubs claimed, "Sometimes conflicts arise between parents about their children, and then the club is often drawn into it even though the parents should really resolve things on their own. The club becomes some sort of third party which they talk to, but they don't themselves talk to each other." In a similar way, it is popular to hire lawyers when challenging planning applications, usually those made by immediate neighbors. Social distance, particularly in relation to people perceived as in some way problematic, is central to the understanding of how the aura, status, and consecrating capital of Djursholm are maintained and developed. As a general rule people are on the alert against all forms of "disrespectful behavior," for instance, in the form of moped-riding youths in the town square; yet addressing them directly would pose a risk of deconsecration.

One important resource for social connections between people in general is, of course, the workplace. In many places people work where they live. In Djursholm, on the other hand, very few of the residents work locally, and even those who do are extremely unlikely to have any colleagues living nearby. That today's inhabitants, apart from children and pensioners, are not commonly seen out and about in Djursholm and therefore do not have much of an opportunity to get to know one another in a spontaneous, informal way, is further added to by the fact that Djursholm, as mentioned earlier, tends to empty out during public holidays, and especially during the summer period. It has always been a place of variation and motion, and not only in recent years, as one of the estate agent that I spoke to seemed to suggest. An elderly resident made the following remark: "My father was always dubious about Djursholm. He felt that it was a transit town. People lived here a few years; then they moved on." There is also a sizable population of expats there, foreign residents living in the country for a few years, and embassy staff. This adds to the transitory feeling. A principal of a school in Djursholm told me: "We have a lot of families moving in. If well-educated foreigners, usually company executives or diplomats, move to this country, they are recommended to come here. This creates a turnover of people, which does not make for a very stable community. On the other hand, the foreigners that do come here are already socialized into living in this kind of community. Often they move from one Djursholm to another."

A teacher at the same school offered the following comment: "On one level this is a highly conservative community where traditions are appreciated as well as certain ways of handling social interaction, good manners, and other social aspects. But on another level it's all very temporary. There's a massive amount of movement, people find new jobs and move, or new people come into the community." The impersonal impression one can sometimes have of Djursholm is also added to by the residents' preference for moving around the community in their cars. Public transport is out of the ordinary, which reduces the interface between people and further increases social distance. It is so much harder to maintain social distance to the people around one if constantly running into them. As was noted earlier, even cycling is not popular in Djursholm, apart from some children and young people. People do like to walk, but this is primarily in order to get some exercise, and not an activity combined with daily errands that might bring one into spontaneous contact and small talk with others.

Particularly neighborly relations in Djursholm seem to be qualified by social distance. Neighbors are quite a unique issue. Because of their close physical proximity, they can gain insights into one another's lives that few others could ever hope to have, which takes on an aspect of awkwardness in a community where the collective aura is based on social distance. And yet neighbors are also in a direct sense crucial for the aura and prestige of one's own address. As in any community, neighbors may occasionally have warm and friendly relations, but because of their proximity, then, they also risk disrupting the fragile relationships that construct the idea of Djursholm. One man put it to me succinctly: "You do not socialize with your neighbors here; that is just how it is." Another person told me: "There's not a lot of visiting going on across the boundaries between one garden and another. We have mainly socialized with the families of other lawyers, mainly the people I have got to know through my work. I think that is the usual way, people know other people through their work. Maybe also the children are an important connection?" And still another person that I interviewed said, "Sure, you can run over and borrow a cup of sugar, but it's not so common. You don't strive to develop ties with your neighbors, as you may do in some other places. Of course, when you first move in you invite the neighbors in for a cup of coffee just to introduce yourself, but everyone knows that's the beginning and end of it. In fact the people you see are work colleagues. Legal families stick together, and medical families."

One person said to me: "I see my neighbors between April and September; the rest of the year I hardly see them. We don't bother each other. The perfect neighbor creates a good atmosphere, keeps the place neat and tidy, but you don't see each other." Distant relations with neighbors are not seen as a problem—quite the opposite. One woman explained it to me as follows: "Saying no to suburban living; that was our thing. When we moved to Djursholm a few years ago I had enormous prejudices. What we liked about the city was the anonymity, but then we realized we could also get the same thing here. The grounds are big here, and the neighbors don't see much of each other, it's not as if people hop across to borrow coffee or anything." Other people I met with had a similar approach: "The large gardens bring a measure of anonymity; you're not in each other's faces like in so many other built-up areas. Neighbors can be a little like relatives; if you're lucky, they're easy to deal with. If they're not what you want it can be hard work. The risk of having to get stuck in a fairly close relationship to people in your immediate surroundings is usually fairly low here, which can be a bit of a relief."

Finally, the prerequisite for the unique social life in Djursholm is clearly the community's layout and geography. Since its establishment, it has been a unique place in the sense that the houses have such relatively large grounds. As one man informed me: "The large gardens here are still very much in evidence. People want to be left alone here." One author wrote in a book published by the historic society that Djursholm was originally planned "with plots large enough for people not to have to see each other." Another author pointed out in an article that the local planning regulations in Djursholm stipulated in 1904 that houses built in the most extensive grounds could not be constructed closer to the road than ten meters, and had to leave a gap of at least six meters to boundaries. In this way the community was based on a concept of individualism. He said that any notion of "a unified and urban construction was neither viewed as desirable or possible. The undulating terrain was rather used to separate one house from another, as if one house wished not to know about the other." One man that I interviewed later sent me an e-mail: "The minimum plot size of 1,500–2,000 m2 certainly contributes positively to good relations between neighbors, because they hardly have to see each other." Another person explained that it was generally disapproved of when people partitioned their gardens to sell off land, as this was detrimental to the social character of the area. Another person went on to highlight how "in Djursholm the houses are generally built in the middle of the grounds, far from the road. This is different from in other places, where the houses are situated along the road. In other words, in Djursholm people did not want to be close to public areas. In the original plans for the area there were even stipulations about fencing towards neighbors and to the street."

One woman who grew up in Djursholm conveyed the following impressions:

The houses here have had more of an effect on me than the people. The houses define life here, create the conditions for a certain kind of life. They are big buildings with large grounds, obviously this must impact on people, just as much as the people impact on the houses. . . . There is a kind of lushness in the grounds; you rarely see these perfectly cut back gardens; there is something free and profuse about many of them. This tells me that there is something inflexible about Djursholm and its inhabitants. . . . People here please themselves, they remain personalities and don't have to adapt to others a great deal. It has probably become a norm and a lifestyle, and it might explain why people like living here. . . . You have a big open area around you here, a large free space. The houses and the gardens are not conducive to spontaneous meetings. Even if Djursholm is very sociable, it is all superficial. You may be sociable, but it is not personal. You keep your private sides to yourself.

When rounding off my interviews with current or former residents, I often asked: Do you feel like a Djursholm resident? Only a handful of them answered yes. One of them said, "Yes, I feel like a Djursholm resident, but of a different kind." One man in his sixties put it as follows: "I have lived in Djursholm for about twenty years. But my school years were spent at a boarding school. Those were the formative years. Because of that I don't fully feel like a Djursholm resident." Another late-middle-aged man felt that "there are very few Djursholm residents. One tends to be something else. And in the summers, Djursholm empties out." Another told me: "I have never set out to become a part of Djursholm; fundamentally I don't even feel at home here. But the children like it. I don't think one ever feels at home here after moving into the area; it's not an environment that creates a feeling of home, at least not if you come here as an adult." But even among the children and young people that I met, spoke to, and interviewed, few seem ready to view themselves as Djursholm inhabitants. On the one hand, there seems to be a feeling of belonging and social identity, but at the same time there is no apparent sense of being a local. This seems especially pertinent for teenagers, who looked almost surprised when I put the question to them. "Djursholm" is a community that creates strong ties between people on a level of social status, but at the same time, on another level, it keeps them separated. Both phenomena are a consequence of the social consecration that defines a leader community.

7

FAMILY LIFE

ROWING UP in Djursholm with parents who have jobs that are
viewed by them, and by the world outside, as evidence of success
and importance, while also providing substantial financial rewards, means that children learn from an early age that they are living in a
special world. Government statistics make it plain, as already shown, that
most of the residents do not have "normal jobs," irrespective of whether
their jobs require a high level of education. Hence, children become aware
from the very start that their parents are "socially significant." This is especially manifested by their absence. Whenever I interviewed children and
young people who grew up in the community, many of them described
how their parents devoted a great deal of time to their work, which in most
cases meant that they were not at home, or that they were away for other
reasons, such as invitations, leisure interests, or overseas travel. Whatever
the particulars, many children in Djursholm do have the functional experience of not having their parents around. As a consequence, they are forced
into an adult mode of behavior by taking charge of their own day-to-day
organization and having responsibility for it.

One young woman made the following assertion: "I suppose I've got
used to the loneliness, got used to Mum and Dad being away so much. But
I'd never leave my children on their own as much as they've done with

me." Another young woman felt, "Me and a lot of my friends have probably become independent quite early because our parents work so much. You end up on your own in the house quite a lot. There are parties all the time. Why go home at one in the morning rather than three, when there's no one at home anyway?" One eighteen-year-old man, in his final year at upper-secondary school, told me the following: "Sometimes I miss the day-to-day chitchat at home, where you just talk about this and that. There's sort of never been time for that, you just go from one activity to another, and Mum and Dad aren't home much. But school has been good in that way. I had a teacher at secondary school who sometimes just let us talk about things *we* found important." Another school pupil said to me: "I've grown up with nannies and child minders; Mum and Dad always worked a lot and traveled." His friend, who also sat in on the interview, added: "Many of my friends have to cope on their own on weekdays; you get used to being on your own." And, as one of the teachers told me: "On the one hand, you could say that these young people have helicopter parents, but often it's just a case of money changing hands. A lot of the parents are away to an extent that some of the children have a tough time as a result." A thirty-year-old woman, who grew up in Djursholm, told me, "Many of the children suffer from loneliness. I've seen it up close—how they are abandoned by their parents. The adults are concerned with themselves. They work a lot, so when at long last they get a bit of time off, they throw a party." Another interviewee who grew up in Djursholm in the 1980s and 1990s, told me: "In Djursholm people prioritize their careers. Where my husband grew up, you just did normal, simple things. When the parents were off work they put their time into their children; that's my understanding of it. But during my childhood, children were often the last thing anyone worried about. We just had to tag along. I very rarely heard the words, 'What would *you* like to do today?'"

These are some of the statements made by staff at the preschools and schools:

Many of our children here have an immense need to be seen, to be hugged. Some of the parents give them too little attention at home, because of all the stress they're under and the little amount of time they have left for their children. We notice that the children often identify very closely with some of the staff, especially if you're just sitting there reading a book, you feel how they just long to be close. Many of the children here actually suffer neglect, not on a level that one could report, it's not about maltreatment or incest or anything like that. It's stress that puts its mark on them, makes them suffer. And loneliness.

(Preschool Director)

Teachers can be extremely important adult role models. In this community where the wheels are always spinning very fast and people don't have much time for their children, the school staff can fill a very important function as adults and role models.

(Principal)

It's sad to have to say it, but I think I know a few of the children here better than their own parents do.

(Preschool Teacher)

Many of our children have a thirst to be loved; they need tenderness. Nannies, who may change every year, can never compensate for a parent who gives the child attention, time, and love. Many of the parents work too much, and they also travel a great deal. Often the grandparents do as much as they can, but they are busy, too, and they also go off traveling.

(Teacher)

Many children in Djursholm are very lonely. Their daily contact with an adult is often with their nanny, and often the nannies are young women from other countries. The parents work a lot or busy themselves with many other activities. One notices this in many of the children, they have a real need for close contact. . . . I think that a lot of the children would like to have more contact with their parents. But they have to put up with it. One could describe it as a debt of gratitude to the parents.

The children know they are growing up in a privileged community which offers them many opportunities, but the price of it is that Mum and Dad have to work a lot. I think that some of the parents also put it like this to their children. The children learn to live with it. In other cases the mothers are homemakers, and then it can go too far the other way. They drop their own children off and they keep a check on everything. The children are hardly left on their own at all. Their presence and control over the children becomes exaggerated, and this is not good either.

(Student Health-Care Staff Member)

I have worked with the richest children in the country. They are very nice, they give me hugs, and they always say hello. But they are very lonely.

(Youth Instructor)

The overriding thing lacking here in this parental group is a basic level of presence. The first year when the child is not yet at preschool, a lot of time is devoted to it, but then once people start working again, many of them don't have the time to just "be there."

(Preschool Teacher)

Obviously, parents in Djursholm love their children in much the same way as any other parents. But simply spending time with one's children is not always prioritized or considered important, because this kind of social interaction is not useful in terms of the social elevation that the community offers. Rather than giving the parent added social and cultural value, an intense level of contact with one's children may even be detrimental. Consecration is based on aesthetic excellence. Children, on the other hand, can be noisy, messy and untidy. The emphasis on early independence may be seen as a part of a child's raising, and is a direct consequence of the lifestyle of the family. This has always been the way things are done in Djursholm, as corroborated by a number of anecdotes taken from historical sources, concerning the relationships of grown-up children to their parents. One resident wrote the following about his parents, two well-known Swedish artists, in a book from 1954 about his childhood in Djursholm:

> From time to time Mother was completely absorbed with her artistic endeavours; when she was working on a new illustrated book, she would be so absorbed by it, that she often distractedly answered, "yes, yes, of course you may," when we boys shamelessly took the opportunity of asking for things, that we would normally have been denied. And as for Father—unless he was receiving someone in need of spiritual or financial support, he would sit in his study, working. And at such times no one was allowed to disturb him or clatter up and down the stairs. If one had rushed into his room to say, "Father, look what I found!" or "Will you help me with this piece of bark" it would have been sacrilegious.

Not only the children but also the parents themselves spoke of how much they must work and how little time there was for daily child-parent interaction. In the following comments I attempt to synthesize some of the parental comments that seem to throw light on the work ethic that many have in common:

> All the men in Djursholm work, and often they work extremely long hours. The women also work extremely long hours, or they don't work at all but then they are still away very much.
>
> (Mother of Three Children)

> Seeing their parents working hard is also good for them; it makes them understand what's required if you want to have a good life. It can't exactly be bad for them, seeing their parents grafting to put bread on the table.
>
> (Mother of Five Children)

> It's not an easy matter to work less. I have a demanding job.
>
> (Father of Two Children)

Certainly I have work in the evenings and at weekends; sixty to seventy hours per week is nothing unusual. It means you have less time with the children; that's how it is.

(Father of Three Children)

I was working a lot when the children were small and growing up. Today I sometimes regret forsaking them.

(Father of Three Children)

One repercussion of absentee parents on the lives of young people is that the latter end up throwing constant parties and consuming high levels of alcohol (according to official statistics, the highest in the Stockholm area). One sixteen-year-old girl said: "There's always someone with an empty house at the weekend, so then we go there." There are several reports in the media about parties that have spun out of control in Djursholm, with absent parents viewed as the cause of the problem. For instance, in one article in the local newspaper, there is a report about an unsupervised party. Twenty people were invited; two hundred turned up. Four girls were the hostesses of the evening. One of them, a fourteen-year-old, explained that the party was supposed to start at eleven o'clock in the evening. The mother, who had given her permission for the girls to have the party, claimed that the only thing for young people to do in Djursholm is party. "Our young people are not offered any alternatives." An employee at a health-care center, who had previously worked with young people in the center of Stockholm, made the following statement:

The most serious abuse of alcohol—well, it's right here, in Djursholm. Is that the price one has to pay for raising one's child here? In fact what causes this is nothing more than poor parenting and parental involvement. The parents can be as committed as they like insofar as being involved in their children's development at school, the friends they have, and so on. But if when all is said and done it's just a long-distance commitment, well, then it is not worth very much. Parents have to be there, both in thought and deed. The fact that young people here drink more

113

than anywhere else in the country points to bad parenting skills in the form of norms and setting boundaries. The children are lonely and confused; they seek situations and groups that offer companionship, and this takes the form of friends and parties.

When I interviewed one woman who had lived in Djursholm for about ten years, she told me, "There's status in having many children here, even four or five of them. You might get the idea that people like children here, but it's not always like that. Many of the children see very little of their parents; people have one or two nannies who take care of the practical arrangements." Another person who had been raised in Djursholm told me, "Prestige is very important, both economically and socially. But there's no time for the children; they are ferried about in a frantic way." Many children in each family is good for the aura of Djursholm, partly as a way of disseminating the community's ideals in the broader world, and partly because the children can be slotted into important social positions in and outside Djursholm. The fertility strategy is about quantity, even if it takes place at the cost of less available care and concern for each child. According to official statistics, 9.3 percent of mothers in Djursholm have three or more children, compared with 3.2 percent for the rest of Sweden.

The loneliness of the children is a consequence of the parents' socially elevated position. The lifestyle of parents simply prioritizes "large" rather than "small" social events—and this in turn becomes a central aspect of how one's self-image is formed and developed in the mold of leadership. For children who learn from their parents' behavior, the absence of the latter implies not only that they must learn to think and act independently but also that they begin to believe that the professional lives of their parents, or their lives in general, are something natural and worthy of emulation. Working long hours, being away from one's children, may admittedly be regarded as problematic even by the parents themselves and could lead to rejection by the children. But it is just as likely to be regarded as the only possible way of living. The distant social relationships produced by such a mode of living are also functional from a societal perspective. Every inhabitant has a role to play in order to maintain the community aura.

Living in close proximity to one's (small) children without the presence of nannies, also strongly implies a lifestyle that is not conducive at all times to consecration. It is rather the case that while living close to one's children creates a lot of joy, it also generates troubles in the form of a lot of apparently trivial concerns, such as dirty laundry, and so on. Children in Djursholm are given much priority and they are considered important—but often at a distance. As a group they are vital for the development of the community and its continuance, but they are also risky in a social sense. One nanny told me, "There are many nannies in Djursholm, and this must be a sign as good as any that people prioritize many other things than their children. It's possible to say that quite plainly without necessarily putting any value judgment on it." Another nanny said, "I'm the one who takes care of daily life, I make sure that it all works, but they do a lot of traveling together. They always go skiing in the winter, often several times. Then it's Dubai, Thailand, and Mauritius. I've come along several times, but the mother and father spend a lot more time with their children when they're away." In other words, the holidays are often something entirely different, as another resident also observed, commenting on a description in a book by his lionized parents: "During these periods—far from all those people, who, at least in my opinion, laid such unjust claims on my mother and father—we felt close in a quite special way, and we came to know and love their simple human characteristics and weaknesses, and to understand that they were by no means superhuman."

Gray, mundane everyday life, with all its trivial troubles and concerns, is something that the good parent in Djursholm would prefer to do without, in just the same way residents are unwilling to go to the recycling station and stand there sorting through their rubbish. By choosing not to be with their children in day-to-day life, but rather putting the emphasis on overseas trips and holidays, where there is an expectation of enjoyment and escape from the dullness of life, the aura and status of the community remains intact. During these trips, the values of Djursholm—the active, positive lifestyle—can be brought to fruition, and the whole experience can work as a sort of training ground, an identity-forming exercise for the children and young people. In other words, it seems as if routine concerns and the undignified aspects of parenting are avoided by paying for services, and finding other ways of lightening the load: and so there will be no need to struggle with overactive or resistant children while putting on their mud-stained rain clothes; getting oneself dirty when dressing them or playing with them outdoors; having to sit with them and revise multiplication tables and fractions, or weeding the garden with them, or even cooking for them in the evening. For such things, nannies, private tutors, and gardening companies can be used. The downside is less social interaction with the children—with social distance as a consequence. Yet, as I have already said, distance is very much functional in Djursholm, where most social relationships have an associated aspect of risk. The often minimal daily interaction with their children is a result of Djursholm's parents having little time for it, and also happens because the required parenting activities do not sufficiently reflect the social status and position that parents wish to display through their residence there.

Parents I met with did speak of a great deal of their engagement in their children's lives—especially these children's involvement in club activities. I have myself been present at matches organized by the local football club or the scouts, and on such occasions I noted the presence of many parents who come along to help out in various ways—and take time to be with their children. One such father told me: "Many parents offer to help as trainers and volunteers during competitions, and they do things like grilling sausages, helping out with the parking, directing visitors, and so on. The activity is reliant on the input of parents." Yet, as has been established, there is normally a lack of parental willingness to help when it comes to their children's leisure activities, which is precisely what one of the organizers at a club that I visited told me: "The parents are spoiled around here. We hardly get any volunteers. They won't help with the barbecue, and things like that. Instead we use them for other things, for instance finding sponsors or setting up committees or project groups."

There are many other signs of lackluster parental involvement, for instance, when the clubs have to offer incentives for parents to put themselves forward as instructors or leaders. One such incentive is offering to put the children of volunteering parents at the top of often very long waiting lists for membership. Other carrots are also used, namely, the persuasive argument that club involvement has positive effects on one's self-development. For instance, on the home page of the scouts, the assertion was made that parental involvement might help "Develop Your Leadership Qualities," in addition to the other more obvious enticement of "spending more time with your child and your child's peer group."

In Djursholm today, there are huge expectations of being *actively engaged* in one's child's life. One mother claimed: "You are expected to live actively, in a committed way. Not to be with your children or at least give them a lift to events would come across as strange. Unless you were traveling or at work." Being "actively engaged" in one's children's activities thereby becomes an expression of the parent's character and morality as a dynamic, highly motivated person. On a club activity day, one father told me, "This is a place with a lot of committed, ambitious people, which you can see just by looking around at all the parents who are here today." A mother explained, "You don't use your time for your house or your garden. Everything has to look good, but you don't put your energy and care into creating a cozy and pleasant interior at home. Instead you let others see to that, cleaners, gardening companies, architects, stylists. You put your focus on the social aspects, even when you go off on holiday." Social aspects, as we have already pointed out, are a significant part of the consecration of people into leaders. A leader does not declare him or herself by being good at gardening or household work or some other specific skill. The operative quality required is a very particular kind of social projection. For this reason, parental involvement in a place like Djursholm is socially driven, and shared parental activities tend to form themselves into social arenas, in which leadership identities are formed and developed.

That the children are separated from their parents for comparatively long stretches of time is, as I have suggested, connected to the fact that in Djursholm it is socially acceptable, and even desirable, to have nannies. Also from a historical perspective, children in Djursholm have been taken care of by adults that were not their parents. My impression of the state of play in the preschools that I have visited is that these institutions are also being milked to the full. Certainly it is not unusual for children to be picked up relatively early (about three o'clock in the afternoon); however, the pickup is usually done by a nanny or an elder relative, as opposed to one of the parents. Even when there is time available to spend with one's children, parents often choose not to do so. One preschool director told me, "For many, many parents on parental leave with one child, who have a second child with us, it's an absolute must that the second child has to be able to attend four days a week rather than three, which is what technically is allowed. They come up with all sorts of schemes, such as enrolling at university or working with their own company, to find a loophole. They absolutely do not want to be stuck at home for two days a week with both children." A colleague of hers at another preschool in Djursholm commented, "Some of the parents have parental leave, but they're determined that their children should come to preschool four days a week, and not just three. They argue about it with us; they argue with the local authority. They should really be making the most of that time with their children." Yet another preschool director claimed, "As a percentage the vast majority of children in Djursholm are at preschool. Even the parents that are at home are not at home with their children." The same person went on to suggest, "People have chosen a certain kind of address where they live, but they pay a high price for it, and they have to balance the books. Their children are not allowed to be ill; every day is a working day, from morning to evening." An employee at another preschool concurred, telling me that many children spent long days at the preschool and rarely stayed at home even if they were unwell: "I think it has something to do with the fact that some of our parents have moved to Djursholm even though their income is fairly ordinary, and they have to work their butts off to be able to pay all the bills. It's tough for those children, they could do with some time off with their parents, but there's never a letup." As I have already reported, a far greater proportion of young children are prescribed antibiotics in Djursholm than in the rest of the country, which could be seen as an expression of the work ethic that holds sway in this community.

One father that I spoke to while visiting one of the preschools told me in this context, "Life here is completely geared up to the preschools. I'd probably guess that most people here have their children at preschool; I don't know anyone who stays at home with their children." Another preschool employee said, "There's an attitude here that it's fine to be away from your children a lot. I mean, quite a few of the mothers are at home, but the children still come here, and there's nothing wrong with that, I suppose. But they want them to come for long days, and all week. Many of them also have nannies who drop them off and pick them up, and take care of them at other times." I look more closely at the world of education in Djursholm later, as I have already mentioned, but for now a quotation from a teacher at one of the schools may be relevant to the discussion here, in terms of the emotional importance preschools and schools may have for children: "Some of the parents expect a great deal from the preschool and school. It is not only about a sense of security and development but about a greater degree of responsibility. But we are not boarding schools, to which children can be handed over. The parents must themselves form the backbone of the children's lives and give them the security and values they need. Schools can never replace that."

The preschools in Djursholm make it possible for the parents to put their time into other things than their children—other institutions can also be seen as important service providers in this respect. The many clubs and associations in the community offer the children stimulation, development, and social interaction, while also generating additional time for parents to pursue their own interests. One of the youth workers in a club had the following comment: "Sometimes I wonder if the parents who put their children here have any genuine interest in the activity, or if it is only about dumping them off." A parent who was very much involved in one of the clubs, suggested, "Obviously there's a concern about fitness and health among many of the parents in Djursholm. But I think it's also a lot about getting the children off their hands. They can get some time to themselves if their children are kept busy. They can even get out themselves, and take some exercise. I'd say that 50 percent of the parents dropping their children off here are wearing training clothes. Maybe they go for a jog in the woods or go down the gym. Others may welcome a bit of peace and quiet at home for a few hours."

Evening recreation activities at the schools are always busy, according to the principals I interviewed, which yet again confirms the image of Djursholm as a community where daily life has little parent-child interaction, because of the parents' demanding work schedules. Several of the sports clubs also offer extensive after-school activities for children and young people. In one article in the local newspaper, the riding stables are described as the biggest youth center in the municipality, especially for girls. On its web page the riding club offers after-school activities, and it has employed two youth workers for this very purpose—this being a chargeable service, with no local authority involvement. The riding club also has a highly active and well run youth section—organized by the same young people that take part in its activities. In a document available on the web page, the after-school activities are described as follows: "Being a young rider at our equestrian club in Djursholm is not only about riding. Here, you can meet your friends in a relaxed atmosphere, you can take care of your favorite horse, or learn more about horse care in courses run by our two specially hired youth instructors. You can enjoy a snack in our cafeteria and take part in events such as the annual Christmas Revue and other activities laid on for the group. Our youth leaders ensure that everything is run in a safe and pleasant way, and that young people coming here enjoy their companionship at these stables." According to the web page, some 150–200 children come to the stables every day, and at weekends the number are even greater. The youth section of the riding club, in association with the youth leaders, organizes a host of activities. Far from all the people that have joined the club participate in equestrian activities, however—a fair proportion are only members in order to take part in the social activities of the riding club. According to information received from the office of the riding club, the association has 450 active children and young people aged between six and eighteen. The number of boys is astoundingly small; in fact there is only *one* active boy older than ten. The riding club further states that most of these young people are in regular contact with the section offering after-school activities. An instructor at another association told me, "The parents want our cafeteria to work as a meeting point for the children after school. We open at two in the afternoon, and then the parents take over at six in the evening." In the tennis club's web site, two of the employees define themselves as "backup mothers" who "know most of the children by name and sight." The women work in the cafeteria and serve food and snacks, while also "keeping everything in order and stepping in whenever there's a need, because many children and young people come to the dining rooms for several hours before and after training."

Following, I present some of the statements made by people who, on the basis of their jobs or functions, come into contact with young people in Djursholm and have reached certain conclusions about their situation:

> For many children the adults have no authority here, one has to manage by oneself. Friends and siblings are the important reference points. This creates a degree of independence. They don't turn to the adults as the first port of call, not to parents or teachers.
>
> (Staff Member, Student Health Care)

> Many of these young people don't go home on their own; they go home with friends and spend time together at home. Often the parents are not at home, but they have each other for company. They do their homework together, or maybe they eat and watch TV. This is also an added security for parents.
>
> (Employee, Djursholm Municipality)

> The children become attached to one another, like a gang that sticks together. The cohesion in the group is very important, it becomes a network for the future. I believe that children here go through things that others can't understand, and it creates a very special feeling of togetherness. They create very tight bonds. They also look for companionship and talk in groups. . . . This is how the children have grown up; they have no concept of any other way of being. But the ones who find it most difficult are the children of new money, the ones who have recently

moved into the area. They can be really arrogant because they're so insecure and they don't feel comfortable. It takes time to gain their confidence, I mean at first they look down on us.

(Youth Worker)

In an environment where many of the parents are absent both physically
and mentally because of the sheer amount of work they do and the level
of responsibility of their positions, children's friends and networks become even more important. One could say the same for poor areas with
high levels of unemployment. There also the young people get involved
very closely because the parents are not there for them. . . . Those who
don't fit into the gang have a hard time of it. There's a certain way of
being and a particular kind of attitude one has to have. In terms of appearance it's very tough. You have to be able to play the game.

(Principal)

However, the existing culture in Djursholm does not only affect the relationships between children and parents. It also has an impact on the interaction between spouses or cohabiting couples. In many ways one might say
that Djursholm is a man's world, at least if one references official statistics
in areas such as education, income, and professional life.[1] Bearing in mind
that Djursholm has a particular kind of professional profile, namely, that
the residents tend to hold responsible positions on the top rungs of corporate life, it is not especially surprising to find that men occupy the best-
paid and most prestigious jobs—after all, the community must reflect the
same trends in this respect as anywhere else in society. Many of the most
distinguished associations, to which leaders from all across the land come
to hold inspiring, illuminating talks, are also intended exclusively for men.
Women, meanwhile, are directed into other forums. One elderly resident
put it as follows: "Many women here are well educated, but they don't work
with anything that relates to their educational background. Instead, their
education has been important as a way of showing themselves off as attractive individuals while they were young. It has been their entry ticket, you
might say, one wants to say, 'My wife is a lawyer, but now we have four

children, and so now it's better that she stays at home with them.' The women get stuck at home; they circulate in their little worlds." A staff member at one of the preschools told me the following:

> Many well-educated women say that they choose to stay at home, but that's a bit of a constructed idea. They actually can't deal with the pressure to perform, having lots of children and offering them a lot of developing and stimulating activities, while also having a career with all that means in terms of demands and performance. But saying, "I can't deal with it" here in Djursholm is not an option. Instead you have to say that you choose to be at home and put your energy into your children and family, I mean in a way it's quite true. But people don't really choose it, they are actually forced into it, because otherwise it's not possible to live the sort of life they do live.

A nanny described some of her experiences of working for two families in Djursholm: "The parents hardly see each other; they don't even sleep in one bed, it seems. The working days are long; there's a lot of travel for the father. Although they're tired, they sit up late working." A woman who lived in Djursholm explained, "A lot of the women go to massage, because then they get touched. Relations in many of the marriages are cold, without love. People don't have time for each other, neither physically, spiritually, nor socially."

Official statistics indicate that the incidence of divorce is lower in Djursholm than in the country as a whole (14.6 percent in Djursholm to Sweden's 22.2 percent). This is not necessarily because spousal love there is stronger than in other places, especially when one considers that spouses probably see comparatively little of one another during the week, because of professional or other obligations. Instead there may be important social—and financial—reasons for staying together. One man told me: "A lot of people here have fairly complex financial situations and family constellations. When assets are divided up it can be quite difficult working out who owns what. There's mixed ownership, old legacies, prenuptial agreements, separate property." A lawyer told me: "Separations here are marked by a lot of contesting about money, and things can get quite heated. People often get lawyers involved. Of course many people sort it out by agreement, but in many cases that is not the case at all. A large number of other players are pulled in, such as the school, lawyers, social services, and so on."

I have heard several instances of women being harder hit by divorces than their spouses. In most cases the men have had by far the higher incomes; in certain cases the men were the only breadwinners of their families. After a divorce, it is rarely the man who moves into an apartment or a terraced house (one woman explained to me that one area in Djursholm was known as "the divorce ditch, where all the women lived who had been kicked out") after the assets have been divided. The aura and status of the man should not be affected; it is the woman who should be demoted. One woman who had lived in Djursholm for ten years explained this to me more succinctly: "The women have a sort of B-grade quality about them; you can sort of switch them once they've had the children. At around forty-five to fifty we have a lot of divorces here. The men get themselves a younger woman. Many women get bitter at that point; they want a man with the same status as before." One woman who grew up in Djursholm but now lives elsewhere said, "The gender roles in Djursholm are fairly pronounced. It's like a trap for women. There are many well-educated women there, who must have had career ambitions. But they've had to give all that up. A lot of them are completely in the dark about their finances. When there's a divorce it's a disaster on all sorts of levels. They know nothing about money, and they don't have a job. In an environment that consistently evaluates achievement and success, they may also end up being looked down on. They don't have much to offer apart from being attractive or maternal." According to one person who had been working for a long time in Djursholm, "The community here is not very equal, despite the fact that many of the women are highly educated. Some of them choose not to work when the children are small, and when they have many children they are out of working life for a relatively long period of time. Typically it's the man who keeps an eye on the finances, and when there's a divorce this may mean that he bulldozes the woman. . . . Usually it's the woman who has to take a hit. For the woman it may be of huge importance to her status to remain in Djursholm, and the idea of having to move away may be very difficult. So people borrow money so they can afford to stay."

The distant relations between parents and children in Djursholm may also apply to relations between young and old. As I have already discussed, people are crucial to one another's social elevation—which also means that they function as mutually dependent resources of greater or lesser importance. When I wander about in the local cemetery I have an impression that the whole idea of the graves is that they should not require a lot of day-to-day maintenance by family or relatives. Many of the graves have been beautifully set into the ground in the form of natural-looking stones. Very few of the graves need regular care, and there is a scarcity of flowers. Several of the graves carry little signs to the effect that they are being looked after by the Parish authority. One man in his seventies told me: "Our children live very active lives; they're always out traveling, and they work a lot. Unfortunately we don't see one another very often. You're pleased whenever you manage to get an audience with them." In my interviews with staff members working for the home-help service or the retirement home or geriatric care in Djursholm, I found a generally accepted view that while families are very concerned about the provision of high-quality care for their elderly members, their personal and tangible involvement is rather thin on the ground:

Many of the families of our patients are pensioners and live hereabouts. Sure, some of them may not be so fit, but lots of them are. There are exceptions, but many of the loved ones don't give their parents any kind of help in their daily lives, for instance, with cleaning or shopping. That is why you have the home-help service, after all. I think many of these children were ignored while they were growing up. You can't expect more of them. One of my patients said to me, "You make your bed and then you have to lie in it." He told me that his son visited him about once per year, although he only lives a few blocks away. I remember another man who told me, "I got so immersed in my work that I forgot about my children." Often the old people try to gloss it over, by saying,

"I'm glad my son got such a good job," or similar. But of course, a lot of elderly people here miss having a closer relationship to their children.

By and large the residents are healthy, they can manage on their own for the most part. Putting the elderly in here is a way of arranging things for them. To begin with, the visits are frequent, then they begin to tail off. People get things set up for the parents so they can go off traveling or work all the time. There's also a social aspect to the old people's home, I can imagine that is how they would see it.

The elders are as a rule very proud of their successful children, but they miss them. The price of their success is loneliness.

Just as the residents buy services such as gardening, cleaning, child minding, homework tutoring, and so on, they also want their elderly parents or relatives taken care of "professionally." In the prevalent lifestyle of Djursholm, based on accepted norms and values, there is no possibility of manual work; nor is it desirable for people to get too intimate with one another. There is an emphasis on distant social coexistence. People must not get involved with tasks that may be regarded as dirty work, nor should they get too close. People's status and aura are best maintained at a distance.

8

A LIFESTYLE UNDER THREAT

O
NE CONSTANT theme when people consider threats against Djursholm's unique culture is the suggestion that it is being built up
and exploited, which would have the effect of watering down
the community's original concept of an exclusive garden city. There is an
anxiety that a larger number of dwellings in the community (especially as a
result of the construction of apartment blocks) might degrade its unique
social character. One man expressed his view on the issue as follows: "Construction of any kind is the most infected question here, anything from
new houses to telephone masts and jetties." One resident wrote in an article published by the historic society in 1944 that Djursholm is not just any
old community; quite the opposite, it is a place where "certain kinds of
owners have congregated, who have not only added a considerable amount
of capital to the municipality and thereby also low taxes, but also a very
particular culture and civility. We wish to retain all this for the future,
yet if the necessary measures are not taken in time, the physiognomy of
Djursholm will inexorably change. In so doing, the community will grad-
ually find itself acquiring a different sort of populace." In other words,
Djursholm is considered to be unique and better in terms of its lifestyle. If
social exclusivity is not maintained by preventing expansion and new building works, "Djursholm as it is today, a place we all love and treasure, will

definitely be a thing of the past." The challenge facing the community, the author goes on, is to ensure that it keeps its "first class house-owning residents and the good taxpayers, who are the only possible foundation for the felicitous future of this place." And so, in the final analysis, it is not the nature of the place, but rather the people in it, that are decisive to it.

If one analyzes the development of Djursholm one can quickly confirm that the inhabitants have been remarkably successful at preventing a gradual development of the area, after the initial construction boom in the early 1900s. One woman explained: "Djursholm has changed, obviously. There's more of everything today. More cars, more buses, and more people. When I was young people used to cycle, but that was also the case in other places. But the town is still the same. It has not been built up very noticeably in the fifty years that I have lived here." Another resident felt that Djursholm "is very special in the sense that it has not grown exceedingly in the last five or six decades." This has been achieved by residents regularly challenging planning applications, and by construction projects being stopped in their tracks, regulations against the partitioning of gardens, and the establishment of nature reserves that have significantly impeded development. For example, in one case where there was an application to build a communal house for four disabled people, several of the neighbors challenged the project in a letter that questioned the benefits of the project from a social perspective. As has already been said, it is a rare thing to see disabled people in Djursholm, and a home for such people, albeit only four such persons, might be regarded as a serious threat to the distinctive social elevation of Djursholm, as implied by its distinctive notion of human behavior.

Yet the greatest threat to Djursholm's unique values and social milieu is not actually a greater density of population, but rather the behavior of the residents, irrespective of how many of them there are. The residents are the very foundation of Djursholm, and they manifest its culture through their actions. The fact that few if any of those that I interviewed or spoke to answered affirmatively my question of whether they saw themselves as "Djursholmers" seems to indicate the level of difficulty experienced by residents to live up to the defining lifestyle ideals of the community. People take a bearing in relation to a norm that obligates them to live as role models, but there is a sense of not quite managing to do so. A well-known Swedish business journalist who was born and bred in Djursholm, describes in his book from 2008 that it can be a torment growing up in a community that is perceived to be privileged, where everyone is believed to go through life with a silver spoon in their mouths. He says that he would not have had any reservations about coming from a different kind of background, and being "the guy who kept studying against all odds, forged himself a career, and struggled all the way to the top!" Performance and success are valued very highly in Djursholm, he goes on. They are part of a norm and an ideal to which most young people aspire, much as he also does himself. And yet it remains a fact, he says, that many of these people will owe their success later in life not to their personal efforts, determination, and skill, but rather to "having the right contacts, the right educational background, and parents with money." This can give rise to a feeling of not having succeeded in any substantial sense. One is expected to be a smart, hardworking person, but any successes in life may not have anything to do with such qualities, leading to a sense of insignificance and worthlessness, according to him, and not at all a conviction that one is a leader— whether or not describing oneself as such.

Many of the people I encountered did in fact express, in a variety of ways, this precise sense of insufficiency in Djursholm, and that the community put them under an excessive obligation to perform:

If you come from Djursholm there are no excuses for not being a success. This is obviously quite a pressure to be under. I never became a boss, and although I am now eighty-three years old I still regard myself as a little boy who is fairly questioning and maybe also insecure about life. In that sense I am a bit of a failure. I didn't achieve much at school either; I just kept out of the way. I failed my finals; I had to retake them. I just wasn't mature enough. It was very irritating to my father; he kept wondering if anything much would come of me. My parents moved to Djursholm for the sake of their children's education, so we would find ourselves decent and respectable jobs later in life. It was a shock not passing my finals, and things continued more or less like this. Of course I have lived well here in Djursholm through all the years, and I come from a good family with a decent background, but my professional life was never anything to write home about, and that, after all, is an important social distinction here. . . . I didn't make the grade when it came to intellectual things. On the other hand, there were others in the same position in Djursholm, but I never managed to make up for it and create anything for myself. Basically I never really took command of myself, I have always been insecure, wondering, and full of hesitancy about myself and life. . . . I often say *give credit where credit is due*. To get some appreciation, to hear that one is good enough, to be recognized for the person you are, I have a soft spot for all that. It has always been important for me to be praised and to hear that I am good enough.

(Man, Eighty-Three)

My parents always told me, "As long as you do your best that's okay." But what does "your best" really mean? Working twenty-four hours per day? Being good at tennis, golf, sailing, and having five children?

(Man, Thirty-Five)

In Djursholm there's always someone who's better, looks better, is smarter, and more successful. I think much more about that now than I used to. Before we moved here I actually never thought about things like that. You compare yourself a lot here, that's just how it is. You can't stop yourself. But it's important not to get carried away with it.

(Woman, Thirty-Five)

The feeling of "am I good enough?" is always there.

(Man, Fifty-Five)

The experience of not being perfect, of not making the grade, is, according to the school staff and youth workers to whom I have spoken, intimately connected with the high activity levels they feel are a defining characteristic of Djursholm. The upshot of it is a sense of stress among children and young people. There is also another related phenomenon of not feeling oneself to be physically flawless. To a large extent this is about striving for "the perfect body," quite simply a body that corresponds to the high ideals to which Djursholm aspires. A physical education teacher told me, "Some of the girls have a very 'refined' diet, meaning that they don't eat enough. If they are training at the same time, things can easily tip over." Another person involved in running the riding club for girls said to me, "Very few people are overweight here, but quite a number are too thin. Often the parents don't seem to notice this. Maybe the mother is also training and dieting all the time and living in a bubble. The horses couldn't give a damn about if you're skinny and a bit of a looker. You mustn't be too thin if you want to ride. Obviously, not too fat either. But the problem for us is often that some of the girls weigh too little."

But possibly the most evident sense of personal shortfall relates to the culture of performance that holds sway in Djursholm, where people are expected to be busy and successful—some of the residents feel that this creates a hard, cold, and competitive environment. In this context, comments have been made to the effect that there is a need for kindness and thoughtfulness and, by this, a positive contribution to a more cozy and easygoing atmosphere so that people can feel that they are good enough *just the way they are*. During one of my visits to an association for young people, several of the individuals I spoke to mentioned that although they had no problems with their schoolwork, and in some cases they even found it easy, they did not feel that they fit into the general social ethos of Djursholm. They viewed this association as a free zone from a social "competitive hounding," which, in their view, was commonplace in Djursholm—and which they had no ability or desire to live up to:

> It's a noncompetitive activity here, a considerate environment where there is space for everyone. Those who don't fit in elsewhere will find a place to be themselves here. It creates new friendships.
>
> (Boy)

You can be yourself here. I wasn't such a big deal at school but in this place I feel I can grab hold of things. I feel I have grown here; my self-confidence has improved in a completely different way from how it used to be in school. There, I often felt almost weighed down, but here it's not at all like that. I'm fine with occupying whatever space I need, talking, and saying whatever I like.

(Girl)

This club is accepting and welcoming, and that's not how things are in the rest of Djursholm. The focus here is on working together and getting to know each other. It's not as hard—and less thrusting. Here you can show aspects of yourself that aren't really possible in other situations. It's really hard-core in Djursholm when you're young. You always have to be cool, the best, gorgeous, and it can easily make you feel like a failure.

(Girl)

You can relax here. You learn to be kind and sensitive and to show consideration. It's like an extra person teaching you how to grow up. You learn how to relate to other people, and how to behave. Before, I used to be more like the flippant guy from Djursholm.

(Boy)

This particular association is not the only free zone in Djursholm for children and young people who feel that the lifestyle there is too demanding and almost out of reach. To these individuals, Djursholm remains "a shining city on a hill," except that it very much remains in the far distance. The municipal youth center has as its mission, to provide a free zone for the young people. A municipal employee explained: "What the youth center offers above all are not a lot of new, cool activities. Young people around here already have everything there is, all the computer games, the lot. Instead, the youth center is a stress-free meeting area, without any performance-related demands, just good companionship. When we have residential camps it's really popular." Another of his colleagues emphasized, "At the youth center we allow young people to be just what they are, adolescents, and not just little adults all the time. They don't have to be purposeful, show grittiness or leadership, be sure of themselves. They can show whatever anxiety or concern they are feeling. It's quite all right to say, 'I can't cope with it.' Here they can relax and stop having to be so responsible all the time. They're so good at home and at school. But here it's different, here they can flip out and be themselves. I think it's quite healthy." He further went on to claim that at the youth center the adolescents can "forget their agonizing about school reports, and their panic about jobs and careers. This is the kind of free zone they don't have in many other places. At home there's a pressure to perform, maybe not in an obvious sense, but generally it's enough just to take a look at how the parents are living. Here they get some human understanding, some empathy. We try to teach them that not everyone can go on holiday several times every year, and that not everyone who's on a lower income is lazy." A teacher at one of the schools said, "The youth center is a unique environment; the kids aren't assessed all the time, and they are not with their parents. This means that they can relax in a different way from at home or at school. At school there's a lot of pressure to be getting the best possible grades and achieving at a maximized level, and many young people also speak of pressure at home. The youth center gives them a zone away from all that, and this is probably its most important function." She further emphasized, "What the youth center can offer is the human part, a social aspect that is not about a firm tone of voice and a list of credentials." One of the young people I spoke to during a visit there described it as follows: "We have a pretty full-on schedule; almost every evening there's something on. The youth center is a good place to come just to hang out. You can take it easy here. At home I'm often on the computer, and then you're in online contact with your friends. It's almost like still being at school." Another adolescent claimed, "Being here is almost like being in a little bubble; everyone forgets about school and classmates. You can't win or lose here." Another of his friends felt, "You sometimes need to just relax, and you can do that here. Otherwise there's always so many activities going on, so much you have to do all the time, and think about. Many of my friends are stressed out. But here you can forget about all that; it's like its own world. You can just exist here." In spring 2014 the youth center, in association with the secondary school in Djursholm, organized a project focused on local young people, which was called "Be Nice." Its keywords were "friendship, love, comradeship, understanding, helpfulness, laughter, generosity, confiding in others, joy, common humanity," and the symbol of the project was a large tree, full of colorful flowers. That these are not the everyday values of Djursholm is revealed by their being highlighted in a project and an organized activity.

The lack of social contact in Djursholm with people who have social problems or are unemployed, disabled, substance abusers, or are just "average income earners" can obviously contribute to a feeling of failure among the residents, because they are constantly surrounded by people apparently *more successful* than themselves. Generally there is an expectation that children should be heading for success, and should have a certain social "sparkle." As I have already established, children hold a central importance to aura and status of the community:

> Some of the children in attendance here don't quite keep up with the others; they're just a little later in their development. And there's nothing odd about that. Parents have different reactions to that. Some are relaxed about it, but others work themselves up and wonder what they can do to get their children "developing" normally, meaning at the same pace as the other children.
>
> (Preschool Teacher)

> There's a desire to remold children who are a bit different. Parents get stressed out if their children don't quite fit in, if they're a bit special. It's important not to stick out. And a lot is asked of them in the schools here. If someone is different there's a risk they may not get through as intended, and that's a worry for parents.
>
> (Teacher)

Children not living up to the norms is a big stress factor for the parents; they start taking certain steps themselves to sort it out, and they grab hold of it in a very purposeful way. Maybe that's something quite unique about Djursholm: if something isn't quite working as it should, or if something is missing, well, people get stuck in and try to resolve it. They don't wait for the authorities to do anything. They deal with it themselves.

(Teacher)

Djursholm is a socially homogenous community with a certain view of normality and divergence that may end up impacting people's sense of self-worth and acceptance, and thereby also their capacity for consecration. This can be clearly seen in the social emphasis on the nuclear family as the central institution. In my many meetings with the residents, I have never seen the slightest reference to "complicated" familial situations such as stepchildren, stepparents, or anything of that kind. Nor have I ever come across any sort of open homosexuality, or so-called rainbow families. After searching on the Internet I have not managed to find any forum for homo-sexual people in Djursholm. There was a link to a "Network of Young Gays in Djursholm," which I tried to open, but the site was no longer active, and all I managed to see of it was the text, "We are young, we are gay, and we are proud! If you're a young gay man or lesbian living in Djursholm, don't think twice, join us now!" One local woman said: "I knew a lesbian girl here when I was young, but she moved away. I don't know any homosexu-als today." A staff member at one of the schools explained as follows: "Djurs-holm is a conservative community that values the nuclear family very highly. There is no way of socializing here if you don't have children; there is no other way of relating to others. I have never met any homosexual individu-als in this community, neither among my colleagues in the workplace or among the pupils. As far as I'm aware, none of my colleagues and none of the pupils are openly gay."

All in all, Djursholm is a community powerfully ruled by its norms, where people do their utmost to live up to the established expectations. The aura of Djursholm is a sort of constantly shining star overhead, on which the residents keep their gazes fixed. As in all small, homogenous communities, the norms of acceptable behavior are narrow. However, divergence in Djursholm is punished with particular severity, because of the social status and prestige that hang in the balance. The nonacceptance in the community for homosexual and transgender people has less to do with any kind of structural discrimination than a straightforward redundancy of such people or families in terms of being able to uphold the prevailing morality, while at the same time they pose a direct challenge to the fertility strategy of Djursholm—the importance of having many children. The disabled are treated in a corresponding manner. That this leads to deep-seated social anxiety and a closely related lack of creative drive among the inhabitants is not immediately noticeable. It is risky in Djursholm to do anything that detracts from the social norm, and, worse still, it is extremely easy to commit social foibles. All the residents present a constant threat to the aura of Djursholm, while at the same time as they are crucial to its continuance.

The high consumption of alcohol in Djursholm is a good example of this. Alcohol is present everywhere in the community. There are no people sitting on park benches drinking beer or booze; rather, alcohol is plentifully consumed at lunches, suppers, on public and private occasions, drinks parties, and during other communal events. Whenever I attended club functions, I often found there was wine and beer on offer, also quite often spirits in the form of schnapps, cognac, or the like. The same went for lunch at the golf club or at one of the restaurants in central Djursholm. In an advert in a local newspaper, one association offers a "Family after Work" event on Fridays at 5:00 p.m., "with snacks and lovely drinks on offer for both young and old." In an article on alcohol consumption in the same edition of the newspaper, reference is made to Djursholm's women as heavy drinkers. A professor of social medicine asserts that highly educated people with good salaries relatively often find themselves in environments in which alcohol is served. And in the readers' section, a letter "Concerned about Rumors of Drunkenness," from a local woman is highly critical of the culture of the alcohol-fueled Fresher's Week, where, in her opinion, drunkenness has become common practice: "And, worse of all, the school provided the premises for this distasteful desecration." The woman goes on to ask: "What does the school propose to do to put a stop to the disgrace of Fresher's Week in future, and how will the school clean up its hallmark as a paradise of alcohol binges?"

One person working in health and geriatric care, expressed the following during our conversation:

> We have many very elderly people here. In general they are very healthy. They have lived a good life. Eaten good food, taken regular exercise, been conscious of their lifestyle. But the major health problem here is alcohol related. People drink far too much; we can see that when we test them for various illnesses. It is very difficult to recognize this just by talking to someone. For example, I think we have been quite bad at spotting overconsumption among elderly ladies. . . . Probably, Djursholm was twenty years ahead of everyone else when it came to this daily drinking. Wine has almost become an obligatory drink with every meal. In some circles you almost have to explain why you are not drinking.

Heavy consumption of alcohol, especially wine and champagne, could have something to do with the feeling among the inhabitants of not being able to live up to the perceived obligations of the environment in which they live. One elderly person told me: "I think one of the reasons why people consume more alcohol in Djursholm is because they suffer from anxiety and the pressure to live up to something. Alcohol is a classic way of self-medicating, after all. Many people try to live up to a certain role, but they don't always manage it." This perspective was echoed by an employee at a health-care institution in Djursholm: "The tolerance for alcohol is much higher here than in other places. Anguish and misery is kept at bay with wine and champagne." What follows is a series of quotations lifted from conversations with some of the residents I have spoken to about their experience and view of alcohol consumption:

> There is a lot of drinking going on here. Partly, there are many events involving alcohol, and partly people have a lot of money.
>
> (Man, Sixties)

The availability of alcohol is a big problem here. Some of us parents can do the rounds and collect bottles and crates of beer, but the kids just make a call, and ten minutes later some dealer has dropped off another delivery. The young people here have the means, they have money to pay for alcohol. And then people have large bar cabinets at home; many keep masses of alcohol in the house. No one notices if a bottle goes missing.

(Woman, Fifties)

There's a social problem here among the young people relating to alcohol, and to some extent also to drugs. Before I understood the realities of it, I reacted much the same as others: "Don't exaggerate." But I was floored by the statistics and some of the stories other parents told me.

(Man, Fifties)

I've been to many parties at my friends' parents. They often invite us younger people in. You obviously get a glass of wine or champagne, and you may get a few more after that.

(Boy, Sixteen)

In our home there's always been alcohol available, I have grown up with alcohol on the table. And that's also how it was in my friends' homes. My parents are very sociable, so we've had a lot of parties, dinners, and so on, where we always had wine. If guests came we'd also have a glass or two at lunch. It's been a quite natural thing.

(Girl, Seventeen)

Djursholm is a highly sociable community where alcohol has a natural place. There's always a glass of wine thrown in, at anything from a parents' evening to a dinner at home. There's no big deal about that; people are more likely to raise their eyebrows if they aren't offered anything to drink.

(Man, Forties)

To be able to party hard and study hard, that's the norm. As long as they manage their studies I have no views on whether the young people drink a bit too much sometimes. I have the same values about myself and my friends. As long as we perform at work, surely it's okay to de-stress with a glass or two of wine?

(Man, Fifties)

Djursholm is an environment that gets you used to alcohol from an early age. You connect it with having fun or relaxing.

(Boy, Eighteen)

In my interviews it was primarily those who *worked* in Djursholm that brought up the subject of alcohol consumption in the community, and, in their view, not only was too much alcohol consumed but there was also a much too "liberal" view of alcohol consumption as a whole, which relates to the sort of social milieu to which Djursholm aspires:

There is an attitude here among the parents that "our children can deal with alcohol; it's not our problem," whenever we bring up the topic of alcohol abuse and young people. They don't think their own young people are a part of that.

(Police Officer)

Alcohol is a very sore point, a pressing question among the parents. There's an unwillingness to accept that our young people have a big problem.

(Teacher)

Why is there so much drinking among our young people here? There are many theories. Availability and peer pressure is one of them. Another idea is that people drink to get over the stress, to cool themselves down. You are expected to drink here. You're expected to be able to drink wine and champagne and be able to talk about it.

(Youth Worker)

The social part is important here in Djursholm, you have to be sociable here to enjoy yourselves and feel accepted. Alcohol is an important aspect of social life. Just look at all the social events organized by adults, at home and in club life. Wine and even spirits are always on offer. There's a good deal of this sort of thing in an environment like this.

(Principal)

I think many parents have a drink to get over the stress. In other places I think people have a drink to get over the boredom. Parents here are very tolerant about the drinking habits of their young people, so there are a lot of parties not only for adults but also the adolescents.

(Student Health-Care Employee)

The consumption of alcohol is not really viewed as a problem among the residents, however. A number of parents have indicated to me during our conversations that they have "full control" over their children's drinking. The parental self-perception seems to have no concept of the negative side effects of alcohol consumption. Wine and champagne are had as a part of the socially elevated culture that the inhabitants are keen to inhabit— while also creating a moment of release from the gnawing self-criticism to which they all seem so disposed. The alcohol therefore has a dual effect: it contributes to the consecration of the community, while at the same time making people feel better about themselves, if only for a short period of time. Questioning the extent to which the residents are capable of *handling* alcohol becomes synonymous with a general challenge on their ability to function as good and decent members of the community. A police officer told me the following: "When we have speed controls outside the schools or to check that people are wearing their safety belts, the response we get is very positive. But when we check people for drinking and driving outside the golf club, for instance, people are not as pleasant. There's an atmosphere of, 'How could you think we'd drink in the middle of the day—you know this is Djursholm!' It seems very provocative to them." An employee at one of the restaurants noted: "Many of our customers like to have some wine with their food, but they don't get drunk. They keep their drinking under control." When I took part in a club event in Djursholm, I was able to confirm that many of the participants drove home despite having had alcohol with their dinner—and this is based on a feeling of being one's own master and someone whose lifestyle is morally impeccable.

The high alcohol consumption in Djursholm should obviously not only be seen as an expression of the residents' need to "take time out" from their many pressing duties. As for young people's drinking habits, these should also be seen as a part of their social education. As has already been mentioned, there are a lot of parties in Djursholm where much alcohol is consumed, and this is based on what the parents themselves have told me, as well as statements from various professional people, for instance, police, youth workers, and teachers. Also, the adolescents to whom I have spoken in Djursholm confirm this, and some expressed their concerns about this on a national radio program on young people growing up in Djursholm that was broadcast in 2010. But another related reason for the partying of young people in Djursholm may have something to do with the intolerant attitude in the community for social variation.

In an interview, one youth worker told me that "there is not much space here for expressions of individuality among the adolescents; it could just be a case of someone dressing a certain way, or having tattoos, or living in a particular way. You have to handle yourself appropriately here. There are many demands on young people and they're expected to stay in line. Drinking a lot of alcohol is one way of releasing some of the social pressure." One of his colleagues had a similar view: "The unique thing about Djursholm is that many of the young people are part of big networks. I am not thinking mainly about their friends, but also their families and relatives. It's not at all unusual to have your grandparents a few hundred meters away, or a gang of cousins, uncles, aunts, and so on. There's always some adult keeping an eye on one. It's not easy just being a young person here coming up with some mischief. So when they start drinking it can easily go off the rails." One teacher declared: "I can understand why our pupils drink so much. I find it odd that they don't drink even more. I almost feel they need to party even harder, so they can rid themselves of all their fear, performance anxiety, and pressure. They need a pressure valve."

As noted, Djursholm is a community defined by its ideas on activity, surging ahead full steam, and dynamism. In a world like this, there is a big risk of intolerance for illness, personal and social failures, and setbacks. People associated with such negatives are seen as a threat to the character and *esprit* of the community, quite simply by being unable to enact the dominant norms and values:

> You get the respect you deserve in Djursholm. It is based on your professional role. If you are a success, people are friendly and interested. If you are unsuccessful or things don't work out, the mood turns icy cold here.
>
> (Man, Seventy)

> In Djursholm people want a lot, people have ideas. You can't say, "It didn't work" or "I didn't have the energy."
>
> (Woman, Forties)

> If something goes wrong here, you have much further to fall. I think one ought to think about that; it's not easy around here if something messes up. You stand to lose so much more than in other communities. Not just money and a nice place to live, of course, but also status, friends . . . and even more.
>
> (Woman, Forties)

> When I grew up in Djursholm, there was a view in my family, but also my friends' families, that you'd look down on those who hadn't achieved as much. There was this disdain for all kinds of weakness or failure, and I think this has affected me and also made me a bit like that. "These people are claiming social security; it's their own fault" was how it went. Or if someone's career had slowed, maybe even because they had decided to prioritize time spent with the children, rather than just work, work, work. Yeah, there was a tendency to look down on people who hadn't fulfilled their full potential. "He didn't manage to go the whole way; he dropped out" was how we'd put it.
>
> (Man, Forty-Five)

No one realized we had problems at home; we managed to keep it under wraps. Or people did realize but didn't say anything. It took a while before I had the courage to open up about it, but then many of my friends told me it was just the same for them. People are so worried about rejection. You never speak about family issues in Djursholm—except maybe divorce—other than that it's a case of keeping the lid on.

(Woman, Twenty)

Even those who work in Djursholm and come into contact with residents in crises or problematic situations often have a feeling that any kind of shortcomings or failures are strongly stigmatized, and for this reason not something that people choose to speak about or reveal:

In Djursholm no less than in corporate life you make the grade as long as you are successful and things are going well. But if you have some problems, people quickly retract their feelers. They are strategic in their social lives; they don't want to be friendly with just anyone, and not spontaneously. They want to know that a person is okay and does not have any problems that might affect them, or just the indignity of finding that they are socializing with a failure. There's a fairly stern judgment meted out in this community when it comes to failure. This is a community with a great deal of surface polish.

(Health-Care Employee)

I think there is a strong expectation in Djursholm that one has to be a successful student, and then to be successful in whatever field. Those who fall short tend to blame themselves; if you don't cut the mustard, that means you're weak—you're worse than others.

(Principal)

Confirmation camps are very popular among our young people here, they get to meet new friends and establish contacts. For those of us who work with young people it's a good way of breaking through some of the boundaries with which they surround themselves. You get very close during a residential camp. After a few days they lower their guards, and then we find quite a lot of young people who are struggling with sadness.

(Vicar)

We come into contact with patients suffering from a sense of fear of social fall, for instance as a result of unemployment or divorce.

(Health-Care Employee)

Parents here have so much to lose if things don't go to plan with their jobs, or if they are socially outed because of something embarrassing. People live at a high level in society, and the fall can be very high. When there was a financial crisis a few years ago, some of the parents here actually killed themselves. And all this affected the young people very gravely, of course. Many people here are living right on the edge of their own capacity, but they show off as much as they can. There's a lot of surface here. When it cracks, it cracks dramatically.

(Youth Worker)

The young people here do all the same shit as other young people. The difference is that if you carry on like that you ruin your family's reputation. If you really mess up, your family takes you out and puts you in a private school. This might include problems such as drugs, substance abuse, and psychiatric illness. Young people of this kind are cared for out of sight. They don't live at home; they're often even sent abroad. People absolutely won't have anything to do with social services or the police.

(Teacher)

Judging by the anecdotes of residents and others, the important thing in Djursholm is to keep various problems and failures out of sight, and this relates to the nurturing of collectively held values (the aura), which otherwise hangs in the balance. Problems remain hidden because of the social intolerance regarding any kind of open dialogue about them. A youth worker at one of the schools pointed out, "The pupils are very well trained on a social level; they are very nice on the surface. But things could be difficult on a hidden level. There's no public bullying here, no swearing or violence or persecution. Rather what you get is people being frozen out, abuse on the Internet, text messages. The whole thing is highly sublimated." A local police officer explained, "The problems are not so visible here; people are good at hiding crimes of various kinds." Another policeman told me: "There are a lot of drugs in circulation here. We keep an intense surveillance on the area, but it's difficult. Unlike in other areas, it also happens out of sight here. There aren't many public places here where drug dealing takes place. It all takes place in the houses, and they're off-limits for us. Police work is far easier in other locations." Open drug dealing in Djursholm would not only be criminal; it would also be socially inconceivable. Therefore, out of respect for the collective identity and obviously also the theoretical risk of being caught, drug dealing has to take place unseen.

I spoke to a middle-aged person who felt that "many parents in Djursholm have far too much belief in 'good old Djursholm.' They don't want to see the problems, do not want to recognize the drinking, the drug taking that are going on, and that these young people are not doing so well. There's a feeling of wanting to live in a sort of bubble of contentment." And a teacher who had previously taught at one of the schools said, "This is a community that idealizes the small-town idyll, a place where people care about each other, where everyone is happy, the children are good and feel great. That's why it's such a humiliation when there are divorces, because then you see how this place is just like any other. Trying to keep up this idyllic image probably also makes people want to hide problems for as long as possible. They want Djursholm to look like a little paradise, protected from the world's evils, populated by smart, good people. But in fact there's a lot of dirt under the surface." An entrepreneur who lived in Djursholm noted, "On one level Djursholm is an idyllic place, and on another level it just isn't. Many people are very stressed, and they run about like crazy." When I spoke to a father that I met at one of the preschools, he told me: "To believe that Djursholm is a perfect environment, with perfect people and perfect families, is obviously not true. There are problems here like anywhere else." Another man, a pensioner, said, "We're living in a wonderful place but of course there are problems here behind closed doors. In other communities the problems are visible in a quite different way."

Another source of potential concern, which may further add to problems remaining hidden and unresolved, has been noted by people in positions of responsibility, such as teachers, youth workers in schools, preschool staff, and medical doctors, the basic gist of which is a reluctance to report anything of a disturbing nature to the social services:

> It's difficult to report parents here; staff tend to be worried about doing so. There's a lot of covering up of bruises going on here in Djursholm, and some children are not treated well. Reporting someone rarely leads anywhere, and then also you run the risk of getting lawyers or other people on your tail.
>
> (Teacher)

> Of course it's something problematic reporting people in Djursholm to the social services. There again it's no different in more vulnerable areas. No school wants to turn against the parents. One of the differences about Djursholm compared to less privileged communities is the verbal ability of the parents, their training in debating, and their capacity for covering up any misdemeanors. People resist by means of their verbal and intellectual abilities.
>
> (Principal)

> I don't have any statistics on this, but I can confirm that my colleagues and I intuitively avoid making any approaches or reports to the social services when we suspect that a child has been mistreated. We're obligated to do so, but at the same time we know there will be strong reactions not only from the affected parents but all the parents collectively. There's a spirit of "keep it in the family" here. Getting the authorities involved is viewed as an attack, far worse than any abuse the child may have been subjected to. . . . Staff that do report parents can end up in a lot of trouble, they can be more or less threatened, and problems

can arise with pretty well all the parents. There's a need for strong support from the top, but the principal is not always so strong. All in all one avoids involving the social services. The attractive surface is maintained, but the children are the ones who lose out.

(Teacher)

Whenever there have been allegations made to the social services, the whole place has turned into a proper circus. The staff feel absolutely oppressed and worried. The parents close ranks and support the parents that have been reported. There's a "team spirit" among the parents.

(Teacher)

As a general rule it is not popular in Djursholm to have anything to do with the local authorities in cases of personal or social problems, whether these relate to a possible application for housing benefits, financial support in case of divorce, and so on—because of a generally held view that public organizations imply disclosure of personal issues. One civil servant made the following claim: "Many people don't seek assistance even when they are entitled to it, for instance, financial support for their homes, or dental care. There are plenty of impoverished widows in Djursholm surviving on very low pensions, and no significant fortunes to speak of. But they don't want to move out of their expensive homes, which are so costly to maintain." A colleague of hers went on to suggest that even with more serious issues, including crime, there was a similar reluctance: "In Djursholm it is considered shoddy to go to the local authority to ask for help, and I am not even thinking of financial support here, but rather support to help deal with problems at home caused by substance abuse, sexual assault, incest, or domestic violence against wives and children."

To reiterate, there is social consensus on problems, poverty, and other concerns not being something that should be aired in public. However, in cases where certain people do get embroiled in scandal, there is social pressure on them to move away and not besmirch or contaminate the aura, status, and prestige of the community. Even when the odd person falls in a moral or social sense, Djursholm must always remain shiny and perfect.

Yet even if clearly immoral behavior, such as physical abuse in the home or incest or the like, can be kept under wraps in the long term, the consequence of this is that personal suffering is placed lower on the scale of concern than the maintenance of the collective identity. In Djursholm, as stated, all people are a source of potential social risk to one another: children, parents, relatives, friends, and acquaintances—the community is under constant threat. One woman that I spoke to, who had divorced her husband and been forced out of their home, had the following to say: "Yes, like many others I ended up living in one of the areas with terraced housing. Everyone knows it is called the 'divorce ditch,' and that it's a place where women live. I lost my old house, but I also lost a lot of our old friends. They probably just felt, 'We don't want to socialize with a loser.'" When seen in this context, it is not so remarkable that the residents of Djursholm choose not to talk about or in any other way show themselves, or any other family member, having any kind of problems. One father of four children claimed: "The name of the game here is knowing how to behave yourself, and even when something negative happens, you're expected to keep mum about it."

PLATE 1

The Castle. Photo by Udo Schröter, CC BY-SA 3.0, via Wikimedia Commons.

PLATE 2

The Upper-Secondary School. Photo by Udo Schröter, CC BY-SA 3.0, via Wikimedia Commons.

PLATE 3

The Chapel. Photo by Janders, CC BY-SA 3.0, via Wikimedia Commons.

PLATE 4

The Country Club. Photo by Holger Ellgaard, CC BY-SA 3.0,
via Wikimedia Commons.

PLATE 5

A Private Home. Photo by Holger Ellgaard, CC BY-SA 3.0, via Wikimedia Commons.

PLATE 6

A Private Home. Photo by Holger Ellgaard, CC BY-SA 3.0, via Wikimedia Commons.

PLATE 7

A Private Home. Photo by Holger Ellgaard, CC BY-SA 3.0, via Wikimedia Commons.

PLATE 8

A Private Home. Photo by Holger Ellgaard, CC BY-SA 3.0, via Wikimedia Commons.

PLATE 9

A Private Home. Photo by Holger Ellgaard, CC BY-SA 3.0, via Wikimedia Commons.

PLATE 10

A Private Home. Photo by Holger Ellgaard, CC BY-SA 3.0, via Wikimedia Commons.

9

SERVICE STAFF

T HERE IS A HISTORICAL division between, on the one hand, the property owners, and, on the other, those who work in Djursholm, denoted as "service staff" by the residents. The service staff may seem insignificant in relation to them, but in fact they are crucial to the self-image and aura of the community. The very notion of *service staff* implies that one category of people is serving another. Excessively simple or practical work should be avoided by good residents, considering the community's prestige and social ambitions. As most of those who work in Djursholm do not live there, a "natural" social boundary and hierarchical order is created. A local authority employee told me: "Few of the municipal employees live here, which must be fairly unique when you look at other places." Service staff remain a very important group of people in Djursholm, partly because of the work they do and partly because they provide a mirror image of what the residents of Djursholm must *not* become—shop assistants, restaurant staff, police officers, civil servants, teachers, tradesmen, and gardeners. Because children and young people do not see their own parents, or those of their friends' parents, performing such roles, they learn early what types of jobs they ought to be striving for. As a result, the service staff perform a function as "anti–role models."

Individuals from the service staff category generally describe Djursholm and its inhabitants from a perspective of outsiders and observers—even though there are a few examples of residents who might also be regarded as service staff, for instance, a handful of preschool and school employees, as well as the odd employee or owner of service-providing companies. However, the vast majority of those working in Djursholm that I met and spoke to do not live there. Many of them have experiences of working in other social environments, and are therefore able to take a comparative view. Their impressions obviously vary, but a common thread in all their descriptions is a sense of Djursholm being a different sort of community. Often there is an initial impression of it as a wealthy and exclusive community, a place to be approached with a certain amount of respect or even awe. A school principal put it as follows: "Coming for an employment interview in Djursholm can be a big thing for some people. It can be quite a leap to start working here." And yet the feeling of being an external observer of a community, in which one has no part, remains even in those who have worked there for many years. Following is a selection of statements as an illustration of this:

This is an elite community; that is how I see it. There are many powerful people here in positions of influence. Many people grow up in families that have power. There are a lot of big-wigs living in Djursholm, these days I suppose it's mainly business executives that move in, and obviously they have fairly specific values.

(Employee, Sports Club)

If I compare with where I was working before, the relationship with parents is more formal here. It's almost like a customer relationship the way you are with them, it used to be more familiar and informal in my other workplace. You got the odd hug and, well, it was more informal. Here there's no proper space for spontaneous and open expressions between parents and staff. You have to be careful about getting personal. There's a distance. And, of course, mainly my younger colleagues may get a little insecure in their relationship with some mother or father that is an important corporate figure appearing on the TV every other day. But I don't actually think parents want to get too close to the staff. They want to maintain a distance, stake out a certain reserve. They are very pleasant and all that, but there's still a distance, which I have not noticed before. As staff we are also a bit guarded about what we say about each other, the whole atmosphere just gets more formal.

(Preschool Employee)

There are very strong images of Djursholm. There are tall gates and hedges, they literally keep people out. There seems to be a desire to show that one has something valuable, something remarkable. And the big houses inspire respect in their own right; they make humans look small, but the person living in them becomes big and powerful. If you live in a place like that, well, there just has to be something remarkable about you. Djursholm wants to be on its own, the whole community is like a *gated community*. And this has been accentuated now even more with the extreme house prices.

(Preschool Director)

One common experience among the service staff seems to be a perspective of Djursholm as a partly isolated world, where people live in a bubble outside the rhythm and terms of the rest of society. In a national radio feature from 2001, a nanny explains that "they [the mothers] have lunch every day with their girlfriends, she goes in to have her nails done, they do things like that, it's just unbelievable. It's so different from how things are in the countryside . . . she [the mother] asked, 'how do you grow potatoes?' I was just shocked, it's so obvious to someone else how you grow potatoes. They have to read up on things before they can do anything." In line with this a teacher felt that Djursholm is a closed world, a bit of a duck pond. "They travel a lot, but they don't have a clue about the rest of the country. Most of the children don't have any friends from outside." And a preschool teacher explained, "Many of our children have never been on a bus or a train, so we train them to do that. The children may well be used to flying around the world, but the everyday things are not part of their lives. So we sometimes take bus trips to train them." A colleague of hers added: "Yes, and when the children travel on the underground, they really stare when they see people with dark skin, or beggars. They probably think that everyone looks like people in Djursholm. This is their world, after all." A youth leader explained to me, on a related theme: "Children in this environment grow into naive adolescents. By that I mean they haven't seen a great deal of the real world. And it can be a real shock to them. As they go into their teenage years, they become aware of the fact that it isn't always a positive thing coming from Djursholm. You have to keep quiet about that when you're out on the town. And that can be an important realization for many people here."

In line with the feeling of being outsiders, which service staff seem to have to put up with, they perceive themselves as subordinated to the residents on a social, economic, and conceptual level, and in a corresponding sense they feel that the residents consider themselves superior to them:

There is a generally disdainful tone about normal work here. If something breaks or you need something fixed in the garden or the house, then you just "get yourself a Pole." It's rare to hear that Mum or Dad are working on the house or that they've helped rake leaves in the autumn. That sort of work is probably not considered important enough.

(Preschool Teacher)

Some of the people in Djursholm that I talk to, give themselves legitimacy by saying, "Well, I have lived here for forty years" or "I was born here."

(Municipal Employee)

The students just get up and walk away from their plates when they have finished. That's why we have put up a sign by the entrance to the cafeteria about removing their plates.

(Staff, School Cafeteria)

Many of the patients here work in health care, which can make our job difficult. They're quite capable of telling us what we have to do, which becomes a real ordeal. But the same goes for the company executives, who keep explaining what they think we ought to do, even though they're not doctors. They watch you the whole time. . . . Some might say something like, "I talked to my friend, who's a professor, and my cousin who's a doctor and it turns out you're right!" There's a lot of control going on in the background.

(Employee, Health-Care Service)

There's really a bit of a superior outlook here. When I was doing a summer job in one of the preschools, for some reason I said to one of the fathers who was picking up his child, "It's always good to have an education" or something like that. Because I was studying at the university at that point. And then he said, "Yes, but it doesn't seem to have helped in your case."

(Preschool Teacher)

That the service staff feel themselves downgraded obviously affects their self-esteem, which must certainly be regarded as functional: for the consecration that Djursholm offers its residents was never supposed to include them, and it is always based on a very clear social differentiation. An article on the tennis club website features an interview with the person responsible for the club cafeteria, a woman who reveals that she lives in another less affluent neighborhood. When asked what she finds most dull about her work, she says the following: "Sometimes I wish that both adults and children could be a bit better at removing their crockery, pushing their chairs back in, putting away their shoes at the entrance, and so on. . . . Although I sometimes behave like an extra mum I wish more people would just understand that their mother does not work here. I feel extra surprised when not even grown-ups can show some humility and respect in that way." The tennis club may emphasize its family values, but it is actually beneath the notice of a good local inhabitant to remove the washing up in the club cafeteria. This sort of dirty work is supposed to be done by service staff living outside the community.

When I have lunches and meals at a fast-food restaurant in Djursholm, where many children and young people go, it is the rule rather than the exception for them not to remove their trays or throw away their discarded soft drink bottles. However, tradesmen and others who come to eat there do take away their trays and throw away the leftovers in a bin placed there on the premises for that very reason. And so we see that even in a cafeteria the children of Djursholm learn who they are expected to be, and are quite capable of comparing their own behavior with that of other groups in the community. In the radio program referred to above, one young nanny described how once she came along to a big party, to take care of the parents' children. She felt she had made an effort with her appearance, but once she got there it was beyond any doubt that she was the nanny. "They all had really beautiful long gowns, sequins and shawls, really over-the-top hairstyles, diamond necklaces, and I was just feeling, 'Yes, I'm the nanny,' surely they're just looking at me as if I'm on a lower level?" One of her girlfriends explained that she felt the nannies were considered to be people who had not succeeded, "It has something of an underclass feeling about it . . . one isn't seen as equal either intellectually or career-wise, one can be used, people don't quite give us normal consideration, we're regarded almost as if we're lower than them." Similar experiences are absolutely reconcilable with the basic norms and values of Djursholm, a socially highly placed community that expects great deeds of its inhabitants. This is even important in order to confirm the prestige of the community. To "only" be a nanny or a café waitress is not viewed as socially successful and does not contribute to the aura and status of the community; as an inhabitant of Djursholm you are expected to "do better" than that. To have any regard for such jobs, or put them on a par socially with oneself, would be a way of fundamentally challenging the codes and lifestyle. When children and young people at the tennis club rise from the table and leave the clearing up to an employee, this is precisely what is expected of them.

In today's Djursholm it is generally believed that local authority employees are effectively hired by the residents, and are supposed to be working for them. This also includes the municipal politicians, a number of whom may also be residents. A local man explained this to me: "If there is one thing we, the residents, don't like, it's power-crazed politicians. In our hearts and souls we're conservatives, but now we gave them a flick on the nose by voting for a liberal party, because the conservatives had become tone deaf. We're the ones who ought to be running Djursholm through our politicians, not the other way around." Another person explained to me that people do not want to be steered; they actually want other people to be steered. "That is why we've had such violent reactions to politicians trying to bulldoze the population here." A parent explained her view of the local council, while talking about the plans of the latter to shut down the municipal youth center: "It was saved by the young people; they behaved in a very professional way. And they had the support of their parents, we are a fairly important group for the politicians after all, there are a lot of taxpayers here."

There are plenty of examples of the fairly direct influence of residents in Djursholm over municipal decisions. In the 1990s the state secondary and upper-secondary school was taken over by a foundation headed by two Djursholm residents. One of the teachers at the school explained the following to me: "The foundation had had its eye on the school for a long time. They managed to mobilize the parents here in Djursholm, and so they started putting pressure on the local council to take it over." An official from the local council told me that the council did not as a general rule want to be the driving force that came up with and implemented the ideas. Instead, it preferred to be a facilitating and empowering player, with the ideas and suggestions ultimately coming from the municipal residents. "The council was not the driver in the creation of the new school, which had been in such a bad state before that," he explained. A colleague of his with many years of experience of working in Djursholm, felt that "if one goes to the local authority in this area, and maybe particularly if one lives in Djursholm, then one has a sense of oneself as a person who is worthy of being listened to and taken seriously. In this municipality I think there is a desire to be very sensitive to public opinion, and whenever this has not been the case, the effects have been punitive. Politicians and civil servants are not 'bureaucratic' toward the residents but actually flexible. In other local authorities it can be fairly rigid and strict." In other words, any suggestion that the service staff might be higher placed than the residents have been highly unpopular. One member of the tennis club suggested, "If the club director were to show up here in a suit and walk around making a big deal of himself, we'd put him in his place right away. In many other clubs it is not like that."

Among the people that I have met that work for various service providers, there is a general sense of the local residents as demanding. A member of the service staff in Djursholm has to count on being checked and scrutinized. A local authority employee said: "Documentation is very important, not least because people demand very exact information from us. And so we have to write down the salient facts carefully. We get a lot of e-mails and telephone calls. Everything has to be responded to in twenty-four hours, which is in line with the municipality's goal of offering a high level of service." An employee in the health-care sector in Djursholm told me that "many of our patients demand to see excerpts from the patient journals. They want to see what has been written about them." A vicar who had previously worked in Djursholm told me in an interview that, during a confirmation camp, while he was pouring away alcohol belonging to two young people from Djursholm, one of them had asked, "Do you have the right to do that?" And when a police officer confiscated a placard with the text ACAB, an acronym for "All Cops Are Bastards," at the graduation festivities in Djursholm, she was herself reported (by the students) and, later, found guilty of misconduct at the district court for having violated the student's fundamental legal right to freedom of expression.

As was earlier stated, service staff, whether a school principal or a road construction worker, are regarded as socially inferior to the residents—while also in practice an employee of theirs. A well-known preacher, who had earlier been involved with the Djursholm Chapel, said: "Here, there is no excessive respect for a person like me. People say what they want to say, no one is insecure about this in Djursholm." Another former preacher felt, on a related subject, that "the congregation is generally very attentive about what I am saying. One has to have something to say, and one has to think about what one is saying. They are sitting there as active, interested individuals. One can't be dogmatic and come up with a lot of simple pointers about how they are supposed to think. Instead I try to open up a way for each one of them to think for himself."

Service staff in Djursholm are a fairly vulnerable group, although, in their own view, they are merely trying to do their jobs. This is especially true of job categories within the local authority, for instance, civil servants handling planning permission applications or overseeing the budgets of retirement homes, or teachers in charge of student assessments, or police officers. For instance, in an article in the local newspaper, a number of residents express their anger at the local authority, which, they allege, has not informed them about the new parking regulations at one of the bathing spots in Djursholm, where, as a consequence, a number of residents have ended up with parking tickets. "To suddenly get a ticket in a place where one has been parking for more than fifty years is incredibly provocative," said one man. The politician in charge of the new scheme confirmed that she has taken a number of calls from irate residents. The politician's answer is to blame it on the parking attendant who has issued the fines (even though this fully complies with the new rules, which the politician has had a hand in introducing): "It's absolutely mad," she told the newspaper. When the youth center was threatened with closure, as reported earlier, young people protested against the politicians. In the local newspaper the proposal was described as a cut caused by the budget the local authority had drawn up. It was emphasized that the parental associations supported the continuation of the youth center—ultimately the civil servants (in other words, the service staff) were blamed for the affair. After meeting with the young people, the politicians decided not to go through with the planned closure.

Following are quotations that describe how some of the individuals that work in Djursholm view their working conditions:

In Djursholm we have private individuals who get annoyed by some deficiency and come to us offering to solve it, for instance, some sporting activity that is not being offered, and so on. You are hardly going to say no to a person who's offering to pay for an Astroturf pitch costing a lot of money. But on the other hand, there's a risk that there will be a sort of expectation from that person towards the local authority. It goes against the basic idea of equal treatment for all under the rule of law.

(Local Politician)

You are always pleasantly treated at first when there is a planning application. They want to create a good contact. But if things don't go their way the tone can quickly change. First they go to the head of the city planning department. Then to the politicians. Lawyers are often involved, although they are often not at all competent when it comes to planning and building regulations, or municipal rules for that matter. Partly it's about scare techniques and showing their influence. But we are a local authority, after all; we have to comply with regulations. You can't just talk your way into a planning approval that runs against laws and regulations.

(Municipal Employee)

Parents often get involved when you are assessing the children's grades, and they often take things further. They don't give up; they can't accept that the teacher's assessment is correct. Being challenged or called into question is just a part of daily life, even by people who are totally ignorant and uninitiated. I have been told many times that I am "taking sides" because I have not given someone's son or daughter the assessment that was expected, i.e., the highest possible grade. The rights of the individual to decide over his own everyday life is very strong here. People find "freedom" important, freedom to be able to make decisions about your own life. Many of the people here also have this opportunity in their working lives. They get frustrated if they run into obstacles. Their freedom to define their own reality is then curtailed.

(Teacher)

The team instructors can't get on with what they are doing. There is so much verbal diarrhea from the parents. Lots of letters calling things into question.

(Head, Sports Club)

The preschool staff have to be very clear about rules; otherwise the parents like to make their own rules. Possibly they are used to making the decisions and having other people adapt to them. But things don't work if everyone has different rules. And we can't back away from that, we'd end up with chaos.

(Preschool Director)

The vast proportion of our citizens are socially functional. They behave in a civilized manner to us. They don't call or yell or make threats. All in all it's quite civil. But pressure can take place in other ways, for instance we may be contacted by a lawyer, or they send e-mails from their workplaces, making sure it's quite clear to one that they are people of substance, company chairmen or doctors.

(Municipal Employee)

When you meet our citizens, there are a lot of foreign expressions and cultural references, for instance, to some performance at the opera. Even more you have a certain style of clothes, which also sends out certain signals. I think it's about presenting yourself as knowledgeable, intellectual. And, of course, it is an attempt to influence you.

(Municipal Employee)

A very particular group of service staff is, as mentioned earlier, the young nannies that work in Djursholm. Nannies do much of the dirty work that the residents want to avoid in their daily lives: dropping off and picking up their children, shopping, laundry, even just spending time with the children. Nannies are also important symbols of the elevation offered by the place. In much the same way as the phenomenon of the housewife, the nanny adds value to particular families, and also contributes positively to the community's prestige and reputation. A Djursholm without nannies would be seen as a waning Djursholm. Despite this, the terms on which they work can be exploitative and anything but "moral." The earlier-mentioned radio program describes how being paid under the table is common, and how nannies can be fired without the giving of notice for the slightest foible. Nannies come and go in the families. One of them put it as follows: "They can use you as much as they want, and if you say anything about it, they can just decide to fire you." In the radio program, there is a description of a nanny who will shortly be leaving, and who must now explain everything to her successor. She explains how the parents want their laundry handled, how certain colors are not to be mixed, that particular garments cannot be tumble-dried, and so on. The proceedings have the formality of a proper job, where the new hand is being shown the ropes by the one about to leave. However, the employer is absent. The "outgoing" nanny explains the importance of communicating clearly with the family, "so things don't get misunderstood, and you really understand them correctly right from the start." Any idea that the new girl should slowly get accustomed to the family seems out of the question. The reporter tells us that she has been given one day to learn the job. The old nanny tells her replacement how important it is to articulate any problems at an early stage, even if "this is really difficult." She rounds this off by saying, "Apart from that they're quite easy to deal with, so I don't think you should have any problems. Really."

The terms of employment come over as insecure and one-sided in the report. My own interviews with nannies in Djursholm highlighted this precise issue. One of them ventured: "Sometimes I feel like I'm the slave in the house, I have to do lots of different things. And they add on things that we never agreed on at the start, like mowing the lawn or unpacking their bags after they have been off traveling. But who are you supposed to complain to? There's no one who can help you. All you can do is stop working for them." Another nanny explained: "They seem to think you should be grateful for even being here, or that people like us who grew up in the countryside have been more or less destitute. Maybe it's a bit like that for some girls from Eastern Europe, but good God, not for us Swedish girls. Some people are grateful, and it means they put up with a lot." The same person also emphasized the advantages of being a Swedish-born nanny. "We know our rights, after all; we speak the language, and we can always pack our bags and go home. Many of the foreign girls have to do really crap jobs, make little money, don't have any leisure time, and sometimes live in bad accommodation. I know of one girl who lived in a little room in the cellar without a window, even. They can't just go home. Even so some of them just get kicked out, into the street. People just say, more or less, 'Hey, you've got two hours to pack your bags.' This is actually not a very pleasant environment; it can be really tough here."

Although many of those that I met who worked in Djursholm took a critical position on the demands and expectations of the residents, there are also several examples of individuals who were deeply impressed by the community and its residents. Many do have an impression of it as a place full of expertise and knowledge, a community populated by the country's elite. Just as Djursholm can function as a social promotion to those who move there, it can do much the same for those who merely come to work. One person who was working in the home-care sector suggested, "Here, people want to know *why* and *how*; all the time you have to be able to explain, and this helps my development as a human being." A colleague of hers felt that in Djursholm most of the people were "economists, entre-preneurs, or doctors," which meant that she was working in a "good and interesting environment." And a teacher at one of the schools felt that "you don't just get bog-standard doctors living here." A shop owner described how she was getting good advice from her customers about how to run her business. "People here ask how things are going. They are interested and knowledgeable about running a company." One person who was working in the health-care sector felt that "parents in Djursholm are updated and know their rights, you are talking to people who know things. They are not intellectually challenged." During my conversation with a leading pol-itician in the local authority, he explained that "in Djursholm people are energetic and involved. This is not a laid-back environment. The general educational level is very high, and this influences me of course." During a conversation with a trainer at one of the sports associations, he suddenly pointed discreetly at a woman walking past, telling me who she was, and adding that "she is incredibly successful." While we spoke, another woman came up to talk about a matter relating to the training. Afterward he also named this woman, offering the additional information that "she has millions and millions in the bank," all of which suggested that he was rather impressed by the financial potency with which he was surrounded.

In an article in a radical left-wing journal, the reporter, who had just visited Djursholm, and who also used to work in the local grocery store there, states that the employees "lived in a silent agreement that we would not discuss the injustices that we were living with, and that it was our lot to serve this most unappealing 'top-of-the-heap' group for bad rates of pay, insecure terms of employment, and awful working hours. The class hatred that so many workers have was conspicuous by its absence. It was rather the other way around. Many people identified with the finer aspects of Djursholm, and took on an attitude and opinions that I had never seen in other grocery stores where I had worked." A caretaker at one of the schools described his job as follows: "Being a caretaker in Djursholm has a bit more status than any other place. Even someone like me can be a part of the image of Djursholm. I am treated respectfully and in a very friendly way by the parents. They are eager to show that we are equal." There are also plenty of examples of how people in positions of power in Djursholm, such as high-ranking civil servants in the local authority, school principals, or politicians, have been invited into the fellowship of Djursholm, for instance, by offers of membership in various associations. As one person told me, "I accepted my membership with a measure of pride." Although he also added, "The invitation may have had certain ulterior purposes." A municipal civil servant stated, "Obviously it is a bit special working in an environment where so many important people live. It's quite something meeting them and getting to know them. Sometimes when I am watching the TV in the evening and I see one of them, I catch myself thinking, 'I was having a coffee with him today.'"

In other words, some people I have met with seemed more or less grateful for the opportunity to work there. One common theme among the teachers that I have interviewed, for instance, is that they are able to concentrate on their main task, this being the actual teaching, rather than putting much of their time and energy into disciplinary matters. To this extent, Djursholm certainly does consolidate their status and self-esteem.

One shop owner explained: "It's a bit of a luxury working out here. No metro, no commuter trains, no gangs of shoplifters. There's hardly anything stolen." A police officer who had previously been stationed in Djursholm among other places felt that "working as a police with young people out there gives you every opportunity of making progress. The parents are pleasant and good, they work and there's no substance abuse, it's an enormous difference from other places." In a newspaper article on Djursholm from 2004, a street sweeper noted, "It's a real pleasure working in Djursholm. The environment is amazing and everything is spick and span. But you have to stay on good terms with everyone." In the same article, an estate agent comments on how "it's a true privilege operating here as an estate agent."

When considered as a common group, such statements become an illustration of the potency of Djursholm, namely, its ability to socially raise up people on the condition that they are capable of acting in accordance with the community's expectations. As long as service staff act as service staff are supposed to act, they will receive their wages in the form of economic capital—and they will also be paid in symbolic capital. A cashier in Djursholm is to some extent something quite different from a cashier in a socially disadvantaged area. This new self-image is formed by the service staff themselves, in their constant meetings with the local residents, in which they are treated as socially inferior and yet also socially superior to people in the same employment categories outside Djursholm. One person working in home care had the following comment to make: "I may sound a bit critical of the customers in Djursholm and how they relate to me and my colleagues, but I do think we all have a lot of respect for them. These are people who have had influence and positions of importance in society. Just being able to walk into their magnificent homes has an effect on you. I do think it affects me. Many times I have thought to myself that it's an honor working for them. You meet so many interesting people." A colleague of hers told me: "It's fantastic working in home care in Djursholm. The customers have seen so much, have experienced a great deal. They have a great deal to tell. They have traveled and met interesting people, they have had exciting, important jobs. I like listening to their stories."

Some of the people began by explaining to me how they initially felt a lot of respect for their new jobs, when they started, but that they relaxed more and more in their relationship to the community. The closer to Djursholm that one gets, the less elevated and extraordinary it becomes. A local authority civil servant put it as follows: "When I first started doing my job here in this municipality, I was struck by how large the houses were in Djursholm. Obviously you meet an environment like this with a certain amount of respect. But over time you begin to realize that those who live here are just ordinary people. They don't always live up to their noble dwellings; let's put it like that." The nanny who was interviewed in the earlier-mentioned radio program explained how at first "I was expecting an enormous house with a pool, all the things you imagine rich people in Djursholm have, well, probably they have a tennis court, a golf course, everything in their grounds. But this was a completely normal house. Big, but normal. Sort of the same kind of kitchen we have at home, maybe a bit bigger." Before this nanny came to Djursholm, she had thought "maybe now I'll be living next door to some celebrity . . . it's a bit cool, I'm the neighbor of *him* or *her.*" But in the end she did not see a trace of any celebrities; instead she had an impression of the community as rather ordinary. In much the same way, the images of Djursholm the service staff had at first when they took on their new jobs contributed to an elevation of their own respectability and honor, unless they did not choose to tell the real story of their latter experiences, in which Djursholm seemed more or less an "ordinary" community. There is an interest from both the service staff and the residents themselves to maintain the generally established idea of Djursholm as a shining, well-functioning, and extraordinary community.

Whenever I went into shops and restaurants in Djursholm, I had an impression of the service as very good—as if the staff members were making a special effort to provide good service. One rarely has to stand in line in Djursholm; as soon as one goes into a shop one is usually greeted with a quick "hello," and there seems to be a desire in the grocery store, the chemist, and in the banks to quickly assist the customer. For instance, when on one occasion I wanted to return an item in a grocery store, I immediately got my money back without any discussion, with a substantial amount of extra money "as compensation for your trouble"—something that I cannot think would happen in similar shops around the country. A shop assistant explained to me that this was "policy," and that problems had to be sorted out "quickly and without fuss." An employee at a health-care center explained, "When you come here we want you to feel comfortable and properly welcomed. We always say hello to people coming in, or sitting in the waiting room. We don't just walk past." In general there seems to be an idea among the employers in Djursholm that one must be flexible and easygoing with the residents, which accords well with the idea of being service staff and nothing more, but also with the additional factor that this also contributes to the consecration of the service staff. In return, they gain the liking, approval, and praise of the residents, which has a positive effect on their own social status. Several of those that I interviewed even struck me as very cooperative and sympathetic and more than willing to add to my questions or suggestions with expressions such as "absolutely right," "I completely agree," "it's exactly as you say," "precisely," or similar phrases.

A departmental head in the local authority claimed: "Our staff have to have the highest possible personal integrity, and obviously they have to be able to resist any sort of bribes from these wealthy individuals. But you have to have an understanding for the unique mood in Djursholm, you must have social competence and the ability to understand the very special Djursholm spirit. If you don't understand that, you're finished. You have to have a fingertip feeling for it, so you can read it." In a similar way, a sports club director said, "You can't just push here. There are lots of wills, lots of little lords and ladies all over the place. You have to listen to them and then find a solution." But this is not only about "fitting in with the community" by being cooperative, as one of the school principals in Djursholm explained to me—service staff also have to behave as service staff in Djursholm. This includes the clothes they wear, their body language, their way of laughing, talking, eating, and so on. In a newspaper article about child minding offered by an agency, the personnel manager of potential nannies in Djursholm explained that in addition to being positive and malleable (which includes the suggestion that one should answer affirmatively if offered coffee by the client, even if one does not drink coffee), nannies should dress in an appropriate manner. The style should be "sporty, neat, classic. Think Ralph Lauren, Peak Performance, Lacoste." Blue jeans also work fine, maybe with "a little blue cardigan. Or a pink top," and, if it makes the child minder look good, "the hair tied up in a ponytail." Then add "a pair of pearl earrings. They symbolize motherhood," the personnel manager says by way of a conclusion. In general it is important to be "reliable, cheerful, and switched-on." One of the nannies I talked to put it as follows: "How one should be as a nanny? Well, never say no; always be cheerful and pleasant and on the ball. Be full steam ahead and never go against anything."

The importance of the social behavior of the service staff to Djursholm's aura and prestige is exemplified by a foundation set up by a local family, which provides financial rewards to staff members in health care, schools, and social services in Djursholm who have been pointed out as particularly approachable and sympathetic. In just the same way as there are prizes and awards for children and young people who behave in a certain way, the same applies to service staff. The reason for this is that, just as with children and young people, this category of people is crucial for the maintenance or even betterment of Djursholm's aura. Prizes are awarded at an annual event, at the symbolically charged venue of Djursholm Castle, to which also high-ranking civil servants and local authority councillors are invited. Thereby it becomes a broadened social manifestation of what the residents expect from those who work in Djursholm. At the same time, this and other events serve to highlight the differences between service staff in Djursholm and other places. In a brochure from a pensioners' association, under the heading of "Who Is the Angel in Your Life?," mention is made of the foundation's awards, with elderly people having the opportunity to nominate members of staff. According to the article, the foundation aims to encourage those "who do something extra for the elderly in our municipality." In a magazine aimed at an elderly readership, I found an article about an auxiliary nurse working in a retirement home who had received a grant of some US$1,500 from the foundation. In the article, the nurse is described as "having carried out her work with empathy and always with a smile on her face"—further, to the expectation of basic medical competence, which the foundation may have difficulties judging, it is precisely this *smile* that is the operative point. In an e-mail received from a highly committed member of a support association to Djursholm's public library, I was told that the finances of the association were sufficiently robust to allow for "small gifts on birthdays and at Christmas" for library staff, as an encouragement for them to keep working for the best interests of the library visitors.

Such gifts, like the grants, are a form of regulating the actions of service staff, with an emphasis on their behaving in a "service-minded way." It is not only organizations that seek to reward a certain mode of behavior among service staff. It is also common for parents to pool their resources to give presents to staff at preschools and schools at the end of the year (which admittedly tends to happen all over the country), and for individual parents to give gifts to staff, for instance, at Christmas. It seems beyond any doubt that a *pleasant* and *attractive manner* is much appreciated in the service staff, which, as we have already observed, also tends to include their dress code and presentation. One nanny told me: "I can tell that they like the way I am. I get clothes and things from them. . . . I suppose they want one to look a certain way, too. The mother in my family has always liked my makeup and hairstyle. . . . When I came home my mother said, 'Oh, you've really changed your style'—except it wasn't really my style." A teacher explained: "In this school you're supposed to be an extrovert and positive in your outlook, not some classic teacher type wearing Birkenstocks. All the women here are very presentable, with chic color schemes, and hardly anyone is overweight."

Several managerial people in Djursholm that I have met have emphasized that the social capacities of the staff are crucial, and they keep this in focus at the recruitment stage. An employee in a sports club told me, "When I was recruited it was a fairly lengthy process, with tests and other things, and it was all very much about what kinds of values I had." One school principal confided she always gave consideration to how a potential employee would fit socially into Djursholm. In addition to formal qualifications and attainments, an important question is the general behavior of the teacher. One preschool director had even observed that "many of our holiday stand-ins, who are usually young women, are highly appreciated. They lack experience and education, but they have a very good way of dealing with the parents, and so they become popular." One shop owner felt that "what it's all about, above all, are the social skills of the staff—not that they're experts at different kinds of wood, textiles, or whatever the case may be." She went on: "It's good to be knowledgeable, but you don't have to be an expert. More than anything what you need here is a way that appeals to the customer. The customer is always right, you have to bear that in mind. If the customer is not happy we take the goods back without any discussion. Don't talk back. Or the customers will talk about you, and the gossip will spread around here like a wildfire. Your name, your reputation, everything." Another shop owner had the following to say: "Maybe people think it's an easy thing, running a shop in Djursholm, just because it's in Djursholm, but that is not correct. You won't get far here just on the strength of a good idea. Everything is dependent on your social skills. You have to keep on your toes the whole time. The customers are very demanding and rumors can start flying really easily." What it is about, according to one estate agent, is "having a good way of relating—it is your way of socially navigating that is put to the test. It's a question of how you were raised, being a successful estate agent in an area like this." One police officer that I interviewed offered the following comment: "When you work in Djursholm, it forms you in a certain way. You're facing a very special climate here. It's not heated; it's polite, civilized, and worldly. You can take things down a notch; it's all about reading the situation. You can't get all tense and flex your muscles and yell at people." A colleague of his added, "As a police officer in Djursholm, you have to be low-key. People around here know about the law, and their own rights, sometimes they even know more than we do. You have to discuss things and build up a common understanding. You absolutely can't raise your voice or try to assert yourself, not even to young people. People have a positive attitude to the police here, but you are always being scrutinized. You have to behave very correctly and sympathetically."

The required social skills are also about being able to match the residents in terms of knowledge and experience. An employee at a company in

Djursholm felt that "you can't just come along like some kid and seem unsure of yourself. You have to have some weight. Not be a *rookie*." In general, according to one employer, "experienced and secure staff are appreciated, people who can face the customers in a pleasant but self-confident manner. You have to have a certain amount of weight here to be able to say no." A civil servant at the local council felt, in this context, that "here, there's a lot of calling things into question, people have opinions. They feel they know best themselves. There's a lot of good in that. But it means we have to stay alert. The challenge is that not everyone is quite satisfied. Which is not good. The challenge is finding a line of reasoning that gets you respect. You can't just fold and go along with everyone." The estate agent quoted above also said, "You have to be yourself here; it's about being who you are. . . . Social competence in my world is about being able to have a discussion about a sale, to be honest and have the ability to say it as it is, if something is not good. In which case you must not also be fairly knowledgeable about your subject." An employee at one of the schools in Djursholm felt that "in order to do well here as a teacher, it's better if you are not a recent graduate. Not because of the children, not because they need extra help, quite the opposite. It's actually about the parents. They sometimes know what they are talking about, but they are always demanding."

Service staff members in Djursholm are expected to be "of a better kind," just as the residents are expected to be "better than average folk." Only the leaders, or, as one might put it, "the best people," are supposedly moving to Djursholm, which in today's economically minded society is confirmed by their ability to buy a house there. In a corresponding way the service staff also have to be the best, which will also tend to contribute to the spirit and lifestyle. For this same reason they must keep exerting themselves. A vicar, who for several years was based in Djursholm, had a sense of "having to deliver" in his vocational work. "You're expected to be on top form at christenings, weddings, and funerals. And you will have feedback; both the rod and roses will come your way. When people are displeased, the rector will know about it." It is about "giving your all," as one shopkeeper put it. A preschool employee echoed this: "You have to have a strong work ethic here; we go to work even when we are feeling a bit unwell. I don't think it's like that in other places. We know the parents have important jobs. We are very involved. We feel we want to do a good job—it's a feeling you have inside. There again, people around here keep their eyes on you. I mean, if I don't do my utmost, my boss will know about it before long. I think the mood brings out a strong work ethic; everyone wants to dive in and do as much as they can in the best possible way." In other words, Djursholm elevates not only its inhabitants but also its employees—on the condition that they behave in a certain way. Being "top-notch," as has been observed, is about being customer oriented and also about one's general behavior.

10

BECOMING AN ELITE

T HE MOST IMPORTANT institutions in Djursholm for understanding the culture and character of the community, and thereby how people are formed into Djursholmers are the preschools and schools— educational institutions with a central role in reproducing the community aura and safeguarding its consecration of people into leaders. These institutions guarantee that the children have a shining, as opposed to a mediocre, future. It is through them Djursholm takes on a sort of embodied importance. These are the places where children and young people spend much of their waking hours, and, especially during their teenage years, the schools fill a crucial social function. As one person put it: "It is school that turns normal humans into Djursholmers. If you have not gone to school here, you'll never be able to feel like a local. I no longer have any contact with friends of mine who did not go to school here." One mother, who had lived with her family for a number of years in Djursholm, told me in an interview:

In general there's a spirit among the parents of "this is our school," which is about being protective of one's school, almost like people in very rural places when it comes to their little village school, which is not only important for their children's education, but to the community as a whole.

A similar view was put forward by a preschool director:

> The preschool is a very important "social connector" for the families. It's not just a matter of picking up and dropping off and going to the odd parents' meeting; it's a lot more than that.

But obviously it is not only social reasons that give the schools their predominant position in the community's pulse and rhythm. Education is the alpha and omega of Djursholm; good grades are crucial for getting into top university courses and, later, attaining prestigious jobs. Excellent grades are also a sort of verdict on the community. If a student fails to live up to the expectations, not only is there a risk of scandalizing oneself and one's family, there is also a broader condemnation from Djursholm as a whole. One father made the following claim: "The children are aware from an early age of the importance of school, not only for the sake of their own future but also for their status and self-esteem. My ten-year-old son is already talking about how he wants to get into the upper-secondary school in Djursholm. It's a sign of success; it means you're someone special, you're smart and you have a future ahead of you." One preschool employee said, "It's important here for the parents that children are properly raised, so they manage well in their lives. It's not unique to Djursholm, but it seems a bit more pronounced here. People have expectations of preschool; they want their children to develop in a certain way. One father made a comment about his two-year-old son, he wanted him to go to the upper-secondary school in Djursholm, and we could make a contribution to that, he felt. I thought to myself, 'Wow, they certainly start planning early.'" When I spoke to a fifteen-year-old pupil during a visit to a school, he told me: "Not going to university isn't even on the radar, I have to fight to get in." As I describe in more detail below, the schools and preschools embody many of the conceptions and ideals that characterize Djursholm. The upper-secondary school is one of the country's preeminent educational institution. Perceived as an elite school as a result of its high entrance requirements and the academic results of its students, it gives further credence to the conception of Djursholm as a leader community.

Most of the parents that I met with were very satisfied with the schools. Their assumption was that stringent entrance requirements and excellent grades are synonymous with good quality. This institutional conception is central to the "added value" that Djursholm offers. If parents were to begin criticizing the schools because of a perceived lack of quality, it would ultimately threaten their own social position and substance as residents. Instead there is a common narrative among parents and school administrations that Djursholm is in a leading position vis-à-vis other schools in the country—yet, more than anything, this is little more than a moral position on how one best organizes the curriculum and teaching practice to attain the best possible results. One parent put it as follows: "The school is set in a wonderful environment. And it has an exceedingly high educational standard. One can only wish that all schools could be raised to the level that exists in Djursholm. If all schools were of the standard that we have in Djursholm, then the situation in the country as a whole would be quite different. The fact that my son's school has been assessed very positively in school ratings proves that it's a quality school." Another parent said, "The schools are very good here. You have very good, committed teachers, and the schools are forward thinking in terms of digital technology, and support for children with special needs." Another parent put it as follows: "We are enormously fortunate to live and raise our children here. In the end you begin to take the high standards for granted, but obviously you shouldn't. When you look at our school, for instance, there's hardly any bullying, no social problems worth mentioning, great teachers, and a dynamic principal." An elderly inhabitant claimed, "My school was defined by its studious pupils. No one failed their examinations. Many received grants and awards. We had highly capable teachers." A teacher said: "Attending our school is a good ticket to one's future."

There is also, in general, among the teachers that I have interviewed, a feeling that the schools in which they work are of a high quality and function well, with competent staff. One of them claimed: "If Djursholm and similar areas have the most ambitious teachers, I mean those who really want to work with education and not just putting their time into problem solving in chaotic schools, it can easily lead to segregation and a self-fulfilling prophecy. The best teachers find their way to the best schools, and teachers who are not as motivated and committed end up in worse schools." Working in a preschool or school alongside colleagues whom one considers to be "the best" will obviously tend to affect one's self-perception, and it logically follows that those who subscribe to such opinion will also start to believe that they are special and better than others. From this perspective it is not so remarkable that staff working in Djursholm's schools regard themselves as role models for other teachers in society. One of them stated, "We are one of the schools that trains the most teachers, and takes in the greatest number of undergraduates for periods of practice and training. We have very high ambition levels in terms of the teaching, and we're popular with the School of Education at the university." One of the principals that I interviewed told me, "It is very popular to apply for jobs here. If we advertise a vacancy, we can get one hundred applications." The general picture of preschools is also overwhelmingly positive. One director made the following assertion: "In Djursholm the preschools are very, very good. I know what I am talking about, I've worked for several preschools in other local authorities. The staff are highly qualified here, they're well educated, and even those who are not specifically preschool teachers are knowledgeable about children's development and what they need to develop in the best possible way."

The conception that people in Djursholm have of their preschools and schools also relates to the school milieus, which many find attractive. Several of the schools are in idyllic positions, often with beautiful landscapes just around the corner, which parents set great stock by. For instance, at the parish house in Djursholm, where there is also a preschool, one can read a description of the place: "With its surrounding garden, [it is] a proper idyll." As I describe later, the preschools have ambitious pedagogical programs, which further contribute to their popularity. Most of the preschools and school buildings in Djursholm look much like any other, but it is not unimportant to the character and culture of the community that the historically important upper-secondary school is such an impressive edifice. The entire campus has a magnificent setting, and many of the roads that lead to it are fringed by beautiful and inviting mansions.

Furthermore, lunch at the preschools and schools (free of charge in Sweden) is of a high order, or at least the premises where it is served are. Many of the schools that I have visited do not have their own kitchens—instead they buy their food from reputable catering firms or local restaurants, a fact that they are keen to report on via their websites. On the web page of the senior years of the secondary school, photos of the cafeteria give one an impression of a café or restaurant, with foaming café lattes and freshly baked carrot cake. Presentation is everything for the elevation of children and young people into full-fledged residents of Djursholm. The school cafeteria seeks to be a socially attractive environment, and thus it can make a positive contribution to the high-ranking aesthetic environment that Djursholm likes to project. I visited a school for younger children, and its cafeteria, named "The Golden Cockerel." The menu in the dining room featuring the lunch of the day for children aged six and up: "Basil fish with white wine sauce and boiled potatoes. Vegetarian: Vegetable cutlets with basil crème and boiled potatoes." One of the teachers told me that the food was very good and well prepared. "It's actually quite an advanced cuisine on offer here. It is even more advanced for the children. I can understand very well that they're not always so keen on it." Nonetheless, if a six-year-old can come home and announce, "Today I had vegetarian cutlets with basil crème from the restaurant the Golden Cockerel," this is not entirely unimportant in a community like Djursholm.

The schools also come across as harmonious and calm. There are no gang fights here, no mentionable issues with graffiti, no vandalized toilets, and so on. In other words, the school milieus are a reflection of the surrounding community. The atmosphere generally relates to a certain level of social and cultural homogeneity among the children. One of the teachers asserted, "Our school is very homogenous, and this creates a certain spirit, a certain kind of culture. There is not a lot of disagreement among the students, and not among the teachers either." Another added: "It's cozy here, a conflict-free zone. People don't have sharp edges." Even noisy student council meetings would be something quite out of the ordinary. As one teacher informed me: "The members of the student council are composed and well behaved." A former pupil, a man in his midtwenties, said, "This is no multicultural school environment. The level of common understanding is quite solid. The school election speaks its own language; hardly anyone here votes for the social democrats."

The rather nondescript art hanging on the walls adds to the impression of harmony. When I visited the upper-secondary school on its Open Day, there were no student paintings hanging on the walls, only bland Matisse posters. When I went through a copy of one of the yearbooks—borrowed from parents—of one of Djursholm's biggest schools, I confirmed that the proportion of darker-skinned children and school staff was very small. The same might be said of the incidence of obesity among the children—the children were mostly slender and blond—their young bodies seemed well adapted to the life that awaited them in Djursholm and beyond. I made a similar observation when I looked at pictures of pupils at other schools in the community published on websites. A picture emerged of a socially and ethnically homogenous world. One of the online school magazines featured a "Fashion" section to present the dress code of the students. There I found many pictures of both boys and girls, published under headlines such as "Outfit of the Week" and "The School's Street Style," which could be described as sporty, casual, and elegant. As I commented earlier, it pointed to the importance of how residents dressed and expressed themselves aesthetically.

The particular social importance of the upper-secondary school is a recurring theme in many of the interviews I made with parents, children, and young people. Frequently it was explained how crucial it was for the children to be accepted there after finishing their secondary education in Djursholm. One teacher put it as follows: "It has shown itself to be traumatic for some young people and parents when their application here was not successful and they had to continue their education at some school outside Djursholm." The school is not only for the acquisition of academic knowledge; it is also a platform for the refinement of social dispositions and relationships. As one of many expressions of this, there is the highly active student body, with its many committees; the common rooms in the school buildings that more than anything resemble living rooms and kitchens in private homes; and various social activities, such as induction week camps, skiing trips, school outings, the staging of musicals, sporting events, and of course the daily social interaction between the students. This is also demonstrated in many photographs in the school prospectus and other information brochures of students engaged in noncurricular activities.

Below, are the views of a number of students, concerning the social qualities of the school:

Our school is like a little community. It's more than a school. We do loads of things together; it creates a strong sense of belonging together. The school has saved many lives; you really get friends here that you can talk to. It's not easy going home to an empty house if you are feeling down. In other schools you are just one of many, but that's not how it is here. Here, everyone knows everyone. Here, you're a person; the teachers know who you are, who your mother and father are, where you live.

Many people feel "we don't want it to end; we want to carry on studying here." It's an amazing feeling of fellowship here, and I actually think lots of people are afraid of what will happen when their time at the secondary seniors in Djursholm is over. But a lot of people do go on to study at the same school afterward, typically the Stockholm School of Economics.

Our school is more than just a school; it's a lifestyle. We do an incredible amount together, and we almost live more or less as if we were at a boarding school. We stay on in the afternoons and in the evenings; it's like a second home. We have a lot of activities, committees, and so on.

You get so close to people here. It's everyone together. You spur each other on. Everyone is fighting to get better, everyone encourages you. Everyone wants to get the best possible grades.

The best parties are when there are lots of people from our school there. We have another social culture than other schools; there's no separation between the sexes, and there's little heated discussion or conversations. Instead people mingle and glide about having fun. It's really pleasant; it gives you a feeling of family.

Many of the parents that I interviewed with children at the school also emphasized the purely social functions of the school. One father explained it to me as follows: "Social life among the students is enormously important, I notice that in my son. It is not just a school; it's a *community*." Another father said, "My children spend long hours there, even into the evenings. It's obvious that they like it." And another parent added, "The students are incredibly committed to their school, and I'm not only talking about the schoolwork. There seem to be committees for everything." When seen in the context of existing family life in Djursholm, in other words, the schools represent an important aspect of the formation of the identities of the children and the young people as Djursholmers. The schools are seen as preeminent, outstanding, and pioneering, thus contributing to the self-perception of the pupils as outstanding and unique. And the pupils are nurtured, rather than left to their own devices—they are absorbed into the general communality, which becomes an important mechanism for safe-guarding the special character and social continuance of the community as a whole.

But there are also critical viewpoints of precisely the social climate in the schools in Djursholm, in which reference is made to the flip side of com-munality, which might be described as exclusion. Social inclusion, which seems a defining feature of the schools, is not always available to everyone. In accordance with the dominant family paradigm, there are clear social boundaries. This, as has already been clarified, is essential in order to "main-tain the membership of Djursholm" through consecration. One woman, in an article about the upper-secondary school in Djursholm during the 1960s, described how many recently arrived inhabitants were exposed to a particular kind of treatment: "The social code automatically excluded new residents until a certain period of time had elapsed, and they had shown themselves worthy of the epithet of 'Djursholmer.'" The social dimension, irrespective of whether one perceives oneself as integrated, is reinforced by means of various communal activities either organized by the schools or by the pupils themselves and their associations and committees. These become important arenas for social confirmation, and exclusion is a serious matter. The student association at one of the schools describes its social and other activities as follows: "In many ways we are a unique school. One of the things we take pride in is the life outside the classroom, which creates the good atmosphere, the so-called Djursholm spirit. Hard swotting and long days are a thousand times easier if you get involved in other, more entertaining, things at school—and at school there's a wide range of choice." One of the principals emphasized how "we work a lot with sports and so on, not just the educational side. This is often a case of team-building activities such as canoeing or barbecues. We compete in LEGO tournaments, which is good for group work. But we also do other things like visiting museums or institutions that seem relevant."

In many obvious ways Djursholm's schools are inspired by corporate ideas in their pedagogy, terminology, and organizational aspects, which in this community are usually seen as a model for success in running services such as health care, schools, and social services. Corporate ideology lies at the heart of many of Djursholm's most central values, and encourages people to develop their autonomous capacities. It is also viewed as a positive value with which to associate oneself—an important ideology underlying the raising of children and young people into leaders primarily in the business sector. Outside the entrance to a school for children aged between six and nine is a sign bearing the following caption: "A modern school for tomorrow's entrepreneurs." In an interview conducted by a business organization, one of the principals in Djursholm described herself as a person with a clear focus on corporate life. She mentioned various previous positions in IT, the banking sector, and in media and pharmaceuticals, and regarded herself as "a positive and encouraging person who raises her colleagues' performance to help them to succeed with their challenges and keep developing themselves. I am politically active, a mentor and a member of charitable organizations working to develop the country's labor market and boardrooms." The board of trustees for the senior-secondary and upper-secondary school in Djursholm is made up of high-level executives from well-known, multinational companies, all of the former with some personal connection to Djursholm.

As a child or young person growing up in Djursholm, then, one is likely to inhabit a world in which due emphasis is put on balance, structure, and, especially, leadership. These keywords, and their tangible application, affect the children and train them into presenting themselves as socially exemplary. This, much like the inculcation of manners and etiquette, is central to the education offered in order to maintain the aura, prestige, and status on which the community has been based since its inception in 1889. Children and young people, as already noted, are crucial to Djursholm, but like all categories of residents they must be trained into observance of a socially desirable behavior. The well-organized structure and spirit that the schools (as well as the clubs and families) strive to achieve, are synonymous with certain ideals that have to be realized.

It is also popular to invite in parents to talk about their (successful) professional lives and, in so doing, how they act as role models for the young people, preferably these people are working in the business community. One of the principals at the schools told me the following:

Many of the parents here are eminent people in the corporate world, and this is a fantastic resource for us. We often invite them in at specific points of the learning process, or to give talks to all the students in the assembly hall. It can be very inspiring to hear a parent's experience of working at the top of, for instance, an industrial company, with all the challenges of a job like that. But also it's about learning about business life as a whole, the challenges, working overseas, and so on. We also ask the parents to let us know if they are interested in giving a talk, and they usually are.

Likewise, one father explained:

> We, the parents, get invited to speak at the schools. The various talks
> give the children amazing impressions, and probably a feeling that any-
> thing is possible. The fact that these parents are also successful at what
> they do hardly makes the experience any worse.

The upper-secondary school also offers lecture series by famous people,
which helps form the students' sense of themselves as future leaders.
While I was working on my study, the school was visited by the internationally known historian Antony Beevor, as well as the Egyptian activist
Sahar El-Nadi. In the school yearbook, reference was made to the board-
room professionals and leading politicians that had come to visit the school.
Students are offered a host of social activities and external events with a
professional edge, aimed at further inculcating an awareness in the
children of how to become decisive, responsible individuals. For instance,
one group of students made a study visit to a school in Nairobi and also
visited the headquarters of the United Nations in Africa. Other students
were engaged with projects and activities such as Innovative Schools, Global
Young Leader, and Life Link. As already said, local associations and companies are involved in the schools by offering prizes and grants for successful students. What emerges from an investigation of the school environment in Djursholm, in other words, is not just a regular curriculum but
various other practices that significantly advance a process of imbuing students with a sense of importance and moral elevation.

In both the municipal and private preschools of Djursholm, there is a
pedagogical approach based on *learning*, which becomes an important
consecrating idea by its contrast to another form of pedagogy based on *free
play*. A pedagogical approach based on *learning* reduces behavioral variation and the social insecurity implied by free play, and creates a more
socially stable environment. One preschool (named "The Pearl") has as its
motto: "A pearl [meaning the child] should always shine with a clear glow,"
the underlying idea of which is about stimulating children's "drive to
learn." The emphasis on learning from an early age makes the community's

children more grown-up and responsible, dutiful and autonomous. These characteristics are generally viewed as vital, and they are crucial to the maintenance of the particular spirit of Djursholm. Following are quotations from employees at preschools in Djursholm concerning the pedagogical focus on learning:

> The parents are looking for learning. They expect letters, numbers, and knowledge. Their children have to learn things. Play is not considered as important, but it's okay if one learns things through play.
>
> (Preschool Director)

> "Free play" here is not the same as "free play" in other preschools where I have worked. Here, free play is more planned and focused on achieving something, it has a goal. And it is important for us to be able to describe what the children learn through their free play, and in this sense even free play is guided by adults.
>
> (Preschool Teacher)

> I think many of our parents think that if you start the learning process very early, maybe when they're no more than two years old, imagine the sorts of results you could achieve!
>
> (Preschool Teacher)

> Learning is more important in Djursholm than in the preschools I worked at before. There, free play was appreciated more, and letting the children be. Here, you are supposed to have clear activities, and preferably people are supposed to come in from the outside, people viewed by the parents as authorities in their areas, specialists such as musicians or writers of children's books. The learning process is centered on numbers and letters and it's all supposed to be preparatory for school entry. Parents are concerned about their children's development even at an age of two or three. They ask if their children are developing normally, when it comes to numbers, the ability to count, draw, sing, and maybe even to read.
>
> (Preschool Director)

Preschools in Djursholm tend to emphasize that all activities should be well organized, and that children should be responsible for their own development. One preschool director told me: "Waldorf pedagogy is not popular here, people don't want any hippy-dippy stuff or weird pedagogical theories here." Instead, all the activities with which the preschool engages itself should be perceived as "meaningful" by the parents according to their norms and values of meaningfulness. One of the teachers explained this further to me: "Social activities for the children are fine as long as we can explain what their purpose is." One of her colleagues emphasized, "It's vital to express to the parents what we're doing from a developmental perspective, so it isn't just viewed as unstructured nonsense." As one of the parents told me in an interview, "What I like with this preschool is that they apply a structure throughout the day; where we had the children before it didn't seem as organized and clear."

The pedagogical ideas in the schools of Djursholm, as one can see for oneself in their websites, are obviously focused on meeting the general goals of the national curriculum. The core subjects are mathematics and Swedish. Reading, drama, painting, music making, and similar "nonacademic" activities are described as means to attaining general educational requirements and good grades in the core subjects—or, alternatively, they are taught because they are presumed to encourage creativity, collaboration, and social skills (for instance, by playing music together or singing in a choir). One of the schools highlights the significance of the aesthetic subjects for academic success and has the motto, "Science and the arts go hand in hand." The school's website goes on to say, "We are convinced that artistic forms of expression, apart from being valuable in their own right, also develop creativity and innovation in the academic subjects. For this reason we strive to offer high-quality teaching in the aesthetic subjects and also rely on certain modes of aesthetic expression as a part of our academic teaching approach."

Aesthetics do play a prominent role in Djursholm. As commented on earlier, art and architecture—even if of a very particular kind—are highly significant. The residents are keen for their community to be aesthetically pleasing. However, an aesthetic education is something quite different from the embellishment of one's surrounding world by means of socially condoned artistry. Aesthetic subjects are about an ability to express oneself through the medium of art. However, aesthetic subjects as taught in Djursholm are generally limited to the facilitation of more academically driven lessons, in which mathematics and language are prioritized. Yet there are other, purely technical reasons why some students should opt for more specialized modules in, for instance, music. One of the pupils I interviewed during my visits commented briefly on this: "It looks good on the CV if you've studied aesthetic subjects, just like if you've decided to do extra sports. A lot of the universities want to see you being involved in those things. It's important to fill out the CV." A similar way of thinking in terms of "CV awareness" is evident in the students' own views of the many social activities offered to them—rather more as means to an end than having any particular value in their own right. Another student told me: "A lot of these committees at school are just bullshit; it's about looking good on your CV. But some of it is serious, like the culture committee, which does some good things." A teacher commented: "We offer a lot of extracurricular activities. School is not just about the educational content; it's also about being active in various associations such as sports, art, music, and politics."

However, any belief that Djursholm's schools offer a genuinely academic environment would be far from accurate. Nor do local residents really expect academic credentials such as reflection, discussion, or analysis. The emphasis on the sciences and on academic learning have more to do with Djursholm's aura as a socially elevated environment than as a general value in itself. The prevalent view of knowledge and insight is very much instrumentalized, in the sense that these are associated with good grades. Repeatedly in my interviews with teachers, it was clarified that what students and parents are interested in above all are results (school reports, grades, or similar)—as opposed to the actual learning process, reflection, or analysis that may lead to such an end. One teacher put it as follows: "Many students here want letters of recommendation from the teachers, to be used in their applications to top universities in the United States such as Yale, Harvard, and Princeton. But they know nothing about these serious academic environments. As far as they are concerned, they're just brand names, more ribbons to pin to their CVs. Their attitude is not serious—they want to pass the examinations, but they don't care about actually knowing something." A colleague of hers had the following to add:

> The strong focus on grades means that there is rarely the opportunity for students to indulge in reflection or risk taking in the form of trying new approaches and heading into the unknown. The students want to know exactly what's required to get a certain grade, meaning the highest possible grade, and if they have not reached that level they want to know exactly what they must do to get there. Most of the parents reason along similar lines. They are not interested in the actual process, the actual learning, or personal development. . . . The only thing that counts is the highest grades. If the student is feeling bad about it all, or isn't free to develop a particular aptitude, or is bored, none of that matters. Nothing but the highest grades as the goal have any weight at all. This blinds people, they stress their way through the process. It's all about requirements and performance, presentations and projects.

Generally among the schools in Djursholm there is a belief that one ought not involve oneself with general knowledge or technical education, for instance, by expecting students to be able to explain grammatical rules or recite by heart the names of all the states in the United States. This is almost equated with dirty work, which is something quite undignified for a resident of Djursholm. One of the teachers put it as follows: "As a student you have to be creative and visionary today, and that is also how it is in the workplace. Being innovative and creative is actually more important than the actual academic course, and having a knowledge of a lot of technicalities." One of the schools, outlining its pedagogical foundations in a course brochure, stated: "Our school has developed a learning environment that is defined by the students applying a scientific working method, an analytical ability, and focusing on problem solving rather than prioritizing detailed knowledge in a number of subjects."

In terms of the pedagogy, then, the emphasis is on social aspects rather than on purely academic and intellectual qualities and approaches—all this in accordance with the founding characteristics and culture of the community. Djursholm's residents are expected to have academic qualifications, but they are not expected to *become* academics. Knowledge is viewed as important above all in a social dimension. In all essential respects it is the person, or his or her manner, that occupies the center ground—as opposed to what he or she actually knows. One teacher expressed the following clarification: "Our students come from families where there are books at home, and libraries are not alien environments as far as they are concerned. But as a rule they are not interested in Shakespeare's plays, only in the brand name of Shakespeare, and being able to say that they have read Shakespeare is more important than any serious reflection on the meaning of Shakespeare's work." During the course of my study I did meet two parents with a critical stance on the pedagogy, based on their impression that the education was too superficial. One of them said, "We did not want our children to go to the upper-secondary school in Djursholm. It's too fluffy there, too 'corporate.'" The other parent put it as follows: "The upper-secondary school in Djursholm is not properly speaking intellectual; it's more like cramming. There's little opportunity for genuine reflection and education."

I have already discussed the social importance of the schools in Djursholm. In several of the schools I studied, the teaching itself is also social, in the sense that it emphasizes and attaches great value to group work and shared projects, rather than individual work and knowledge acquisition. The emphasis on "fun" teaching, one of the trademarks of the upper-secondary school, is also at root a sign of a student-centered learning process; in this, the primary role of the teacher is not to disseminate formal knowledge but rather to act as a facilitator of a certain climate in the studying environment—to continuously help generate a "wow factor," with a corresponding level of enthusiasm and joy among the students. As one of the students explained, the most important thing is that the teachers are "pedagogical and good at teaching . . . . rather than just being good at their subjects and well qualified." Another student emphasized in a school questionnaire, to which I was given access, that "a good teacher" is a teacher who is creative and stimulating:

> I am not a teacher by profession but I like the art of teaching and I am always trying to see how I would improve a lesson, if I find there's something that doesn't appeal to me. Sometimes it is hard, and I know the idea is that a teacher should always come up with a lot of creative stuff that's supposed to be ground-breaking. But often it's not needed, sometimes a PowerPoint presentation with a few humorous moments is enough. Teaching is an art form, and if a school is going to be the best, you need as many Picassos, van Goghs and da Vincis as possible. . . . Without good teachers there can't be a good school.

Later I move on to aspects of the relationship between teachers and students. However, at this moment, it should be emphasized that "fun teaching," which is based on the students' ideas of what is fun or not, challenges the authority of teachers as traditional providers of information, passed down from the lectern. This pedagogy is dressed up in the popular concept of "entrepreneurial learning," which, according to one teacher, is about how "nothing untried is wrong—the children are allowed to improvise their way forward." Or, as another teacher put it, "they have to continuously think anew, try different angles" and "be inventive." One of the principals explained that entrepreneurial learning "is not mathematics or writing, it's an approach, a way of looking at the world which is all about testing things out, trying new things, grabbing hold of what you want, pushing boundaries, and challenging them." Another employee at one of the schools felt that "being entrepreneurial" is about accessing knowledge in unexpected ways. "We teachers don't always have all the answers."

The pedagogy implies that the students are trained in an active approach, which accords nicely with the existing norms in Djursholm, but it is also about manifesting to the students that no one is superior to them. Teachers are reduced in a genuine sense to service staff, who, through their enthusiasm and guidance, should help the students reach their goals. The image of adults that students acquire through the teaching environment is a confirmation of their own social status and ability. One principal clarified to me that "the children have to solve the problems themselves. They have laptops. The teachers don't provide them with answers and facts; instead they encourage the children to find out for themselves. It presupposes an active, engaged attitude among the children. The teachers facilitate the collection of knowledge, but the children have to drive the process for themselves." The main result of attending school, then, is hardly an academic approach with intellectual insights—more an inculcation of social skills:

> A pupil matriculating from our school has learnt things that cannot be measured or assessed. It's an attitude to himself and his surroundings. It's a can-do approach, a curiosity, a willingness to try new things and stretch the boundaries, to explore and open up new lines of thinking.
>
> (Principal)

> The students here become employable, and it's not just a matter of their high grades. They gain a self-belief, a way of looking at themselves. They have a natural sense of their own participation, and an outlook that seems to say, "I have something interesting to say." "Words are silver but silence is golden"; that saying doesn't exist here. Here, the students learn to convey a message, and they expect others to find it interesting. . . . The children are encouraged to express themselves and think, "I have a certain value as a human being; that is why I am allowed to occupy a position." Their parents encourage them to do so, and we give additional support to this attitude. And that is an important factor in achieving success. When employing people, one tends to choose those who express themselves clearly, in a confident way. That is why it is so difficult to advance beyond the limitations of your own class. This outlook creates security, self-assurance. But when it goes wrong, even against all expectations, then it can go very badly wrong.
>
> (Teacher)

We have certain courses that refer to "leadership," and that's a word with many positive associations in this place. But then we also run courses in subjects that are tangential to leadership without emphasizing the term. For instance, we teach people how to collaborate effectively and organize themselves in teams. And we also have courses in rhetoric, where it's all about conveying a certain message, and generally just communicating. Public speaking is something we train our students to do throughout the course. You could simply say that we train our students into shouldering positions of leadership in society.

(Teacher)

Children need a social ability, a certain way of finding things out for themselves. They don't have to be able to reel off the names of all of Europe's capital cities; instead they must learn to handle the codes of society and life. We have some subjects that may possibly not be so very important, such as history and religion. But then we also have subjects that are crucial, such as computing. And yet teachers don't learn anything about computers at teacher training colleges.

(Principal)

In the world of preschool education in Djursholm the social ability of the children is also prioritized, but obviously on another level. Here, it is a matter of their ability to socialize in groups, play with other children, and so on, which admittedly are also considered important abilities in many other preschools in the country. One of the preschool directors I interviewed made the following statement: "The most important thing is the social outlook. Reading and writing will anyway be learnt at a later stage. The most vital thing is to be able to function in the group, to be able to receive instructions, handle conflicts, and so on. From our perspective it is important to have functional children, not studious children." A colleague of hers explained, "When we meet the parents to discuss progress, it is often the social aspects we talk about, how the children are doing in the group. The parents are very concerned about whether their children have friends, and if they are friendly to other children. Also that their children show consideration and are popular, that is also important. We work a lot on the social aspects here, we try to develop the children into sociable individuals who enjoy interacting with others." In other words, the emphasis on learning in the preschool marketing does not mean that the social aspects are less important—quite the opposite. The idea is that children are not raised into what one assumes would be introspective, antisocial academic specialists. In general, the important thing is for preschool to make a contribution to the development of socially functional children, based on society's norms and values:

> We want our children to have a sociable and civilized behavior when they're eating; we want them sitting properly and not running about, not talking with their mouths full, and so on. The social aspect is very important here for the learning process, for instance, learning to stand up in front of others and talk. Actually we produce some very nice kids here, with a good social foundation for school. Having the courage to talk in front of others is important. We practice that through various role-play games, musical performances, and so on. For instance, we have a game called "the secret bag." The children have to put their hand into a bag and pick something up and then tell the others what it is. It's a very good exercise that works in a playful way.
>
> (Preschool Employee)

During an interview, one forty-year-old woman who grew up in Djursholm looked back on her preschool days with gratitude: "We learned a lot of things at preschools that stood us in good stead later in life. We learnt to shake hands when we got there, and we were taught to think that everything can be solved if you stay cheerful! Those things make life much easier. I mean it's all in the Montessori pedagogy, the whole thing of learning to be responsible." One preschool director concluded our conversation with the following assertion: "Parental expectations of the preschools in Djursholm include table manners, a good attitude, style, and development. Not storage. It has to be an evolutionary process; there needs to be drawing and singing. People expect social competence already at preschool level. The idea is that you should go to museums, to the chapel at Christmas, and so on." Ultimately, the focus on social ability in the educational approach in Djursholm is about how to navigate in future professional environments. Such environments are basically considered to be corporate—an area where such qualifications are deemed essential.

The earlier-mentioned emphasis in schools on group work and presentations are further examples of how children and young people are trained in communication, particularly when this is about speaking in front of others. One fourteen-year-old pupil explained, "We learn a lot about holding speeches in normal, day-to-day teaching, it's all about getting them to listen and be convinced about what you want to do. It's about getting people to do things you believe in, such as running a basketball team." One teacher told me, "There are courses here that are exclusively about presentation technique. But all the courses and subjects already include a lot of presentations and project work, even in the sciences. People are trained in their ability to enthuse others and convince those in their surroundings." The presentation training has clear aesthetic and social dimensions. As a presenter one is forced to think about not only *what* one is saying but also *how* one is saying it, and how one appears while doing so. A presentation becomes a sort of display of all one has learned, in terms of values, as a child of Djursholm—and this is a significant educational aspect for further development. On one of my visits to a school for children aged six to nine, I listened in on a training session before a performance to the parents. The specially contracted singing coach emphasized to the twenty or so children that "this is really important" and also said, "If you can also insert a little smile, it will make it perfect." The comments made were less about the actual singing: the choir had to express itself primarily through movement, and not their voices—the social rather than the musical attributes were in focus. The principal explained to me that a great deal of classroom time had been devoted to this. The children were not merely supposed to sing; they were also to smile, look happy, clap their hands in time and make synchronized facial expressions—all to make a certain impression on the no doubt proud parents. As an analogy, one could say, implementation is less about the music and more about what sort of image of oneself one can project. The typical adult resident is an expert at assessing precisely this. As a child and young person in Djursholm you are taught to communicate in an aesthetically pleasing manner. In a junior year at one of the secondary schools that I visited, a member of staff told me how "we have a game called Show and Tell, which is about how every child can choose a theme and then give a presentation on it to the class. We do this in all age groups. It's about stimulating the child's ability to autonomously present a narrative—for instance, a talk on the lives of squirrels. It creates a certain level of proficiency in speaking in front of a group. A lot of the presentations are quite professionally done, with Power-Point slide shows." A colleague of hers added: "It's quite common as a part of classwork to give presentations of assignments, for instance the children may read out stories they have written. Often they make very professional presentations, you can tell this is something their parents are good at." An employee at another school for younger children told me, "I have an impression that the children are supposed to know a lot, and that it's important for them to show what they know, and display their social skills and leadership. That is why we have so many talks, performances involving the children, theater and musicals. The idea is that the children should learn to stand in front of others and convey some sort of message. Several of the parents have suggested that the children should perform in front of their friends and teachers using a microphone, so they also learn to handle a microphone." In other words, it is not only about training oneself in rhetorical presentation but also one's own presentation through dress and body language. On the stage, in front of others, the children become aware of how others see them. The crucial thing is not to "be oneself"—preferably one should be like all the other inhabitants of Djursholm.

11

JUDGMENT AND FEAR OF FAILURE

N MANY WAYS the schools in Djursholm might be described as performance focused, which is reflected in the academic results and entrance requirements for the local upper-secondary school. This whole culture is a reflection of the surrounding society and its worship of activity, dynamism, and professional and financial success. And yet the performance-focused culture also idealizes a certain lifestyle, in which a human being is expected to do "grand things" and then, for that same reason, be a "grand person." Consecration in Djursholm occurs in several ways, but it is rarely free of charge. The children are expected to work hard, and this is how they are elevated. In general I came across a feeling among the students I met that good grades are decisive for one's future while also an expression of one's personal character—therefore also one's morality. A person performing at a high level in society is assumed to be a morally elevated person, a role model, and a paragon. One of the students put it as follows: "In the olden days you could get through the door just on the strength of your family name. My dad was probably the last generation for that. Now only hard work counts. Of course, the odd contact can help me out, but only a bit. Before it was all fixed up for you. These days you have to have an academic qualification to be successful." One parent took the following view: "Not getting an education, that doesn't exist in Djursholm. If you don't educate yourself, people think you're unwell."

In an article in a daily newspaper, the upper-secondary school in Djurs-holm is described as a performance-driven school, in which the students struggle to achieve the best possible grades. One of the assistant principals comments in the article: "Many people come to this school with a convic-tion that they are top students, and they can get despondent when things don't go to expectations. We often point out that you start on a whole new level here, and a lower grade is not a catastrophe." Another article on the school looks at the general utilization of computers. One of the students commented in an interview: "In the upper secondary it's not good, for example, if you get ill. But if you do, you can read the teachers' PowerPoint presentations on your computer at home"—presumably from the sickbed. One of the school's founders explains in a business magazine that students can get stressed out by the fact that "here, everyone is the best" and there is a widespread angst about performance. Once again we see how the con-ception of Djursholm's schools as elite institutions clearly focused on performance is important for the social elevation that the community of-fers its inhabitants. There are also plenty of instances of how students view themselves as an elite. On the website of one of the student associa-tions, one can read the following: "Some of the most ambitious and high-performing students in the country attend our school"—and then, even more tellingly, the students, "with few exceptions, are the best in their subjects." In an information video about the intermediate classes of a secondary school in Djursholm, one of the students describes how "I think you learn more here, you learn things better. I don't know why, it's fun to learn. You work better somehow." And a student at a Djursholm school writes as follows in the school magazine:

> We all strive to do our very best and we get there in so many different ways. When you look at the high graduation marks people achieve at the upper-secondary school in Djursholm, we can draw the conclusion that most succeed. The feeling of achieving something that makes you proud of yourself is indescribable, but unfortunately the feeling of having failed is absolutely devastating. Sometimes you don't quite get there, and at times like that it's not so easy accepting the situation and

moving on. It's about finding your motivation again, because before you know it there's another examination to start revising for. School has been a place where I have been given the chance to develop myself. I am now in the third and final year, and sometimes I catch myself feeling jealous of the younger students who have more time ahead of them here than I do. I'm not saying I can't wait for the graduation, only that I wish time had passed a little more slowly, so I could have enjoyed a little more some of the things I have missed because of the high pace in my everyday life.

Several of the employees at the schools in Djursholm, whom I have interviewed, also recognize that in the schools where they work there is a clear emphasis on performance:

Ninety-five percent of our students will probably be in the top five percent in other schools, meaning the proportion of people that are going for top marks.

(Teacher)

The students base their whole self-esteem on performance, and it breaks some of them. As a rule the students are stressed out, they all want the best possible grades, actually nothing else counts at all. A friend of mine working at a school in the countryside told me that the students there just aim to pass, and get through the whole thing in one piece. But with us it's only top marks that matter. It's tough being a teacher here; the students almost seem to believe that top grades are a human right. Anything but top grades needs to be explained. There's a lot of pressure to achieve very good results.

(Teacher)

As a student at this school you are always under scrutiny, and I am not thinking here of the usual sort of scrutiny in the form of regular lectures and classroom presentations, tests and tutorials, but also the pressure coming from parents, the way that teachers and other students see things, and so on. It causes a lot of stress. But there's no way of slowing down the pace out here. All our students want to get into the best upper secondary schools.

(Teacher)

One person explained, "There's nothing odd about studying here. You're always hearing, 'Everyone's at home doing their homework right now, so that's what I'll do too.' There's positive pressure about studying, swotting. People spur each other on; it creates a sort of peer pressure, which means that the parents and teachers don't have to be on your back all the time." One student said, "There's a heck of a pressure on us, but we help each other. We help each other between classes and between academic years. The pressure makes you closer to each other. It's an advantage; it prepares us for working life, where there's also a lot of demands about your performance and how you have to be able to work with others and function as a group." The student went on to say:

It's a demanding time; a lot of pressure is put on you. At home, your friends, the teachers. Everyone wants you to succeed; everyone has to do their best. Parents want everything tip-top, also between friends there's pressure to succeed. Even the teachers expect it. They often call us "the best" and "the elite," so we have a lot to live up to. . . . You don't really say much about those who are not coping, but there's a silent understanding about their situation. It's tough here; anyone can fall like they've done. . . . If you start deflating, losing your pace, and not managing as well as you were before, the best help you can get is from the teachers. They always see you; they keep an eye on your performance. They can help me if I start losing the edge; they're incredibly committed. Last term things weren't going as well, and my mentor [teacher] had a talk with me, and I got support and encouragement to work harder. Now my results are good again.

A teacher confirmed that "the students spur each other on and trigger each other; they keep an eye on each other's reports." A virtual classroom is maintained through social media, around the clock. "The twenty-four-hour student is a reality here with us," another teacher told me. "Most of the people here have all the latest technology, which facilitates a constant online presence, and they are in nonstop contact with other students and teachers." And, in this sense, the students are never quite away from the school: it is a constant presence in their lives. Many of the teachers I spoke to told me that they were even in contact with their students in the evenings and on weekends. One of the school's websites points out that it is a highly modern institution, as the students and teachers work with the help of computers. A principal suggested to me, "Here in Djursholm, I have not met anyone who feels negative about the use of computers in the teaching process, quite the opposite. Partly, computers are regarded as a 'modern' aspect of school, which is a good thing in itself. And, partly, computing is viewed as a facilitator of higher grades because of the possibility of interaction between students, getting feedback from teachers after school, more efficient coordination in team projects, and so on. The students are online the whole time, they have the latest computers, the latest mobiles." The constant online connection also means that schoolwork can be tackled even if one is at home, off sick—and this becomes yet another expression of the expectations on residents to show extraordinary qualities. One fifteen-year-old student told me the following: "We do our homework together via Skype. And it does happen that you're in the class digitally even when you're ill at home, and the teachers don't find anything odd about that." Many of the students I spoke to felt there was competition between them to see who performed best, which created pressure. One seventeen-year-old girl said: "It's very tough in school; everyone works really hard." One of the principals commented, in this context: "The students are focused like arrows, they put a lot into their studies and work a great deal. They have lofty ambitions, but there's a cold feeling, a lack of close relations between the students. It's extremely *competitive*." And a teacher I spoke to felt there was a tendency among the students to put one another down and make one another look silly in order to make themselves look good. "It's a fight for status. If someone makes a fool of himself or isn't successful, it's often blamed on the others."

A general view among the students was that the grades one ends up with are basically derived from motivation, engagement, and input of work, all of which underline the individual's sense of responsibility, character, and capacity. And, as in Djursholm, all social relations and human relationships are tinged with risk. This was how one student put it, in a discussion on course work on the topic of "How Our School Could be Improved," to which I was given access by a teacher: "In my view, it is very rarely a lack of knowledge or a student being 'bad' that leads to poor results and a less successful education; it has more to do with each student's motivation and will to get engaged in course work that plays a central role." A fellow student wrote: "I'm totally convinced that most of the students here have the capacity to get the highest possible grades in many subjects. The reason why many students don't is that their commitment fails." One student claimed, in an assignment, that if she were the principal, she would create an elite school, "where the students consciously choose to go to school in order to attain the highest possible educational level. To create motivation among my students, I would run a course where they were informed about how the brain is plastic in its structure, and how we have the ability to affect our intelligence and our brains' capacity from an early age by training it in the very best way and exercising it in different ways." The emphasis on individual ability accords well with the founding ideology of Djursholm, and is ultimately about individual morality: excellent educational results are a product of will, and thereby also of lifestyle. Those who achieve the highest grades are not only considered intelligent, but above all they must by definition be living virtuously. In a corresponding way, the unemployed are regarded as unworthy. Unemployment in a community like Djursholm is not primarily a result of external factors, but is viewed as the outcome of poor ability, a lack of employability, and so on—in other words, of bad morals.

Whenever I spoke to students and former students from Djursholm's schools, many of them described a feeling of insufficiency, which can be explained by their constant self-assessment of their work as good or bad— which is also a judgment on the way they are living their lives. One woman of about twenty, who had embarked on a degree course at a university, claimed, "These two years since I graduated from upper secondary have given me much more, I get to meet different people, and to see different things, and I feel more confident. Although school in Djursholm is such a small world you don't feel very secure there. You are always unsure whether you are good enough. But now when I look around I realize that I am good enough, and actually, that I'm quite good." Very much in line with this statement, there is generally a pressure among the students to succeed with their education and attain excellent grades, which at the same time become a receipt of their value:

> Some of the students completely break down when they don't get the grades they were hoping for, and if they also have to take criticism from their parents it can turn into a fairly difficult situation to handle. It's no fun seeing your students crying, but some of them are really not used to any kinds of setbacks. And occasionally they have far too high expectations of themselves.
>
> (Teacher)

> If things don't go their way, if, for instance, they don't get the appreciation, the results, or the marks they had been expecting, it is not unusual for them to start crying. That's both boys and girls. The inner pressure is so strong, and the expectations of success sometimes so unrealistic. If things don't go as they had been thought and planned, well, then they have a really hard time dealing with it. Some also get angry.
>
> (Teacher)

Teachers and principals that I interviewed in Djursholm felt that parents as a general rule had high expectations of their children's educational achievements; hence, the pressure to study was not only coming from the students themselves. This was sometimes even true of preschool children. One preschool teacher told me: "Parents want to see progress in their children, and preferably that their child is one step ahead in areas such as reading or writing skills. Some of the parents want to coach their children, they start reeling off the alphabet with their two-year-olds." One teacher whom I interviewed in a report on the seniors in secondary school felt that the big problem in Djurs-holm was not a lack of motivation or commitment among the students, as is often the case in other Swedish schools, but rather "the anxieties caused by either the students themselves or their parents applying excessive pressure about achieving top grades." A principal told me that "there is a terrific amount of parental pressure on the students," and a colleague of hers at an-other school said, "The parents keep pushing even if the child is not tal-ented. But surely it's good to put pressure on children? Surely it's good to make some demands?" One teacher had the following to say on the topic:

> That parents are putting pressure on their children is beyond discussion. At meetings when I see the parents, I often hear, "Surely my son can do a bit better if he only tries harder?" All the time there is an expectation of achieving something even better. But these students are already doing much more than anyone should ask of them. They don't always feel they make the grade, precisely because there's an idea here that more effort is needed. *Good enough* doesn't exist here.

No, *good enough* is not something that defines Djursholm; rather, it is a strive for excellence. Parents making demands on their children, and maybe even putting pressure on them to perform in their schoolwork, is an ex-pression of the importance of *becoming someone*. And yet, ultimately, school is not viewed as crucial because it offers the possibility of attaining goals of this kind through intellectual achievements, but rather because it offers essential social training and consecration through the top grades that are required in order to excel, and thereby also to lead. Excellence, based on a concept of a superior lifestyle and thereby also better morals, takes the form of the existing activity culture—by the terms of which the students are expected to be committed, enthusiastic, and generally "busy."

> When I call the parents to let them know that their children should go home, it's not unusual for them to say, "She can stay a little longer; she may get over it in a minute." The parents usually don't want the children

to go home; they're worried they may miss important schoolwork, and they also see themselves as irreplaceable at work.

(Employee, Student Health)

Often the children are sent back to school too early, even though we stipulate that they should stay home for forty-eight hours after they have got better. Last week I had a boy coming in the morning, pale and tired. He had thrown up the evening before, but not in the night or in the morning. And then his mother brought him in. When I called her up she said, "But he's fine now." He sat with me; he was tired and sluggish. I'm sure she wasn't very pleased with him when she came to pick him up a few hours later.

(Employee, Student Health)

A mother of five children, all of whom were attending one school or another in Djursholm, put it as follows: "We ask a lot of our children; we want them to get through upper-secondary school with top marks. Why? Well, because if you have top marks you can choose. They don't have to go for a demanding academic education later, but they have to have the possibility." Another parent said, "My daughter started going to a school outside of Djursholm, which had a good reputation. But she didn't like it there; she wanted to come back to Djursholm. She didn't find the teachers very good, and the pace was too slack." Another person who had moved out of Djursholm explained: "My children went to stable schools in Djursholm without trouble or social problems, where people require certain things and do not just accept everything as it is. In Djursholm you have to behave yourself and perform even as a child. Demands like that are not as clear in other places, for instance, in the neighborhood where we live now."

As mentioned earlier, there is a general conception in Djursholm that the schools are superior to those in other places. This idea is based not so much on the parents being able to assess the actual content of the curriculum, but rather on the fact that the students seem committed, enthusiastic, and high performing. As I reiterate later, performance does not always take the form of superior intellectual grasp as expressed by top grades, but is often made up of a combination of social excellence and communicative ability. On the other hand, there are some parents who have expressed concern about the culture in Djursholm of pressurizing students. One of them asserted: "The children have a lot of homework. They start studying English at a very early age. They have masses of work even at weekends. It feels as if my daughter is getting stressed out by all this." Another parent said: "It's actually not so easy being a parent in Djursholm. The school puts a lot of pressure on them. I can't help my daughter with her homework when it's chemistry. She wants a professional person helping her. Many of my friends have been hiring tutors for years to help their children. The pressure to study which many young people feel, I also feel as a mother." Another parent told me the following:

> We parents believe that the level is sometimes higher than the upper-secondary curriculum; it quite simply gets too difficult and complex. Often our children and young people are regarded as more mature and competent than they really are. Some of the teachers are impressed by the drive and adult manner of the students, and so they treat them like adults. But they are not adults. . . . There are also parents who are worried about school being too difficult.

Irrespective of whether it is the teacher or school, the parents, or the students themselves who contribute to the ramped-up pace of study, the result is the same: the students have to orient themselves according to a norm of not being expected to become intellectual experts able to report at a detailed level on articular subjects—but rather, having the capacity to sort, organize, and handle their lives, or, in other words, to become brilliant leaders of themselves. Clearly, the downside of this can be feelings of insufficiency: in striving to achieve a norm of excellence, complete success cannot always be guaranteed, and from time to time it will be qualified.

One teacher told me that "several of the children are stressed out; the high pace is making them feel bad." A colleague of hers felt that "there is a kind of frantic quality in this community, an exaggerated drive to be doing things." Another teacher made the following assertion: "The most common dysfunction among our children, if you could put it that way, is that they're overactive, stressed, and speeding. It's very common." A headmaster at one of the schools explained, "We train our children to reflect, rest, and sit down. We actively train them to just enjoy doing nothing. Many of them find it difficult. I think the parents ask far too much of them." One teacher told me: "Stress, that is what our students feel when it seems to them as if 'there's one path for me in life' and they can't live up to the requirements of that road, or that they're not happy, quite simply. This road in question is described by words such as success, academic education, career, and is often about working as doctors, lawyers, company executives, economists." In an article in the local newspaper, it is claimed that a third of the students at the upper-secondary school suffer from stress. An employee at a student health-care unit at one of Djursholm's schools told me that "the commonest problems I run into are stomachaches, headaches, anxiety about performance. There are quite a lot of stress symptoms among the children. Many of them have masses of leisure activities plugged in. Several worry about how to make the 'life puzzle' add up, with all the musts, demands, and expectations."

One teacher felt that the pressure experienced by children and young people in Djursholm was certainly related mainly to school. "But at the same time there are a lot of helicopter parents when it comes to more practical things, like getting lifts and being dropped off. There are no demands on the children in terms of making their own way to and from school." This is because logistics, unlike the actual schoolwork, are not socially consecrating. The intense pressure arising from school is a consequence of its critical role in Djursholm's aura and cultural capital, expressed through the behavior of the children. A colleague of hers, on the other hand, felt that Djursholm was not unique when it came to performance. "Children are always under pressure from their parents to perform, but it may be a case of different kinds of performance. Focused on different things. To do well academically is important, and not disgracing one's family by failing at school. There are definitely high demands here, but I don't know if you see more stressed children here than anywhere else." The stress among the pupils was primarily social and largely about becoming *someone*, with excellent grades regarded as decisive in terms of this ambition. This stress is the price of social consecration: striving for elevation is a story that in many respects causes pain to those who wish to live it.

Students and parents expect a demanding school environment—the teachers do, too, and this is largely about confirming the status of the schools as elite places in which both preschool and school staff members in Djursholm stand out as role models for their colleagues in the rest of the country. The schools and preschools are also crucial institutions for the reproduction of the basic norms and values of Djursholm. As a principal explained to me: "Our teachers have a varied background, many have international experience and have worked in corporate life. They all have very high ambitions and expect results."

One eighteen-year-old student had the following to say: "The teachers are always leaning on us to be more committed, they're really pushing us towards top grades, they seem to take it for granted that this is what everyone wants, which is a bit weird. That is always their yardstick. Is it not good enough if the teacher helps the students get decent grades? All the teachers want the students to get the very top grades." One teacher took the view that the teachers' stringent demands for student performance was fundamentally about the pressure *teachers* were under from their superiors. "I believe that the school administration wants the school to be, and be seen to be, a top school, and a lot of effort goes into maintaining that image. A vital part of it is obviously about getting very good academic grades in the top year." The academic consecration in Djursholm, as described earlier, is based on a perception of the schools as excellent; top grades among the students are in this context absolutely essential. The schools contribute to a performance-based and competitive environment—the consequence of this being that Djursholm emerges as a shining, highly functional, and morally superlative world.

On the whole, a high-performance lifestyle is expected and idealized among Djursholm's students. A teacher made the following suggestion: "In Djursholm people expect themselves to be very virtuous and dynamic, to be A-grade people. This affects the children, who are also expected to be A-grade. They have to be the best at school, the best at sports, the best at music, have excellent general knowledge, be pleasant mannered and polite, speak several languages, know how to handle themselves, have traveled all over the place, have a lot of friends, and be involved in things." My impression, having taken part in various classroom situations at the school—from core subjects such as language and mathematics, to sports and dietary science—is that the students were really involved in their school work in the sense that they seemed *active* in the classroom, as an expression of their social commitment. For instance, when I sat in on a geography class, more or less all of the children were extremely keen to answer the teacher's questions—without any signs of timidity or even insecurity. And when I had the opportunity of telling a class of seven-year-olds that I was writing a book about Djursholm, several of them put up their hands and let me know that they wanted to be interviewed. One teacher felt that "even in the classes where our less gifted students come for extra math tutoring, everyone is really on the ball." When I sat in on a mathematics class I was able to confirm the assertion for myself. This was what I wrote in my notepad:

> The pupils make their class contributions in front of everyone, they don't sit there quietly and the answers don't have to be drawn out of them. Even when they don't know what they are talking about they keep talking. It's so natural for them to share their opinion and enter into discussion. At this level in mathematics there is not much to discuss, but they discuss it nonetheless. The pupils seem very sure of themselves, and they believe in their own abilities. When they put up their hands they do all they can to be picked, they wave and gesture. They really want to answer. Thoughtfulness, reflection, and silence are less in evidence.

One teacher told me: "Our students have opinions, and they like and appreciate being listened to. One pedagogical trick that I often use is, I ask them, 'What is your opinion about this?' It usually leads to a class full of enthusiastic, involved students. Most of them respond to being asked what they think. You don't have to draw it out of them at all. They quite clearly prefer classroom discussion to being taught."

The articulate, dynamic, committed, and apparently high-performing student is idealized in Djursholm, and all are encouraged to live up to the image. A project-based, Montessori-inspired pedagogy is prevalent in both preschools and schools, where the concept of "entrepreneurial learning" is popular—as mentioned earlier, this is an approach that emphasizes the social behavior of students, rather than tangible knowledge and expertise. The positive ideology of Djursholm underlines an enthusiastic, cheerful, and committed approach to studies and the acquisition of knowledge. As a teacher it must certainly seem more challenging to work in this kind of environment, rather than in a more skeptical and critical classroom, where attitudes seem tinged by a lack of motivation and failing interest. An enthusiastic, active, and absolutely never indifferent approach might be described as a crucial virtuous outlook in Djursholm, as well as being increasingly in demand in today's workplace, and in many areas of the higher education system.

In general, school staff take the view that the students from an early age are striving for prominent positions in society, which explains their drive and commitment to their studies. This striving is about the desire to be normal in Djursholm, to fit in, be accepted, appreciated, and liked. One teacher put it as follows in our conversation: "Our students are under terrific pressure to get good grades, and get into the right schools. Everything has to be 'spot-on.' I mean, getting into medical school is pretty tough. You can't just relax and let things take their course, or go along with the process and let that be the important thing. Everything is carefully planned here and organized, the goals are clear and precise. . . . You have to excel here." A colleague of hers emphasized: "The pressure on these kids is huge, and they also put massive pressure on themselves. Only top grades count. All other grades are seen as a failure. Parents are so used to being the best, being at the top, that this also defines the way they relate to their children. And the children also quickly learn to take this approach on board; only the best is good enough and you have to get to the top, otherwise it's a failure." Another teacher made the following statement: "Our students want to get into the best courses; nothing else exists for them."

When, in my interviews, school employees described their students' goals for their higher education and future careers, the types of courses that came up were mainly in areas such as economics, law, technology, and medicine. Aesthetic education attracts very few, which, given the norms and values of Djursholm, is hardly surprising. One of the teachers made the following assertion: "I have met many highly talented people who, had they been in another environment, would certainly have gone on to study at art institutions, for instance, subjects like graphic art. But in this place it would create a clash with the expectations of a career. 'That's not the sort of thing you go for,' is probably what people would say. We don't educate any musicians, artists, or dancers here, despite the fact that in every year we have several talented individuals. Instead they pursue theoretical and classic academic careers." A colleague of hers explained: "The small number of people that go for the aesthetic side, often think about studying at some international design school where you often have to have contacts to get in. I am thinking of areas like fashion and design." Another teacher shared her impressions of the career choices of Djursholm's children: "A career as a librarian hardly even exists in the conceptual universe of these students. We don't produce future humanists or cultural scientists, rather we tend to churn out lawyers, doctors, and media and corporate people. . . . But while the parents don't see librarianship as a high-status job, I do think they regard it as an admissible job and education." A vicar working in Djursholm claimed: "The young people here are formed by the rational, not the abstract or the inexplicable. Being a clergyman means that one cannot always come up with rational answers or advise someone in a rational way. I think this seems too vague for these youngsters. And it's also badly paid."

Whatever sort of education the students opt for, they are quite clear about the need for very good grades, because they will generally be trying to get into the most prestigious courses. And even those who do not dream of having a first-class academic education under their belts, will still tend to have quite prevalent ambitions to achieve social and economic excellence. One principal informed me, "Even while they are juniors at secondary school, the children speak of having good jobs or becoming professional athletes. There's an awareness that one has to get to the top, either in careers or in sport." A teacher at the same school said, "Between first and third grade, when the children talk about jobs they tend to have something in mind like being singers, performance artists, or professional hockey players. It's only later that they start talking about being lawyers or company executives. I hardly ever hear anyone say, 'Truck driver, police officer, painter, welder.' So even though the dream jobs may change as they get older, they are always aiming very high!" A colleague of hers at another school felt that "in many other places the young people and their parents are happy enough if they get through school and pass their examinations. They hope for a job, nothing remarkable perhaps, but a decent enough job. Here you have to go to Stanford, and become a doctor or a lawyer. People don't worry about passing their exams, they worry about not getting the very highest marks possible." When I go to a mid-secondary school class and have lunch with the students, a couple of the boys answer my question about their future, telling me that they want to make a lot of money. Their teacher commented: "When students are asked what they want to be, they often answer that it's important to get rich and have a job that pays a very high salary. I can understand them. If they want to carry on living in a community like this, well, then they have to get rich. I also think their attitude is that 'everything is worse than Djursholm—nothing else will do.' That's why money is an important question for them at an early age. They know they need money to live the only lifestyle they know, which they probably also think is the only right and proper one."

In one of many questionnaires, I targeted all the students in year six at one of the schools, as well as all students in year nine, and the third year of the upper-secondary school in Djursholm. There were no statistical ambitions about the questionnaire; rather it was a way for me to gauge student attitudes in relation to a number of questions. There were fifty responses from year six. Sixty-three students in year nine responded, and ten students responded from the upper-secondary school. Among other questions, I asked, *What do you want to do for a job when you grow up?* in the questionnaire for year six, and *What do you want to work with in the future?* in the questionnaire addressed to the older students.

The answers provided by the schoolchildren and the young students were about prestigious jobs, which accorded very well with the answers described above. Professions frequently mentioned in their answers included the legal, medical, and veterinary spheres. But there were also other jobs mentioned, such as business, stockbroking, and similar others. Among the younger children there was a broader range of jobs, such as in the music industry and in dance. One example was a girl who wrote: "I'd like to be a dancer, or a singer or an actress. I'd also like to be a fashion designer." Another girl specified: "Fashion designer, model, photographer, actor, something I like and enjoy doing!" Several of the younger children also make it clear that they'd like to make plenty of money. One boy emphasized that he wanted to "make a LOT of money. Work at a nightclub," while another declared that he would like to "invent something and be able to make a living of that. And then I'll be financially independent." Other children merely said that they wanted to be successful, without attempting to define this more closely. A small number of the children were unsure of what they wanted to do in the future. However, one of them did add: "I don't know what I want to do for a living when I get older, but once I do know I'll do everything I can to succeed with it." Some of the girls stated that they did not want to work; they would prefer to stay at home and be housewives.

One of the questions to the young people in year nine and the upper-secondary school was, *What are your expectations of yourself?* I have selected here the ten first answers in the web-based questionnaire that they answered:

I expect of myself that I do the best I can, that I am always well prepared in my studies, and pleasant to my classmates, teachers, and school staff.

That I get top grades in every subject and I can finally make my dad proud.

I expect that I will manage to get good grades. I work a lot at school and I try to get everything correct in tests and examinations.

To perform as well as I can.

My expectations of myself are that I will be able to spread happiness around me and show people who I am, so that teachers and others can understand my way of "thinking." My expectations are that I will be able to fulfill my goals, which above all means good grades.

To keep up in class and do well in the tests.

I expect of myself that I will get the best grades I can, so that it feels as if I've done my absolute best at the end of my school years.

I expect myself to work hard and never give up.

Not to be lazy and to do my best in every situation.

I expect to take responsibility and take on board new knowledge and use this in new situations. I also expect myself to be pleasant to others, because this makes for a better atmosphere.

A proportion of the students pointed out in the questionnaire that not only were high grades important to them—they also aimed to develop relevant social skills that could be decisive for their future professional roles and life in general. For instance, one person wrote: "In addition to the professional expertise that is obviously required, I must also have good social skills and the ability to listen, talk, and relate to other people," while another student explained that the goals to which he or she aspired "are not only about a good educational level and intelligent motivation, but also social skills."

Children and young people in Djursholm are *destined for higher duties*— and they know it. As has already been described, there is an awareness among Djursholm's residents that they belong to a social elite, and with this comes a sense of having the right to express their opinions and, so to speak, pronounce on the state of things in society. However, it is all very much about having self-belief and faith in one's own ability, both of which are based on a perception that one is living in a way that is morally exemplary. In an article, a teacher in Djursholm expressed a sense of how the students "more or less across the board [are] equipped with a self-image that allows them to grab hold of whatever they want. . . . The students here are the same kind of students that I have come across in other schools—but here they are calmer, and more secure, and, to a certain degree, stronger. They can cope with being themselves as individuals, and standing up for their own points of view. Their self-confidence may be imbued from home, someone believes in them, supports them, takes an interest in them and their education. Quite clearly they have a good home environment." One teacher that I interviewed made the following claim: "I come into contact with all sorts of students here, in terms of intelligence and talent. But they have one thing in common: a very good level of self-confidence and a belief that everything is possible and everything will work itself out. This holds true both for the students who are not especially gifted, and those who are." A colleague of his went on to say that "while the classes are still in progress, they keep working to achieve top grades. Even when things have clearly fallen apart they keep fighting. There's a belief that things are going to work out, that nothing is impossible as long as you really exert yourself and do your very best." The children's belief in their own abilities comes into play at school; moreover, it is already evident at the preschool level. One preschool teacher told me, "The children have incredibly good self-confidence and a belief in themselves and their abilities. I had to laugh the other day when we were at swimming school with a group of the children. They thought that just by showing up at the swimming class they would be able to swim. We had to tell them, 'You are here to learn; that's why you are here.' They just think they can do anything."

12

TACTICS FOR SUCCESS

A S HAS ALREADY been discussed, one of the most crucial questions for parents and children in Djursholm are the school reports, which are a significant aspect of the consecration offered by the community to its residents and lead directly to influential roles and identities in society. What follows are statements on school reports and their significance, made by a number of teachers in the community:

> Children in the lower and intermediate years of their secondary schooling are much the same as any other children. But once you get to senior secondary and upper-secondary level that sort of ideology no longer works. Those who are not strong students are more noticeable, and it gets more important to maintain appearances. The final grades do not only assess your knowledge; they also decide your value as a person. Those who don't get very high grades aren't considered as smart. People differentiate between one child and another. . . . Top grades mean everything. On the one hand they are important in a career sense, as without them you won't get into certain courses. And on the other hand, it has social importance here.

> The students are very aware of how many points are required to get into this or that upper secondary course. They put themselves under a lot of pressure.

We often have to say *good enough* to our students, and "you've done your best and that's wonderful—it's fine," but it often feels like you're talking to deaf ears. Only top grades count. If people don't manage that, they are enormously disappointed.

Top grades are important not only to the individual student and his or her family; as I mentioned earlier, they are greatly significant to the entire community of Djursholm. One teacher put it as follows:

> The school has a reputation for academic excellence, which is also quite true. For that reason there is certainly a level of expectation and pressure on the students who get in here, that they must achieve very good results. A poor academic showing in a school of high performers is a hard blow to the self-esteem. . . . The school wants to maintain its image as an elite institution. How would it look if schools in Djursholm had large groups of students that didn't even pass, or if the schools were very average? It would not fit with the self-image of the community. Everyone—students, parents, and the school—are working on maintaining the high grades.

As a rule, the teachers suggested that higher grades achieved by the students could hardly be explained by the idea that Djursholm's students were more gifted or intelligent than other students. Quite the contrary, one of the teachers even claimed that this was nothing but a well-established myth. She claimed, "When they have to do national reading and writing tests, they get frighteningly bad marks. . . . Which makes one ask oneself, how is it possible, despite this, for these students to end up with such high marks?" A colleague of hers put it as follows:

> In terms of pure knowledge, this is a fairly average school. When we run national aptitude tests, we're very much on an average level. The children here are not outstandingly clever. Many of my colleagues here in the teaching staff often say, "Oh, we have so many good students here." And yes they are, they are good, and they are quick and polite and they know how to behave and how to make a good impression. But in

terms of the actual knowledge they have at their fingertips, they are not so different. In addition to that, we do also have quite a number of children with learning difficulties, who would have fallen quite far behind the others if we had not ploughed a lot of additional resources into their teaching. . . . I have worked at several other schools around the country, and I think this is a school much like any other, but among those of my colleagues who have only worked here, there is a feeling that this school is unique, and that the students are outstandingly gifted.

One reason for the high grades in Djursholm is obviously the hard work that is put into achieving them—the commitment of the students. As noted, Djursholm could be described as a performance-oriented culture with a focus on education, which means that one is prepared to struggle to achieve high grades. Nonetheless, there are other significant explanations for the academic success of the students, which have less to do with their intelligence and diligence and a good deal more with the social abilities of their parents. The latter may be viewed as consecrating *tactics for success*, which are about various "shortcuts" to make education (as a result of high grades) confirm the social status of individuals that have grown up in Djursholm. Such practices are clearly not aimed at getting students or parents to recognize the excitement of serious intellectual or artistic pursuits, in fact they have a good deal more to do with entrepreneurial attitudes and morals. Just as the established pedagogy of Djursholm helps form socially dynamic rather than reflective or analytical students, the "shortcut" practices reinforce the same tendency. What this fundamentally creates is a purely antiacademic attitude, which develops and focuses on other attributes.

There is a general expectation that the schools in Djursholm are of top standard—ultimately manifested in the grades obtained. Staff members, primarily teachers, are a key factor in this context—and thus, in a certain sense, are the most important asset of the community. A teacher expressed this as follows: "There's pressure on us as teachers, from the school head, from students, from parents, and also there's the pressure we put on ourselves, to achieve top grades. If you don't give someone very good reports there's a great burden of evidence on you, which can be quite hard work, and sometimes you have to take a lot of crap from angry parents. As far as the school is concerned, its reputation will start to wane if the grades start coming down."

There is a commonly held feeling among the teachers that I have spoken to, that the parents and also to some extent the students are influencing the grading of students in the school reports:

The grading culture is more about setting people free than putting them behind bars. If there's a balance between a grade A and a grade B, you should be giving an A. That way you avoid arguments. The parents here make no bones about turning themselves into activists. If you don't give their children top marks, there's a reaction. All the teachers know about this, of course. If you give someone a C in another local authority, the parents are happy enough with that.

Our power as teachers over the students is that we report on their progress and in the more senior classes we assess them. I think that part can get frustrating, for instance the school reports are so much subject to negotiation among students and parents.

Every year as we get closer to the school reports the teachers start getting stressed out, especially during the spring term when the final reports have to be written up. Some teachers have come out of it really badly, the stakes are high after all, maybe with a place at the upper-secondary school in the balance. Of course you do get influenced by that.

Many of the parents here are so professional and good at running and handling people, they can just chew us teachers up like little morsels. That's also what they do in their jobs. They're quite capable of going in hard and giving a teacher a hard time if she's a young woman. When it's about your own child, things can get quite subjective. They run the whole gamut of possible responses from threats to manipulation when it's about getting the teacher to award a higher grade. Some teachers have ended up in trouble.

During my years as a teacher here I have occasionally run into parents who, in a variety of ways, have let me know that they are lawyers. This might for instance take place by their e-mailing me, so that I could see their job titles. Obviously this is a form of coercion. I actually called the National Bar and Law Society, and they said it is not okay to send out e-mails with their professional titles on them, when it's about their children's schooling. We are public servants, as teachers. It is improper influence. . . . Obviously the parents' jobs have an effect on you. Knowing that the child's father is a road construction worker, or the chairman of a large company, does change the way you talk and reason about the child's development. Many of our parents have professions that are all about influencing their surroundings according to their own interests. They are made for this.

One teacher stated, "Today, it's the actual learning process that forms the basis for assessment and school reports. Certainly you also write reports according to results, but it's just as important how students got there by analysis and reflection. I believe that the residents of Djursholm are blessed in his respect. They have been trained to verbalize, to present themselves in a certain way. Many times I have caught myself thinking, 'Goodness, how clever they are,' but possibly if they were assessed using a different method one might reach a very different end result." The evaluation criteria now in force, which emphasize the learning process, may obviously result in relative advantages depending on the pedagogical approach in a given school. As described earlier, in Djursholm there is a popular pedagogy where the social and communicative behavior of the students is placed in the foreground, rather than, so to speak, emphasizing the ability to conceptualize about actual knowledge. The setting of grades could obviously also be affected by the ability of the students to discuss and call assessments and school reports into question. Another teacher stated, "The children are very good at negotiating; they are articulate. Obviously one can be influenced by this, and maybe even raise a lower grade to a higher one for some assignment." Another teacher that I spoke to felt that "sometimes you get bombarded by various arguments about why the marking was done incorrectly, and at times like this it is important to stand your ground." One teacher told me that "the students know how to assert themselves, to negotiate advantages for themselves, for instance, deadlines for tests or handing-in dates."

The recurring question among the teachers that I have interviewed, which, in their view, impacts their working life, is the whole issue of the demands and expectations of the parents, which in all significant aspects is about the students having the best possible educational development, which then, by definition, must be concluded by very high grades. There is a general understanding among staff, both in preschools and schools, that parents are highly interested in everything—from what food is on offer to the school environment to the pedagogical approach—all of which can be understood in the context of the schools having to reflect the values of Djursholm and contribute positively to its "status aura." One preschool director claimed that "parents are very involved in the performance-driven aspects at preschool, they have a lot of views about the pedagogy and other things." Their involvement, in many ways, is a reflection of the existing skill set in Djursholm. One teacher explained this further: "When earlier I worked at a school in a more ordinary area, the parents were quite capable of getting involved, quickly repairing a playground or something else that needed fixing. By this, I mean that they fixed it in a practical sense. Here, the parents would never put on blue overalls and start hammering at something. But they are very good when it comes to engaging with the local authority."

A colleague of hers felt that "parental involvement is selective and limited. Anything that is difficult and negative they draw back from, for instance bullying, social problems at school, alcohol. They don't even want to touch those things. They prefer to connect with positives, which means the studies. Negatives they avoid." One principal told me: "The parents have a lot of knowledge and resources. They are well informed and up-to-date, so they're highly involved in every detailed aspect of our activities. They want to participate, they want to be kept informed, and they also want to feel that they can have some influence. They are looking for a clear development plan for their children, and they're keen for them to hit their targets, and for the whole process to be followed up with development programs, progress meetings, and so on." On the other hand, one preschool director commented, "In local authority quality assessments we usually get poor results for our provision of information, even though we put so much into it. But the parents demand even more, they want a really detailed level of insight." Parental commitment is also manifested in the fact that they tend to show up without fail to all events organized by the pre-schools and schools, as well as the regular progress meetings with individual children. One employee at a preschool told me the following: "Usually both parents come to the progress meetings. They want to know. We usually schedule the meetings for maximum convenience for the parents." A colleague of hers observed, "When the parents come in for various activities there's usually a lot of mingling. I reckon it's sort of popular to say, 'Last week I went to the school for the Open Day.' It shows that you're involved."

The schools are crucial to the process of consecration in the community, partly by their accreditation and social categorization of the inhabitants, and partly also by their function as vital social training institutes in how to *become* residents of Djursholm. Against this background it is not so very strange that the parents should wish to involve themselves in the day-to-day running of the schools—especially in how the teachers conduct their work. The parents I spoke to were also aware that their involvement and interest in preschool and school affairs was in many cases considered rather overbearing by the school staff. One father admitted as much to me when he made the following comment: "There's a fairly well-established insight among the parents that we can be a difficult group for the teachers to handle. Demands are made, and we interfere. As people we're used to calling the shots, after all, and I'd say that we generally see ourselves as fairly competent. But when it comes to our own children, we forget about normal boundaries and we keep pushing and demanding nothing but the best. I suppose it's quite human." Another parent explained, "The teachers are under enormous pressure to deliver the best results for the children. It's hard for them. When a particular child falls short, parents do accept that it isn't the teacher's fault, although that suggestion will probably also be mentioned. But if a whole class doesn't deliver, well, then it's the teacher who is failing. Teachers are expected to be alert, high performing, and skilled. The stress levels must be fairly high for them." Another parent told me the following: "When I moved to Djursholm with my family, the first parents' evening was a total shock for me. It was like a lynching, and the principal was weeping. Afterward it was explained to me that this was an extraordinary evening, but still. It was a first impression worth taking note of! Parents here are very involved, and a minority of them really can behave at times like a lynch mob."

The parent collective can be seen as a force directed primarily at teachers on questions such as the leadership and running of the schools; the students also exert influence in their capacity as young "members" of Djursholm. The teachers occasionally have a sense that the students are behaving in a socially superior way and taking liberties with them. However, in Djursholm this cannot be seen as an instance of bad manners; it should rather be seen as an expression of children and young people being aware of their value *as residents of Djursholm*. One teacher told me: "When I drive into the school it annoys me that the students don't get out of the way of my car. They are well mannered in a certain sense, but also very conscious of their own worth." When I asked, in a questionnaire for children and young people, what in their view constituted a good school, I was treated to mostly long and carefully reasoned answers centering on teacher commitment, pedagogy, pace of study, assessment, and so on—all of which suggested anything but indifference. Students in Djursholm have always been aware of their value—to a very great extent the community may even have been established for the sake of the children, even if for no other reason than their importance as resources in the social connections between adults, and the status and aura of the community. In this context, it is not so very odd that children and young people should feel important in the school environment, and take the view that, in fact, the teachers ought to be listening to *them*.

The often highly developed social and communicative ability among Djursholm's children and young people obviously affects their relationships with staff members in the preschools and schools. One teacher affirmed that "the students are educated, articulate, and polite. In a way it is good. The parents and children know what their rights are, and what we, the school, are duty-bound to do for them. In many other schools I'd say the students and parents more or less go along with what they are told. It is not like that here." Another teacher explained that his colleagues at his school had a special relationship to the students, because of an assessment system that gave the students the possibility of evaluating the teachers. "This is not exactly a question of the teacher's competence, manner, and style, more a case of assessing 'variations in the teaching,' and so on. But certainly it is a case of giving students the chance of expressing their views about particular teachers." In the following quotations, I sum up a number of views among teachers of their relationships to the children and the attitudes of the latter to the classwork:

There is a general attitude of "I have a right to get top marks," but that just cannot be right. I think that children and young people here are used to having everything their own way, and they're not accustomed to any problems in that respect. I also think they're used to seeing themselves as very competent, and most of them are. But when they meet others with the same attitude, and when some are better than they are themselves, problems can arise. They don't always reflect very much on their own attitudes.

If the students don't think you are a competent teacher, they complain. And what do they complain about? Very rarely it's about the actual course work, because they don't have the knowledge to assess that. They're not in a position to judge whether a teacher is competent in a given subject. It's more about one's manner, one's performance, one's style.

If the students don't get what they want, they start moaning and this could even lead to Mum and Dad coming in. Some of my colleagues handle this by trying to be very "customer oriented" and accommodating. But I think this is counterproductive. The allowable boundaries are always being moved forward. . . . The students are spoiled at home. They get what they want, in order to avoid conflicts. And then there's this attitude of, "I'm a customer, school is supposed to serve up what I want."

When you give a student the wrong school report, as the student sees it, you first have the student's hissy fit, and then the parent's.

I spoke to one teacher who felt that the status of teachers is generally low in Djursholm. According to him, teachers are nothing less than "service staff" in the sense that they coach the students into getting good results. "The parents often seem to think that their children are highly gifted, incredibly driven, and so on, and that the teachers are supposed to be there as a resource to rely on whenever there's a need. And they have to be on call. . . . Knowledge and expertise are not really so highly valued in Djursholm. A person like a librarian is not an authority in this community. The same thing goes for a teacher. Our teachers are not trained in leadership, which puts them at a disadvantage here." That employees at preschools and schools often feel socially inferior to parents and even students, is ultimately about economic realities, which are regarded in Djursholm as important indicators of people's value. A teacher explained this to me: "Parents and students have a psychological advantage over the teachers. We have low salaries and clapped-out cars and we can't afford exclusive holidays on the other side of the world. This creates problems in the relationship. Everyone is aware of it." One of his colleagues stated: "You can tell that these kids are walking around with a month's salary on their backs."

Indeed, teachers are expected in a variety of ways to give students maximum support during the school years, after all their crucial purpose is nothing less than the creation of genuine Djursholm residents. They are also expected to be available in the evenings and at weekends—at one of the schools that I visited, the teachers were given a "Twitter course" for that very reason. A teacher explained that "we are online continuously, I work a lot from home and I often have contact with the students in the evenings and sometimes even at weekends."

In certain ways the relations between staff from preschools and schools on the one hand, and parents and students on the other, can be likened to a battle for control, direction, and authority, which ultimately is about how Djursholm should be further developed, seen, and described. The heads of the schools in Djursholm are often of a mind with the residents themselves—the ties between the parental groups and the school leadership is manifest, and they are sometimes also unified as "residents." Furthermore, every school is dependent on its academic success in order to be regarded as a winner. As has earlier been mentioned, the teachers are a key factor in this, not least in their role as the examiners and assessors of grades. One teacher gave me an example of how this can lead to situations, where the parents take *de facto* control: "I remember a class meeting to which parents were invited, where things got rather unruly because the teachers did not manage to take control of the discussion. One of the fathers, a prominent corporate leader, stood up and said 'I'm taking over here!' Then he ran through all the school's problems as if he was making an analysis of a company, and rounded it all off with five or six 'focus areas' for improvement. All the parents just sat there with the jaws hanging open—and they loved it."

The attempt of parents and also students to influence teachers and even principals when it comes to student assessments, should not, however, be regarded as immoral. Quite the opposite: in Djursholm such behavior is perfectly moral, and even highly appropriate. The community expects involvement and dynamism and, furthermore, there is a sense of social one-upmanship in relation to the teachers, who in a purely hierarchical sense are subordinated to the residents. Dissatisfaction about a school report is not, as already explained, rooted in any particular insights into the student's academic capacity or factual grasp, but rather in his or her social behavior. A poor school report, irrespective of the subject, becomes synonymous with a critique of the individual's character rather than intellectual attributes. This is a provocative matter in Djursholm, when considered in relation to the image of the dominant lifestyle. A decent, rather than an excellent, grade in mathematics, for instance, is not more of an evaluation of a person's knowledge than a judgment on certain human and social qualities. Given that the residents perceive themselves as socially exemplary, and as lifestyle role models and paragons, any other grade than the very best possible is highly problematic and difficult to understand. Parental interference in the setting of students' grades also becomes a classic leadership tactic, which the children/students can observe and learn valuable lessons by. As a leader you are expected not to be passive in the face of difficulties or disappointments, but active and entrepreneurial. A number of approaches can be utilized: threats, flattery, pleas—all to achieve one's purpose. Pressure from parents and students can therefore be viewed as an important *tactic for success;* a complementary factor alongside the students' tangible efforts in his or her studies.

Another possible explanation for the high grades in Djursholm might be summarized by recourse to the simple idea of cheating, which seems a fairly well established practice in the schools in the community, at least according to a novel about Djursholm, published in 1927 by a well-known Swedish author who lived there. In it, we read how the son of the family—the subject of the novel—talks to his school friends shortly after graduating from the upper-secondary school in Djursholm:

> They all expressed their high-minded disdain and sublime contempt of the examination they had just sat through. And they were all eager to point out how exquisitely limited their learning was. Through their school years they had cheated, bluffed, and dodged, they claimed. The thought

of it gave them a deep sense of satisfaction. It seemed that none of them were on a very high level in a moral sense. Which may not have been entirely their own fault.

In an issue of a school magazine from Djursholm, one can read a period description of school life in the years between 1913 and 1917. There was particular emphasis on how quickly students learned to get high grades:

> Cheating was a much appreciated sport as long as it was conducted elegantly and not disclosed. Clumsy, disclosed cheating was harshly judged and considered indecent. Earlier tests were purchased, and they considerably eased our homework with translation tasks. We did not greatly reflect on how our vocabulary would not be improved by employing this short cut. Our idealistic head master introduced unmonitored examinations for a time. This was a paradisiac state of being for us, who were already lumbered with moral defects. Any required help was available from more talented friends for the solving of inexplicable mathematical and physics problems, older friends in higher classes were generous with their help for the younger. All this took place by means of discretely exchanged slips of paper from the pockets of our overcoats.

In a community like Djursholm, where factual knowledge is not as a rule regarded as valuable in its own right, but where rather the acquisition of certain social abilities is idealized, cheating is not considered immoral or problematical—there is no risk of desecration to the community if it does not come to light. To cheat and in this way "handle a problem" becomes more than anything an expression of (high) morality and successful leadership. It is not excellence in terms of knowing something that Djursholm expects. What it values is social ability. One man in his eighties who had had his schooling in Djursholm and afterward spent most of his life living there, explained to me that "cheating was very common. Cheating your way to a pass, well I'd say everyone did that, otherwise nothing would have worked. But we felt it was immoral to cheat your way into getting top grades. It was a silent rule. One wanted everyone to pass, no one was supposed to fail to matriculate from the upper-secondary school."

Several of the teachers I spoke to also claimed that there is widespread cheating among the students:

> You push the boundaries here. You act with bare-faced cheek, without shame. You take a chance. That's probably the way it is in many other schools as well. There's a lot of cheating here, maybe not so much worse than in other places, but the difference here is that some of the students can afford to pay others to write their assignments. . . . What's interesting is that it just doesn't add up with the idea you have of students in Djursholm. You think the students are so smart and good here, and sure, they work hard. But they also cheat a lot. It's a clash with the ideology of "I have succeeded because I am smart and I have tried very hard."

> When I've taken part in sports days I've sometimes noticed some of the students cheating. I've asked them why they do it. The answer I've had is, "What difference does it make if you don't get caught?" It's a moral outlook that worries me if it also applies to the actual studies, that so long as you don't get caught then cheating is quite all right.

> We have had cases many times when a student has done something stupid, and we find there is no parent there we can talk to except on the telephone. They go away for a week and sometimes longer. Then you realize just how alone some of our students are, and no wonder they make mistakes sometimes. Who is going to explain to them what's right and wrong? . . . Take the cheating, for example. You can't just blame cheating on a bad moral outlook among the students. The cheating culture is a result of the morality that is established here in the families and the community. It's all about success, and you have to use all means to reach your goals. And if on top of all you have parents that are away a lot, then who is going to give the child guidance about what's right and wrong? . . . The student is only trying to live up to the expectations of

his surroundings. That our students don't see cheating as anything bad or unfair is itself an expression of all that.

Obviously cheating is very common in this kind of environment. The students are no smarter than anywhere else, but the demands on them are much higher. Cheating is one way of getting by here.

Cheating is very common here. For example, people buy essays. Of course, we try to detect cheating by using certain computer programs, but it's not enough. This is a cheating culture, and it is helped along by the fact that so much of the teaching is about essays and projects. One of the students I caught doing it said to me, "But everyone is doing it." If there's a window of opportunity in the system, they use it.

You know here that you can break the little rules to earn yourself big benefits; that is a part of the student culture here. No wonder there's a lot of cheating, not massive stuff but nonetheless. I would be willing to stick my neck out and say the students here who don't come from Djursholm don't have the same attitude, at least not when they first come here. There's a certain way of looking at right and wrong in this community. I don't think that what we regard as cheating is viewed here as cheating. Instead it's something creative; it shows that one wants to make progress, *no matter what.*

There is a very strong feeling here of entitlement, in other words, something one feels one has a right to. Students at this school have a feeling that they have a right to brilliant grades and glowing school reports. If it doesn't work out that way, they are not worried about finding the back door. It is not seen as immoral. The immoral thing is to refuse them what they are entitled to, namely, top grades.

In my interviews with school staff members and generally in conversation with the residents, the view is often expressed that many children and young people in Djursholm suffer from dyslexia. The introductory text on the upper-secondary student association's website contains a number of grammatical errors (italicized below), which are more or less illustrative of this: "Some of the country's most *ambicious* and high-performing students study at our school. The activities of the student association have *fluctated* over the years, but today the activities are *succesively* increasing, and the association is now, like the school, a pioneer in all its areas with few exceptions. Today, the association is one of the country's fastest-growing *studant* councils." Helping students with dyslexia is something of a specialty for schools in Djursholm. In a school web page, the following text appears, emphasizing that "a well developed use of language has decisive importance for successful studies and intellectual progress. . . . At the beginning of each academic year we investigate reading skills, vocabulary, and spelling, in order to ascertain how best to give support to students on the basis of their knowledge level. We find students who need extra support, and we are therefore able to help them from the very beginning." In an article in the local newspaper, a founder of one of the schools commented that "above all we want to put our efforts into literacy. Many pupils with reading difficulties are not noticed until they are seniors, which is far too late and causes unnecessary suffering." The upper-secondary school in Djursholm also profiled itself from an early stage as a school *for* dyslexics. In a publication to commemorate the ten-year anniversary of the school, one of the founders describes how, since the very beginning, they "worked very consciously to facilitate learning for students with dyslexia or other learning problems." For many years the school had a so-called dyslexia quota, which meant that students who had been certified as dyslexic were admitted alongside the normal intake. One teacher explained the following: "As an appendix to your school report you could inform admissions that you had dyslexia. In other words, those with poor school reports would have a note about their dyslexia. An assessment would then be made by us and after that we would admit a number of students under the terms of dyslexia quota." The then principal claimed in an interview that it was a "question of equality" and that the system could be seen as a product of the fact that "there are board members in this school who have dyslexia." For many years the chairman of the board of governors of that school was a well-known man from the world of Swedish business. In a newspaper article, he is described as an unschooled but financially successful entrepreneur, whose difficulties with reading and thereby also studies have tormented him throughout his life. He set up a foundation and provided an endowment for a dyslexia prize. Clearly he also took his concern for dyslexics with him into his role at the upper-secondary school in Djursholm.

A local authority employee made the following claim:

The senior and upper-secondary schools in Djursholm are interesting. They were set up by two parents in Djursholm who wanted their own school, an elite school. In this way they were fulfilling a tradition in Djursholm. The old school had also been started by a resident in Djursholm and it became an exclusive school for those with the means to live in Djursholm. . . . Today you can't charge fees; anyone can be admitted. But all of the children of the founders had dyslexia, and so they got into the school because of the dyslexia quota that they introduced. In this way the school kept the same exclusivity as the old school. The dyslexia quota quickly became incredibly popular. The parents saw to it that their children were diagnosed as dyslexics, until it had got to a level where the school had to put a stop to it, by only accepting diagnoses from particular organizations. . . . The whole thing with dyslexia has become a bit of a social boundary that is especially evident in Djursholm.

As far as the schools are concerned, then, it seems that the medical diagnosis of dyslexia can contribute to shutting out certain groups of students and offer others an exclusive and smooth entry ticket. In the current Swedish educational environment, with any children and young people entitled to apply to schools in Djursholm even if they do not live there, there is obviously a theoretical risk that the schools in the area get taken over by more academically excellent and smarter students from outside the community, yet lacking in "adequate" social dispositions and abilities. In cases where high grades cannot be offered, a dyslexia diagnosis has been a door opener for "socially acceptable young people," in addition to other practices mentioned above.

In general one might say that a dyslexia diagnosis is not an especially stigmatizing social encumbrance, and hardly at all in Djursholm. It is often presented as an almost positive attribute, a condition associated with creativity, engagement, and leadership. Many famous decision makers and corporate leaders have spoken openly about their problems as dyslexics.[1] Several residents that I interviewed also mentioned their dyslexia in positive terms. One man suggested the following: "My blindness to words means that I have to think in new, unexpected ways. Where others hit the wall I end up finding the right way. Dyslexia is a fantastic creative force. Of course it can be hard work in particular situations, but in the right environment dyslexia is not a handicap, quite the opposite." Another man explained, "Dyslexia is not necessarily a handicap, especially not if you are a leader. Maybe dyslexia is a precondition for becoming a successful leader? You can make different connections and be forced into new, creative solutions. You combine things differently. The dyslexia creates a creative vein. Quite simply you have to think in a different way."

The dyslexia diagnosis offers a medicalized solution to a person's shortcomings in terms of their lack of ability, intelligence, and diligence. Instead of a person appearing *worse* in a purely social sense, he or she can actually look *better*, bearing in mind the learning impediment the person in question is apparently struggling with. Students in Djursholm are expected to be the best in the country, the role models of all students. If they cannot manage this on the basis of their knowledge alone, the dyslexia diagnosis offers a welcome helping hand. One teacher put it as follows: "Getting a diagnosis, for instance dyslexia, which is by far the commonest, is not stigmatizing. There is good self-confidence here, and positive self-esteem, and a diagnosis of that kind does not harm to all that."

The dyslexia diagnosis is also described as a "layman's diagnosis," a condition that both students, teachers, and parents can easily "notice." One teacher claimed: "Dyslexia is common here, and it's also the easiest condition that teachers can recognize, without any medical training. ADHD and Asperger's, which we also get here, are harder to see as a layman." Given the general pressure for performance and good results, there is obviously the opportunity of blaming "the failure," such as not getting the very highest marks, on one's dyslexia. A specialist pedagogue remarked: "There must be many ambitious parents here who see to it that their academically underperforming children get diagnosed as dyslexics. It's quite okay being a dyslexic; many people here are openly dyslexic. It's quite okay having that problem." Several of the teachers that I spoke to also suggested that the dyslexia diagnosis can be explained by its way of liberating the individual from moral responsibility for indifferent academic performance:

> We're up to our necks with diagnosed students. "Why not a grade A?" Instead of just saying it the way it is, that the student is not good enough or doesn't work hard enough, they produce a diagnosis for him. Once you have a diagnosis, you also have an explanation for a relatively poor level of performance. Above all you can make demands about additional resources, which, in the longer run, will result in higher grades. It's not at all stigmatized, being a dyslexic here.

> If the child falls behind, does not hit targets or seem as driven as his or her friends, then sometimes the parents want their child checked for dyslexia. Which means that one is not considered stupid even if things aren't going well in school. It's important here to come across as smart and intelligent. If one doesn't come across this way, which is the case for several of the students, it has to be explained in some way.

> As soon as things don't go exactly to plan, as soon as the tiniest thing interferes, both students and parents get very concerned. If the problems persist, meaning if the results are not the best possible, they want the child checked for dyslexia. Often this is not a case of any large-scale or serious problems. Just a couple of slightly lower grades are enough to start people thinking along the lines of, "Maybe dyslexia?" No wonder we have so many dyslexics. There's a huge nervousness here about not getting top grades, not succeeding.

Being diagnosed as a dyslexic, then, is relatively popular among the students or former students I spoke to. Hence, the dyslexia diagnosis, alongside the ability of parents and students to influence the teacher to award higher grades, is an important *tactic for success*. The diagnosis enables a transfer of the typical weaknesses of the (corporate) leader, namely, reading and writing, to the (corporate) leader's strengths, namely, social and communicative ability. But above all, the dyslexia diagnosis lightens the load of the schoolwork and can have a positive effect on school reports. One man who grew up in Djursholm put it as follows: "I am dyslexic. At school everyone wanted to become a dyslexic; it gave you loads of advantages. You got as much help as you wanted. I know lots of people among my friends who are dyslexic. Some were more dyslexic than others. Any other diagnosis than dyslexia might cause funny looks." A student said, "Dyslexia is not considered an ailment here. When I was at another school in the municipality there were hardly any dyslexics, but there are lots of them here. I mean, you almost get a bit jealous of the dyslexics, they get so many perks. . . . In my group of friends there are several who have dyslexia, but they really don't have any serious problems with reading or writing. They make some mistakes now and then, but who doesn't?"

The dyslexia diagnosis means that, as a student, you are entitled to take examinations orally rather than having to write, and rather than having to read one can have texts read to one. This accentuates the relationship between teacher and student and puts the student's communicative and social ability at the center of things. The fact that as a dyslexic one can have more time to complete the examination is also significant. In a government report it is stated, "It is not a statutory requirement that a student must have a formal diagnosis in order to be eligible for differential treatment in national examinations." In other words, as a student one does not even have to be formally classified as a dyslexic; it is enough to have dyslexic symptoms. According to the report, examples of differential treatment include "more time to sit examinations, the possibility of using a computer, editing one's text using speech synthesis, having certain instructions and tasks read out to one, and being able to provide answers orally." The school's earlier introduction of a dyslexia quota, its generally dyslexia-friendly culture, and the expectation that staff and particularly teachers should be particularly supportive of students with alleged dyslexia problems can all be seen as aspects of an institutionalized system in Djursholm designed to enable

weak or average students—irrespective of whether they have any real reading or writing difficulties—to achieve top grades. In this, they will be
further assisted by the communication skills of their parents, as well as
their own powers of persuasion. The dyslexia diagnosis enables students
to take examinations orally rather than in written form, and this may be
particularly advantageous for the students, in view of their social skills and
confidence-inspiring ability to present themselves in the best possible
light.

Whatever the method by which the high grades are achieved, it can be
said that the schools in Djursholm are defined by a clear drive to succeed.
All students are expected to develop positively and achieve high grades.
Students and parents, as well as schools and principals, orient themselves
in relation to this norm, and this is a factor in how the schools function in
an organizational, cultural, and moral sense. In this context it could also
be the case that a dyslexia diagnosis has a functional aspect in Djursholm.
It may even be problematic to indicate that a certain student has a problem
with his or her studies. As one teacher claimed: "If a child is having problems, it often takes time for parents to accept it and believe what we are
saying. I think this must be different from in other places, where parents
are possibly not as well educated or in such high-status positions in society.
Probably it is something shameful here, to have a child who is not developing as quickly as the other children in an educational sense. Or maybe
parents just find it difficult to absorb the fact, because they could never
have imagined such a situation." One of her colleagues felt that many of
the parents perceived their children as "A-grade," meaning that they were
very clever and ambitious. And in this sense it was even harder to point to
problems and shortfalls, or criticize the child at all. "The reaction you often get is, 'There's nothing wrong with my child.' Instead the problem is
shoveled across to us, on the teachers or the school as a whole. You have to
have some pretty good arguments and evidence to break down those kinds
of perceptions. As a rule it's really hard; it's hard for them to see that their
children may have some issues, or that they're simply not top-notch
students—they're just ordinary students." Another teacher commented,
"Saying to a parent, 'Your child is having problems' may result in you

having a bucket of cold water emptied over your head. It's difficult having those kinds of problems, and that is why I believe some children don't get the help they need or only get helped once it's impossible to ignore it any longer. There's a spirit of *no problem* that affects me as a teacher, but also parents and the students. In the end it's the student with the problem who suffers because of the prevailing climate." The community as a whole expects excellent grades. "Poor students" jeopardize the reputation of the schools and Djursholm as a whole, in addition to the price paid by the student and his or her family, in the form of damage to social status and weakened career prospects. In a leader community, the aura is everything.

13

LEADER COMMUNITIES

The Rise of the "Consecracy"

M Y STUDY of Djursholm suggests that the consecration of people into leaders is expressed through a perception of them as trend-setters and moral paragons, human signifiers for how others should think and act. To affect the world by the creation of norms and values is far more important than the application of technical rules and bureaucratic instructions. By this I mean to say that the formal merits, knowledge, competence, and intellectual abilities of leaders are not in the foreground; rather it is their lifestyles. As C. Wright Mills emphasized more than half a century ago when describing the typical American chief executive:

> The characteristic member of the higher circles today is an intellectual mediocrity, sometimes a conscientious one, but still a mediocrity. His intelligence is revealed only by his occasional realization that he is not up to the decisions he sometimes feels called upon to confront. But usually he keeps such feelings private, his public utterances being pious and sentimental, grim and brave, cheerful and empty in their universal generality. He is open only to abbreviated and vulgarized pre-digested and slanted ideas. He is a commander of the age of phone call, the memo, and the briefing.[1]

This underlines, as Konstantin Lampou has stressed, the importance of moral virtues, for instance, in the form of courage, fortitude, a sense of fairness and moderation, greatness of heart and generosity, a pleasant and appealing manner, and toleration.[2] Indeed, Max Weber claimed that social order is based on certain conceptions of legitimacy, which, in turn, depend on the ability of various "status groups" to maintain particular lifestyles. Insofar as it is all about living a certain kind of life it is also a matter of organizing and designing the latter—one could further elucidate this by distinguishing between the concepts of *lifestyle* and *style of life*. The latter is central to the process of legitimizing power and influence, with various status groups in society being the bearers and interpreters of (dominant) norms and conventions. According to Weber, a society can be stratified according to class or according to status, where the latter, in comparison to the former, is based on lifestyle as well as esteem or honor. Weber claims that status is positive or negative social prestige, which is manifested in terms of lifestyle, lineage, education, and so on. Hence, money and occupational position are not enough in their own right to earn a certain social status.[3] In his study of an elite boarding school, Ruben Gaztambide-Fernández makes the following point:

> Status hierarchies are not simply reproduced through the transference of economic resources, but also of the symbolic materials and subjective dispositions that are required to demonstrate membership in particular status groups. In other words, having access to economic resources alone does not give a person elite status; rather the ability to demonstrate particular behaviors, dispositions, knowledge, and aesthetic choices is essential in order to assert particular kinds of status-group membership.[4]

As already suggested, *aura* is an important part of the terminology in use here, but in studies and analyses of leaders and leadership it has tended to merge into the background of what Weber called *charisma*, which has now become popularized. Aura and charisma are not the same thing, however. *Charisma* relates primarily to a leader's generally accepted personal qualities, and bears no relation to established social institutions. *Aura* is a collective identity. Charismatic people often become leaders as a consequence of their personal radiance and aura. Yet, by the acquisition of a collectively defined aura in the form of consecration, even mediocre, entirely "ordinary," and uncharismatic people can become leaders. In just the same way that a crudely fashioned chair can be turned into a work of art, a quite ordinary human being can be turned into social art. From this perspective, leader communities could be regarded as "aura factories," or, as one might also put it, "aura societies." What I mean by this is that some environments can be regarded as leader communities not on the basis of intellectual superiority or their educational level, but rather through their social culture and lifestyle.

According to my analysis the area that I have been studying is not a leader community on the basis of excellence in knowledge, intellectual expertise, and superlative analytical capacities. It is true that its inhabitants are exceedingly well educated and that they attribute their success to hard work, intellectual ability, and formal merits, which are significant factors in their ability to have leadership roles. Yet ultimately it is not their formal qualifications that are the decisive factors in their influence. To this extent, Djursholm is not a meritocracy. It is rather a leader community in a moral sense, by means of the lifestyle that is constantly being created and recreated by the inhabitants. Its experiential superior moral character acts as a principle of distinction and legitimation, as it poses as the moral vanguard of the nation.[5] As a form of social organization, it is therefore something I would like to refer to as a *consecracy*—a society that leads by means of its aura, brightness, and radiance.[6] When Alexis de Tocqueville analyzed America in the nineteenth century, *aristocracy* and *democracy* were two central analytical ideas for him.[7] Tocqueville perceived America as a democracy—by his definition, this was an egalitarian society, in contrast to an aristocratic social system. Admittedly he conceded that there were hints of aristocratic expression in America, yet as a unifying analytical idea Tocqueville believed that democracy was by far the best way of describing and interpreting American society. In accordance with Tocqueville's methodology, I suggest that consecracy, coined from the term *consecration*, is a more effective way of understanding Djursholm than the concept of meritocracy.

Like probably many other leader communities, my area of investigation is influenced by meritocratic virtues and ideals, but these are not what give the community its unique character and definition. It is consecration that sets it apart and gives it form—this being the creation of a certain aura and prestige to confer high spiritual value on the community. A meritocracy is a society based on the conception that an individual's social value consists of what he or she has achieved in terms of knowledge, qualifications, and abilities. Despite an often imposing academic background, a typical resident of Djursholm is hardly fundamentally different from an average citizen when it comes to intellectual ability. Obviously there are important exceptions, but Djursholm's residents are much like any other persons and cannot be said to have any significantly deeper insights into the world. Shamus Khan expressed this well in his analysis of students at an American elite boarding school: "Perhaps the point is not really to *know* anything. The advantage that St. Paul's instills in its students is not a hierarchy of knowledge."[8] Similarly, Robert Jackall observed the following in his study of senior corporate managers, which is a group of persons that typically corresponds to a country's economic elite: "For most managers . . . future chances in an organization, after the crucial break points in career are reached, are seen to depend not on competence nor on performance as such. Instead, managers see success depending principally on meeting social criteria established by the authority and political alignments—that is by the fealty and alliance structure—and by the ethos and style of the corporation."[9]

In a consecracy such as Djursholm, it is not regarded as abnormal for parents to repeatedly question the competence of teachers, particularly when it comes to grading their children; or for pupils to cheat and take shortcuts in their studies; or when schools diagnose academically less able children as dyslexics. Michel Pincon and Monique Pincon-Charlot make the following case in their examinations of the higher classes in France:

Reading is one of the most solitary cultural practices in existence. Thus it is not a very social activity. However, the relationship of the grand bourgeoisie to culture is above all social: cultural activities are among the forms of socializing proper to the group. . . . By contrast, groups less favored with economic capital but well endowed in cultural and educational capital will value reading above all, one of the cultural practices most accessible from a material standpoint.[10]

Hence, the typical leader community does not earn its preeminent position through traditional meritocratic principles. Yet a consecracy is built on the idea that an individual's social value is based on his or her aura, brightness, and radiance, in which practical knowledge in all essential respects is about excellence in how one *relates to the world*—as opposed to what one knows about it. What sets a leader community apart is that it is *radiant*, not least because social problems are repressed or ignored, but also because people do not spend their time on (trivial) everyday activities that might hazard the collective aura. They do not, for instance, dress, eat, laugh, drink, take walks, and so on, in a manner that might be perceived by others as vulgar or devoid of style. Many people in Djursholm have the community to thank for their social value and social status, rather than their intellectual capacities, their diligence, or their commitment to greater ideas. This creates a particular kind of loyalty to the community. There exists a collective consensus not to speak ill of one's neighborhood, and the collective covers up any problems for as long as it possibly can. The inhabitants are engaged in a struggle to make themselves radiant, and they seem to manage this more or less—which is crucial to the ability of the community to appear in the eyes of the surrounding world as an exemplary place with the right to admonish, prescribe, and provide moral guidance.

Leader communities are all to some degree formed by consecration, but some are more clearly consecracies than others. There do exist intellectual and cultural leader communities with a greater component of meritocracy than in economic leader communities. As Pincon and Pincon-Charlot have shown in their studies of *la grande bourgeoisie* in France, every elite group has its spatial location.[11] Social identity is defined by contrasting lifestyles, and, in the case of leader communities this is not about excellence in skill or knowledge, but rather excellence in manners, by which not only the behavior of a human being is vital, but also his or her body's physical appearance.[12] Leader communities are *corporeal*, a way of walking, standing, eating, and moving—quite simply habitus, according to Pierre Bourdieu.[13] They do not only offer living facilities in a technical sense. They are actually a way of life. To this extent they offer a number of almost magical stages through which ordinary people are consecrated and imbued with a certain aura. In all significant respects this is about evolving their social expression. They are characterized by a striving for aesthetic excellence in terms of buildings, public spaces, and restaurants, as well as the inhabitants themselves. They purpose to engraft a feeling of grandness, nobility, and majesty onto its inhabitants, while also seeking to be virtuous, honorable, moral, and noble. Indeed, there is something religious about the community that I have examined, something holy. This holiness does not emanate from any religious rites but is encompassed by social actions that have an almost religious meaning.

Leader communities consciously work to create an aura around themselves, their nature, their buildings, and, especially, their residents. By living there, one can express, at the same time, social prestige and status, financial worth, and cultural capital: these coordinate as the multidimensional expression of wealth.[14] Often these communities can point to a long line of people whose lives and doings might be described as exemplary expressions of the intellect and artistry, and yet, as has already been argued, their leadership character is not based on more competence or innovation or artistic excellence than most other communities. Rather it is the communities themselves and the elevated social qualities of the residents that create the leadership position. As a consequence of the inhabitants' careful aesthetic nurturing of themselves and their social milieu, as well as their well-developed social and communicative abilities, they seem more insightful and confidence inspiring than others. An urbane mode of living permeates these places. In all essential respects they are aesthetically driven societies, by their insistence on manners and behavioral aspects, which, in turn, are closely related to human morals, ways of living, and ethics. Societies of this kind also strive to be aesthetically elevated, with beauty, agreeable art and architecture, and so on, at the center of everything—and where, as I have already argued, every possible kind of dirt or problem has to be ignored or swept under the carpet.

The aura that marks leader communities is, by necessity, an aura that requires distance. If one gets too close to them, they are no longer quite as radiant. The artist Andy Warhol once said, "When you just see somebody on the street, they can really have an aura. But when they open their mouth, there goes the aura. 'Aura' must be until you open your mouth."[15] An essential but simple aspect of consecration must therefore be about social separation, which, in the case of a place such as Djursholm, is also tangibly geographical. Merely by moving to such an environment, one manages to distance oneself from other groups in society. The new arrival instantly changes from being a "normal person" into something new, which he or she could not have been described as before. By this distance from the "vulgar crowd" and its trivial concerns, the new resident acquires a redefined character. The most fundamental and crucial mechanism of consecration, then, lies in separation from the general public, and from the rest of the world. Entry barriers to leader communities are admittedly high, as a consequence of the property prices there, but once new arrivals are comfortably settled, the elevation can begin, provided that they are committed and willing to learn.

As an effect of their residence there, they acquire a value that rarely corresponds to their intellectual abilities or formal attributes. Essentially, this is about their aesthetic mode of expression and behavior. These areas offer people the opportunity to dress up their background, polish up the odd provincial accent, change their surnames if there is a need to do so, wear the garments favored by the higher social classes, eat different food, move in society in a different way, and so on—all of which become pivotal social markers for the higher level of influence in society that these people often aspire to. People living there do not necessarily have more challenging professions than others; nothing substantial about their work (or their education) points in an obvious way to anything that might naturally set them apart in a meritocratic context. Quite the opposite—even an admittedly profitable job as a financial analyst may come across as gray and uninteresting. If one can avert one's eyes from money as a mode of social reward, the inhabitants as a rule tend to be successful in their careers in a rather unremarkable way—in Djursholm only a very small number were recognized as leader figures before they came to the area. This is why the actual life there is so vital to the social ambitions of most of the residents. With the passage of time, the lifestyle acquired as a resident is what makes one a leader.

The process is far from deterministic and free of criticism or hesitation among the inhabitants. The sense of unworthiness with which many of Djursholm's residents are burdened, illustrate the demanding nature of becoming a part of this world. The possibility of becoming socially legitimate and a generally accepted leader is dependent on certain cultural processes, rituals, and ceremonies, and this is largely about conferring people with a certain "status aura," in other words an aura based on their lifestyle rather than any knowledge or skills they may possess. A leader community consecrates an executive elite, that is, a decision-making, opinion-forming elite not only distinct and separate from other groups in society but also recognized as such by the latter and often even considered worthy of this position.

Indeed, in leader communities there are a significant amount of symbolic capital locked up in wealth, culture, and social relationships. They could even be described as a form of symbolic capital: symbolic of a certain taste and particular customs and behaviors intimately associated with success, leadership, and responsibility. Yet the symbolic capital, the aura, is extremely fragile. It is constantly at risk of destruction or devaluation as a consequence of irresponsible or immoral actions. The residents are at the very heart of the process of creating and maintaining the aura of these areas. People there, including those who simply work there, therefore have to be educated in how to behave in a way that is suitable to the social elevation of the place. The greatest threat comes from those who have sufficient economic resources to buy a home there, but do not have the capacity to live their lives in a socially acceptable manner. In leader communities, as in all communities, there is a moral hierarchy, which stipulates that certain people behave "more morally" than others.[16] For this reason, staying in control of the borders to the outside world and the territory of the community themselves, are not only central to the consecration the community offer their inhabitants but are also a prerequisite for the continued momentum of leader communities as a model of the ideal life.

But are the virtues and ideals that define leader communities really unique to such places, and thereby a way of explaining their elevated social position? It appears to be the case that people's social and communicative abilities, their aesthetic qualities, their way of moving, dressing, and behaving, are taking on greater significance in working life and other social contexts. *Employability* and *social skills* are terms that are being accentuated both in higher education and the labor market as a whole. What Ervin Goffman referred to as *presentation of self* has without a doubt become more important in a neo-liberal world, where people are expected to display an active, entrepreneurial, and energetic lifestyle.[17] Employability, in all significant respects, is about how one behaves, and not in the most important sense about what one knows.[18] Consecration processes have always been central to the social elite, but maybe these activities are now being taken over or assimilated by the general public. In a leader community such as Djursholm, it has long been the case that *presentation of self* is elevated into a norm of everyday life; in everything from an individual's patterns of movement, smell, intonation of speech, clothes, to the outward decoration of buildings, style, and other architectural qualities. In an era where meritocracy as a life ideal is still taken for granted by most people, consecracies lay claim to a leading position as symbols of a higher moral approach to life. Meritocracy always runs the risk of excessive emphasis on formal or "intellectual technicalities," whereas consecracy lays its focus on larger themes.

But if consecrating virtues and ideals are gaining broader significance in society as a whole, might there also be some justification for believing that Djursholm and similar communities' time of importance as social role models may soon be over? In much the same way as Weber spoke of the "routinization of charisma," meaning that the radiance of the individual becomes a general norm, one might speak of the "routinization of aura."

Either that, or they will be strengthened by remaining a social primus inter pares among many other consecracies. In any case, by living as a resident of a leader community, one has the opportunity of being transformed into an attractive citizen in the neo-liberal society. Society as a whole is evolving, with leader communities at the forefront, away from an emphasis on meritocratic principles for social advancement, influence, and power, to one of consecrating virtues and ideals, in which the importance of formal competence and factual knowledge have been substituted for social skills and aesthetic radiance.

The concept of consecracy is an alternative to meritocracy when interpreting contemporary society. It is not only certain environments that can be described as consecracies but potentially also society as a whole; this provides a basis for discussion of, for instance, how future political policy on education and the labor market should be conducted. If we wish to become a society of consecration, higher education has to form its students as if they were living in a place like Djursholm; the same ideals would have to be applied in the marketplace. It might be regarded as cynical if a society, which has up until now regarded itself as a meritocracy, stops putting primary emphasis on formal qualifications, knowledge, and competence, preferring instead to focus on people's social behavior, aura, and radiance. Yet our capacity for individual leadership, an ability now expected in all of us and especially in children and young people, is constantly emphasized. Such development could not only be regarded as cynical but also as extremely risky. In a typical consecracy, most of the leading people have no more substantive knowledge than anyone else—and in many cases maybe even less so. In all essential respects their ability to lead is based on a certain kind of social behavior and the embodiment of a particular lifestyle that is regarded as morally elevated. In this sense, consecracies are hazardous social entities. As I have already stressed, aura is always a fragile entity. If one gets too close to it, there is a risk that cracks may form. A consecracy is always a hairsbreadth away from losing its leadership position and reverting to a much more ordinary, or even mediocre, social grouping.

Meritocracy is fundamentally bureaucratic but also, for this same reason, based on fairness. It is constructed by means of rules and norms to which everyone can relate, and the idea of it is that everyone should have a chance of succeeding, whatever their background. This is not the case with consecracy, which is composed of segregation, separation, and social differentiation. In a consecracy, the operative point is not what you know, but *how you are* as a person, and the sort of lifestyle that you are pursuing: how you talk, how you move, how you dress—also your physical body. Meritocracy relies on human knowledge for its substance. Consecracy is concerned with people's aura. It is very much as one of the elder residents of Djursholm told me: "Imagine when they find out that I'm a faker—I don't know anything! But, you know, everyone worries about that here." In an "aura community" the economy is based on people's social skills rather than their knowledge or qualifications. Certainly it is true that also meritocracies can pass over and ignore certain groups, indeed Michael Young, who coined the term, regarded it with much critique and skepticism.[19] However, the alternative in the form of consecracy as a dominant future social format is considerably worse. Meritocracy offers the better foundation for a society's economy, and it offers people better prospects of integrating and making a living. And yet the fundamental question is far more down-to-earth. For instance, I would assume that every person who is struck down by a serious illness would prefer to have a doctor acting on the basis of knowledge and proven experience rather than a less competent but in other ways aesthetically, communicatively, and socially excellent person.

The era of consecracy is now, but is it possible to safeguard the future importance of meritocracy, in order to guarantee the equal rights of all people to work and social advancement—and provide the underpinnings of a strong, egalitarian, and dynamic economy? Possibly. What is needed, more than ever, is the development of criteria in the school system and in higher education for reasserting the value of real knowledge in place of the emphasis on social skills that seem to dominate the (economic) elite's schools and universities. The expectations on teachers at schools and universities have to be redefined, so the latter can once again become professional knowledge institutions rather than training institutes offering coaching and social mentoring skills. We need a syllabus intent on the development of intellectual and analytical capacities in the students. And we urgently need a critical outlook in social sciences and humanities departments, to refocus on the strict demands of meritocracy. Qualifications, knowledge, and ability would then be the fundamentals of people's employability, social advancement, and social influence in society.

If my analysis in this book has been accurate, I believe there is every reason to discuss consecracy as something that will one day be dominant over meritocracy—and what the economic, political, and social implications of this will be. For this reason there is a continued need to study and analyze elite environments such as Djursholm as leader communities, whether they are located in Europe, China, the United States, or elsewhere. Not only are they worth studying and understanding on their own merits; above all they can be understood as role models, and, as such, they give shape to norms affecting a far greater number of people than merely those who live within their boundaries.

ACKNOWLEDGMENTS

MANY PEOPLE in Djursholm or others with connections to the community have taken the time to meet with me, both for interviews and more spontaneous meetings and conversations. Some of the residents or individuals who work in Djursholm have been particularly involved in helping me access members of this community, and I am especially grateful to them. I have received generous invitations to various social events, and I attach particular value to the many meetings I have had with local residents in their own homes. I have also been welcomed in Djursholm's associations, companies, preschools, schools, youth center, chapel, restaurants, and cafés, to share in people's daily lives and hear about their experiences. I want to thank the councillors and politicians in the municipal council, school principals and nursery heads, restaurateurs and shop owners, representatives of associations, and others in similar positions, obviously also the employees and association members that I have met. I experienced the people I interviewed as being open and confiding in me honestly. I deeply appreciate the commitment that has been shown in helping me understand this community.

I also wish to thank the Swedish Foundation for Humanities and Social Sciences and the Jan Wallander and Tom Hedelius Research Foundation for their funding of this research, as well as my friends and colleagues at various university departments in Sweden for their helpful and constructive comments while pursuing the project. Likewise, thanks are due to organizers of and participants at seminars and workshops where I was given the generous opportunity to present my research. For the realization of this book, I am particularly grateful to Carl Cederström, Peter Dobers, Johan Hansson, Hans Hasselbladh, Konstantin Lampou, Christian Maravelias, Petter Sandgren, Per Skålén, Mitchell L. Stevens, and Richard Swedberg. A special thanks to my translator Henning Koch, who offered valuable comments on the text as he worked on it.[1] I am grateful for the opportunity to publish the study with Columbia University Press and would like to thank editorial director Eric Schwartz and his team, as well as two anonymous reviewers, for their helpful comments and criticism. Copyeditor Robin O'Dell reviewed the final text carefully and suggested a number of valuable linguistic and stylistic improvements.

Finally, I am indebted to my wonderful family: my wife, Maria, and my sons, Gabriel, Samuel, and Johannes.

LITERATURE

Alvesson, M. 2011. "Leaders as Saints: Leadership through Moral Peak Performance." In *Metaphors We Lead By: Understanding Leadership in the Real World*, ed. M. Alvesson and A. Spicer, 51–75. London: Routledge.

Andreotti, A., P. Le Galès, and F. Moreno-Fuentes. 2015. *Globalised Minds, Roots in the City: Urban Upper-Middle Classes in Europe*. London: Wiley.

Anteby, M. 2013. *Manufacturing Morals: The Values of Silence in Business School Education*. Chicago: University of Chicago Press.

Atkinson, R. and S. Blandy, eds. 2006. *Gated Communities: International Perspectives*. London: Routledge.

Baltzell, E. 1958. *Philadelphia Gentleman: The Making of a National Upper Class*. Glencoe, IL: Free Press.

Barnard, C. 1938. *The Functions of the Executive*. Cambridge, MA: Harvard University Press.

Beaverstock, J. V., P. Hubbard, and J. R. Short. 2004. "Getting Away with It? Exposing the Geographies of the Super-Rich." *Geoforum* 35:401–407.

Bendix, R. 1960. *Max Weber: An Intellectual Portrait*. Berkeley: University of California Press.

Blakely, E. J. and M. Gail Snyder. 1997. *Fortress America: Gated Communities in the United States*. Washington, DC: Brookings.

Bourdieu, P. 1984. *Distinction: A Social Critique of the Judgement of Taste*. London: Routledge.

Bourdieu, P. 1996. *The State Nobility. Elite Schools in the Field of Power*. Stanford, CA: Stanford University Press.

Bourdieu, P. 2001. "The Forms of Capital." In *The Sociology of Economic Life*, 2nd ed., ed. M. Granovetter and R. Swedberg. Boulder, CO: Westview.

Bourdieu, P. and J.-C. Passeron. 1977. *Reproduction in Education, Society and Culture*. 2nd ed. London: Sage.

Brooks, D. 2000. *Bobos in Paradise. The New Upper Class and How They Got There.* New York: Simon and Schuster.

Burns, J. M. 1979. *Leadership.* New York: Harper and Row.

Carlson, S. 1951. *Executive Behavior: A Study of the Workload and Working Methods of Managing Directors.* Stockholm: Strömbergs.

Chase, S. 2008. *Perfectly Prep. Gender Extremes at a New England Prep School.* New York: Oxford University Press.

Cookson, P. and C. Persell. 1985. *Preparing for Power: America's Elite Boarding Schools.* New York: Basic Books.

Courtois, A. 2015. "'Thousands Waiting at Our Gates': Moral Character, Legitimacy and Social Justice in Irish Elite Schools." *British Journal of Sociology of Education* 36:53–70.

Dalton, M. 1959. *Men Who Manage.* New York: McGraw-Hill.

Domhoff, G. W. 1974. *The Bohemian Grove and Other Retreats. A Study in Ruling-Class Cohesiveness.* New York: HarperCollins.

Durkheim, E. 1973. *On Morality and Society.* Edited by Robert Bellah. Chicago: University of Chicago Press.

Elias, N. 1994. *The Established and the Outsiders.* London: Routledge.

Elias, N. 2006. *The Court Society. The Collected Works of Norbert Elias.* Vol. 2. Edited by Stephen Mennel. Dublin: University College Dublin Press.

Fitzgerald, F. 1981. *Cities on a Hill.* New York: Simon and Schuster.

Garsten, C. and K. Jacobsson. 2003. *Learning to be Employable.* London: Palgrave.

Gaztambide-Fernandez, R. 2009. *The Best of the Best: Becoming Elite at an American Boarding School.* Cambridge, MA: Harvard University Press.

Gerth, H. H. and C. W. Mills. 1946. *From Max Weber: Essays in Sociology.* New York: Oxford University Press.

Goffman, E. 1959. *The Presentation of Self in Everyday Life.* New York: Anchor.

Goffman, E. 1961. *Asylums. Essays on the Social Situation of Mental Patients and Other Inmates.* New York: Anchor.

Granfield, R. 1992. *Making Elite Lawyers: Visions of Law at Harvard and Beyond.* New York: Routledge.

Hay, I., ed. 2016. *Geographies of the Super-Rich.* London: Edward Elgar.

Holmqvist, M. 2008. *The Institutionalization of Social Welfare: A Study of Medicalizing Management.* New York: Routledge.

Holmqvist, M. 2015. *Djursholm—Sveriges ledarsamhälle.* Stockholm: Atlantis.

Holmqvist, M. and C. Maravelias. 2011. *Managing Healthy Organizations: Worksite Health Promotion and the New Self-management Paradigm.* New York: Routledge.

Holmqvist, M. and A. Spicer., eds. 2013. *Managing 'Human Resources' by Exploiting and Exploring People's Potentials.* Research in the Sociology of Organizations. Vol. 37. Bingley: Emerald.

Howard, A. and R. A. Gaztambide-Fernandez, eds. 2010. *Educating Elites: Class Privilege and Educational Advantage.* Lanham: Rowman and Littlefield.

Jackall, R. 1988. *Moral Mazes: The World of Corporate Managers*. New York: Oxford University Press.

Jahoda, M., P. F. Lazarsfeld, and H. Zeisel. 2002. *Marienthal: The Sociography of an Unemployed Community*. London: Transaction.

Kanter, R. M. 1977. *Men and Women of the Corporation*. New York: Basic Books.

Kennedy, M. and M. J. Power. 2008. "'The Smokescreen of Meritocracy': Elite Education in Ireland and the Reproduction of Class Privilege." *Journal for Critical Education Policy Studies* 8:223–248.

Khan, S. R. 2011. *Privilege. The Making of an Adolescent Elite at St. Paul's School*. Princeton, NJ: Princeton University Press.

Khan, S. R. 2012. "Elite Identities." *Identities: Global Studies in Culture and Power* 19:477–484.

Khan, S. R. 2015. "Changes in Elite Education in the United States." In *World Yearbook of Education 2015: Elites, Privilege and Excellence: The National and Global Redefinition of Educational Advantage*, ed. A. Van Zanten and S. J. Ball, 59–70. London: Routledge.

Khan, S. R. and C. Jerolmack. 2013. "Saying Meritocracy and Doing Privilege." *Sociological Quarterly* 54:9–19.

Koh, A. 2014. "Doing Class Analysis in Singapore's Elite Education: Unravelling the Smokescreen of 'Meritocratic Talk.'" *Globalisation, Societies and Education* 12:196–210.

Kusserow, A. 2004. *American Individualisms: Child Rearing and Social Class in Three Neighborhoods*. New York: Palgrave.

Lamont, M. 1992. *Money, Morals and Manners: The Culture of the French and the American Upper-Middle Class*. Chicago: University of Chicago Press.

Lamont, M. and A. Lareau. 1988. "Cultural Capital: Allusions, Gaps and Glissandos in Recent Theoretical Development." *Sociological Theory* 6:153–168.

Lamont, M. and V. Molnár. 2002. "The Study of Boundaries in the Social Sciences." *Annual Review of Sociology* 28:167–195.

Lampou, K. 2002. "Traits and Skills for Managerial Leadership: A Virtue Theory Approach." Occasional Paper 2002/3. Uppsala: Department of Business Studies.

Lareau, A. 2003. *Unequal Childhoods: Class, Race, and Family Life*. Berkeley: University of California Press.

Le Wita, B. 1994. *French Bourgeois Culture*. Cambridge: Cambridge University Press.

Luthar, S. 2003. "The Culture of Affluence: Psychological Costs of Material Wealth." *Child Development* 74:1581–1593.

Luthar S. and C. Sexton. 2004. "The High Price of Affluence." *Advances in Child Development Behaviour* 32:125–162.

Martin, W. 2015. *Primates of Park Avenue: A Memoir*. New York: Simon and Schuster.

Maxwell, C. and P. Aggleton, eds. 2015. *Elite Education: International Perspectives*. London: Routledge.

Mintzberg, H. 1973. *The Nature of Managerial Work*. New York: Harper and Row.

Mills, C. W. 2000. *The Power Elite*. New York: Oxford University Press.

Peters, T. J. and R. H. Waterman. 1982. *In Search of Excellence. Lessons from America's Best-Run Companies*. New York: Harper and Row.

Pincon, M. and M. Pincon-Charlot. 1989. *Dans les beaux quartiers*. Paris: Seuil.

Pincon, M. and M. Pincon-Charlot. 1999. *Grand Fortunes. Dynasties of Wealth in France*. New York: Algora.

Pincon, M. and M. Pincon-Charlot. 2002. *Voyage en grande bourgeoisie*. Paris: PUF.

Pincon, M. and M. Pincon-Charlot. 2007a. *Les Ghettos du Gotha. Comment la bourgoisie defend ses espaces*. Paris: Seuil.

Pincon, M. and M. Pincon-Charlot. 2007b. *Sociologie de la bourgeoisie*. Paris: La Découverte.

Pow, C-P. 2011. "Living It Up: Super-Rich Enclave and Transnational Elite Urbanism in Singapore." *Geoforum* 42:382–393.

Richardson, I., A. Kakabadse, and N. Kakabadse. 2011. *Bilderberg People: Elite Power and Consensus in World Affairs*. London: Routledge.

Rivera, L. 2016. *Pedigree: How Elite Students Get Elite Jobs*. Princeton, NJ: Princeton University Press.

Rodenstedt, A. 2014. *Living in the Calm and Safe Part of the City. The Socio-Spatial Reproduction of Upper-Middle Class Neighborhoods in Malmö*. Doctoral diss. Uppsala: Uppsala University.

Sandgren, P. 2017. *Globalizing Eton: A Transnational History of Elite Boarding Schools since 1799*. Doctoral diss. Florence: European University Institute.

Schleef, D. 2006. *Managing Elites: Professional Socialization in Law and Business Schools*. New York: Rowman and Littlefield.

Scott, R. 1969. *The Making of Blind Men: A Study of Adult Socialization*. New York: Transaction.

Stensgaard, P. and M. Bernsen. 2011. *Hellerup. Historier fra reservatet*. Copenhagen: Gad.

Stevens, M. 2009. *Creating a Class: College Admissions and the Education of Elites*. Cambridge, MA: Harvard University Press.

Stewart, R. 1967. *Managers and Their Jobs*. Maidenhead: McGraw-Hill.

Swedberg, R. 2005. *The Max Weber Dictionary: Key Words and Central Concepts*. Stanford, CA: Stanford University Press.

Swedberg, R. 2009. *Tocqueville's Political Economy*. Princeton, NJ: Princeton University Press.

Tocqueville, A. de. 1998. *Democracy in America*. Translated by Henry Reeve. Hertfordshire: Wordsworth.

Van Zanten, A. and S. J. Ball, eds. 2015. *World Yearbook of Education 2015: Elites, Privilege and Excellence: The National and Global Redefinition of Educational Advantage*. London: Routledge.

Veblen, T. 1994. *The Theory of the Leisure Class*. New York: Dover.

Warhol, A. 1975. *The Philosophy of Andy Warhol*. Orlando, FL: Harvest Book.

Weber, M. 1978. *Economy and Society*. Edited by G. Roth and C. Wittich. Vols. 1 and 2. Berkeley: University of California Press.

Weber, M. 1991. *Critical Assessments*. Edited by P. Hamilton. Vol. 2. London: Routledge.

Weber, M. 2001. *The Protestant Ethic and the Spirit of Capitalism*. London: Routledge.

Whyte, W. F. 1943. *Street Corner Society: The Social Structure of an Italian Slum.* 4th ed. Chicago: University of Chicago Press.

Willis, P. 1977. *Learning to Labor: How Working Class Kids Get Working Class Jobs.* Farnham, UK: Ashgate.

Young, M. 2008. *The Rise of the Meritocracy.* London: Transaction.

APPENDIX

THE ETHNOGRAPHIC STUDY

N SEVERAL RESPECTS, my study has been inspired by Alexis de Tocqueville's masterpiece *Democracy in America*, which was first published in 1835–1840. The creation of Djursholm in 1889 was based on the American model, in all its star-spangled, utopian glory. Djursholm too was colonized by people who escaped "the old country"—although their exodus was an intranational one, driven by wealth and privilege—in stark contrast to the 20 percent of Sweden's population who emigrated to the United States from the mid-1800s to the 1920s in order to escape poverty and lack of opportunity and freedom. Tocqueville, much in the same way as I have tried to do myself, set out to explore an environment that had escaped extensive sociological attention. Richard Swedberg describes Tocqueville's method as follows: "Collecting facts on whatever topic he was studying was a true obsession for Tocqueville and was closely related to his ambition to be an original thinker. . . . Tocqueville's basic rule, when it came to the collection of data, was *anything goes*—that is, any way to collect data was fine as long as it resulted in providing him with the facts he needed. . . . He interviewed people, sent out questionnaires, studied laws, and pored over legal commentaries, government documents, different types of statistics, and quite a bit more. Tocqueville also *observed*—listened with eyes and ears—whenever he could and wherever he was." This is what

I have tried to do also. Overall, priority has been assigned to the empirical material, not to the ideas; an approach Max Weber formulated as "theory must follow facts, and not vice versa."[1]

Hence, the study on which this book is based has a certain academic context, in which my professional identity informs my conclusions on the community, because of the methods and working procedures I have chosen in the implementation of the study. Yet, as has already been suggested, my personality, social background, and the neighborhood itself are significant in my interpretations and the manner in which this book was written. Being a professor in management at a prestigious university was clearly a door opener in a community populated by an economic elite. My basic command of the social codes of the area, a result of my upbringing and education, probably also played a significant role. In addition, living in a neighboring community almost as wealthy as the area under study probably made access even easier. My address was regarded by several people I met as a kind of seal of approval. David Brooks, author of the book *Bobos in Paradise: The New Upper Class and How They Got There*, described his relationship to the group of people he studied and analyzed (Bobos). The quotation below is analogous to my own relationship with the community I studied and the people living there:

> These Bobos define our age. They are the new establishment. Their hybrid culture is the atmosphere we all breathe. Their status codes now govern social life. Their moral codes give structure to our personal lives. When I use the word *establishment*, it sounds sinister and elitist. Let me say first, I'm a member of this class, as, I suspect, are most readers of this book.[2]

My study was implemented by the following methods:

FORMAL INTERVIEWS

Formal interviews consisted of meetings and conversations with people, set up by prior consultation (usually e-mail). In all, 207 people were interviewed. They fell under the following categories: *local inhabitants*, people who lived or had lived in the area, and *employees*, people who worked or had worked there. The first group consisted of 128 individuals. At the planning stage of the interviews, I did not attempt a rigorous breakdown of age and gender in the target groups, but I did try to maintain a reasonable balance. Many times, inquiries about further individuals to include in the study were made as the interviews drew to a close, at which stage I rounded things off by asking for introductions. To a certain extent, then, the sample was formed in relation to those I had already met. A number of individuals came back spontaneously after their interviews to suggest other people they felt I should meet. In other cases I took the initiative myself, especially when interviewing well-known local residents. The interviews were mostly conducted one-to-one, but in certain cases I saw husbands and wives or cohabiting couples at the same time, with or without their children. I also interviewed adolescents separately.

With local inhabitants, I consistently tried to approach a variety of them, including (a) recent arrivals, long-established families and individuals, including those individuals who had left the area; (b) children, teenagers, and young adults; (c) parents/middle-aged people; and (d) the elderly/pensioners. I found that most of the men and women of working age (between sixteen and sixty-seven) were active in the labor market, but a relatively large group consisted of housewives. I never attempted to interview people from any particular professional category or educational background. As indicated by official statistics, the population is largely made up of graduates with high-ranking positions in the world of finance, business, and commerce. A small number of unemployed men were also interviewed. In certain cases, interview subjects played a dual function: on the one hand, I interviewed them as private individuals; on the other hand, they were spokespeople for institutions and organizations, such as the community's chapel, the lending library's support association, the scouts, or the tennis club.

In the group referred to as *service staff* (seventy-nine in all), I set out to meet individuals holding down a variety of jobs in the area: nuns at the convent; tradespeople and market gardeners; police officers; au pairs; preachers at the chapel; shop and restaurant staff; self-employed people; estate agents; school staff (see more below); employees at various associations (for instance, the golf club, football club, and riding club); local authority employees (for instance, at the public library, departmental heads at the municipal council, employees in various local authority departments including the social services department, the technical office, the education office, etc.); and those working in the health service (pharmacies, health centers, dentists, care in the community staff).

Particular attention was focused on preschools and schools, where meetings with all kinds of staff members were requested: heads and pedagogic staff at preschools; principals, assistant principals, teachers of various subjects (both theoretical and practical) at secondary and upper-secondary level—but also extracurricular staff, special-needs assistants, those working in student medical services, school caretakers, administrative people, and librarians. I interviewed the principals and headmasters of almost every school and preschool in the area, including both private and public institutions. Seven of the schools were studied in-depth, with regular visits, as well as a large number of interviews with employees across a number of categories, as specified above. Generally, when establishing contact with individuals in the *staff* category, I first approached the principal to ask for an interview with him or her and then other employees after that.

Usually the interviews lasted forty-five to sixty minutes, and all were undertaken with an assurance of confidentiality, on the understanding that there would be no recording. This was especially important when meeting individuals in the staff category. After each interview I typed up my notes in a plain Word document. In other words, quotations presented in this book are not direct quotations from tape recordings, but rather reported speech annotated during the interviews. In certain cases where it has seemed possible to identify a person, I have made minor adjustments to protect that person's identity, such as changes of gender or age. The phase of my study at the time of each interview, to a very great extent, affected the questions I asked—obviously also my choice of interviewees. In the early stages of my study, questions tended to be broader in scope and more generalized than at the end of the project. To a large extent they were about getting interviewees to talk freely about their experiences of the place in relation to their own backgrounds (for instance, whether they had recently moved to the area or were raised there). Later in my study, when I wanted to deepen my understanding of certain issues that had been flagged earlier, such as the consumption of alcohol among young people, I chose more targeted questions.

Another group that I interviewed were the representatives of political parties in the municipality, as well as certain individuals that had made inquiries about the neighborhood (particularly journalists).

INFORMAL CONVERSATIONS AND INTERVIEWS

Informal conversations and interviews mean spontaneous meetings and discussions with the people I met in streets and squares, libraries, shops, and restaurants, at parties and social occasions, on the beach, at the tennis club, and so on. These individuals were either from the *local inhabitants* or *staff* categories. It is difficult to estimate how many conversations took place, but they must certainly run to a considerable number over a five-year period. In a small number of cases, my identity as a researcher was not known in these situations; however, most people were well aware of what I was doing, for instance, at dinners to which I was invited by private individuals and associations. These informal conversations and meetings, which continued throughout my study, were an important supplement to the formal interviews. They added to my overall impressions of the dwelling. They were especially useful during visits to schools and preschools, when I was able to talk informally to staff, parents, and children, or to children and adolescents during breaks or at the end of the school day. I also struck up informal conversations with a variety of people while visiting associations such as the tennis or golf club.

OBSERVATIONS

Between 2010 and 2015 I frequented the area intensively, in public places or as a visitor to local associations or at events to which I had been invited. Additional observations were made in the many homes I visited to conduct interviews, dine, or attend social events. Over the course of these five years, professional and private visits to the area occasionally merged. In my role as a researcher, I was there with my family many times—also with one or more of my children for an excursion on the weekend or during school holidays. On a few occasions, I went to restaurants with the children, and then compared my impressions when eating at the same restaurants without the children. Certain places required the presence of my children, for instance, the visits I made to playgrounds. I visited Djursholm by day and night, weekdays and weekends, and in particular I tried to be there for public ceremonies such as National Day celebrations, the Christmas market, and so on. For research reasons I also took walks and went cycling or jogging in the area. The way in which I was received, as a private individual, a parent holding a child by the hand, or a professor working on an assignment, also refined my perceptions of the community I was studying.

QUESTIONNAIRES

I distributed a number of questionnaires in preschools (for parents) and schools (for children and adolescents), as well as traditional online questionnaires. These questionnaires did not have any statistical ambitions, but they were used as backing material for my interviews and conversations with respondents of various categories.

ARTICLES, BOOKS, WEB PAGES, AND OTHER SOURCES

My understanding of the neighborhood was considerably broadened by reference to various written online and off-line sources—anything from articles written by professional journalists, to obituaries and birthday greetings in local newspapers. I am a long-established subscriber to blogs, and, via Facebook and other social media, I informed myself about events and activities held in places such as the youth center. The publications produced by the local history society, the archive of which has occupied me for many hours, were especially important sources in this context. As noted, all written sources in Swedish, such as articles in newspapers, historic texts, blogs, and so on, are not specified in this book; see instead my Swedish text (Holmqvist 2015).

STATISTICAL MATERIAL

As a part of this study I ordered statistical material from various Swedish government departments on, for instance, the income and wealth of the inhabitants, the types of crimes for which they had been prosecuted, and what medications were prescribed to them. These specially ordered statistical materials often provided information to back up impressions formed on the basis of other sources.

NOTES

PREFACE

1. See Pincon and Pincon-Charlot (2002).
2. All written sources in Swedish, such as articles in newspapers, historic texts, blogs, and so on, are not specified in this book; see instead my Swedish text (Holmqvist 2015).
3. See Bourdieu (2001) and Bourdieu and Passeron (1977) for an examination into the various definitions and conceptualizations that exist of the concept; see also Lamont and Lareau (1988).
4. Contemporary sociological texts on elites are largely concerned with how education contributes to producing and reproducing elite groups: e.g., Anteby (2013); Chase (2008); Gaztambide-Fernandez (2009); Granfield (1992); Howard and Gaztambide-Fernandez (2010); Khan (2011); Maxwell and Aggleton (2015); Stevens (2009); Rivera (2016); Schleef (2006); and Van Zanten and Ball (2015). What these rich accounts bear in common is that they advance our understanding of how privilege and status is made possible for some people and its moral, social, and political consequences. Schools are organized settings, and some of them, such as elite boarding schools or elite business schools, appear as ideal environments to foster national and international elites: they are often geographically, culturally, and socially isolated places making them appear as "total institutions" in Goffman's (1961) sense. They offer distinct ceremonies and rituals that their members contribute to reproducing, and they often have an articulate goal to foster a future elite (see Sandgren 2017). But the making of elites is, of course, not limited to the formal context of schools and similar settings—it includes a much broader context. A number of studies propose how members of elite groups share distinctive tastes and lifestyles that are defined to a large extent by cultivated, aesthetic dispositions, and how these in turn contribute to producing and reproducing social differences: e.g., Andreotti,

Galès, and Moreno-Fuentes (2015); Baltzell (1958); Domhoff (1974); Pincon and Pincon-Charlot (1999); and Richardson, Kakabadse, and Kakabadse (2011). Few if any, studies have so far focused on how elite groups live in tangible geographically distinct places, and how their communities affect their identities and selves as elites; see, however, Pincon and Pincon-Charlot's (1989, 1999, 2007a, 2007b) examinations of exclusive neighborhoods in and around Paris; cultural geographers' studies of the "the superrich" (e.g., Beaverstock, Hubbard, and Short 2004; Hay 2016) and sociological studies of "gated communities" (e.g., Atkinson and Blandy 2006; Blakely and Gail Snyder 1997; Rodenstedt 2014). In relation to my study, these do not, as a rule, offer any comprehensive ethnographic account of the lifestyle that dominates elite environments; nor do they analyze them as "leader communities." There are even fewer accounts about the effect of their community surroundings on children, in terms of creating identities and perceptions of themselves as future elites. As Bourdieu (1984) has repeatedly stressed, children growing up as future leaders learn that they are part of a privileged class at an early stage. To this extent, the potential of elite schooling in forming fundamental elite characters may be somewhat limited. As, for instance, Stevens (2009) has pointed out, those entering prestigious schools, often come from prestigious environments. Lamont and Molnár (2002, 172) argue: "Having an extensive vocabulary, wide-ranging cultural references, and command of high culture are valued by the school system; students from higher social backgrounds acquire these class resources in their home environment."

5. See Holmqvist and Maravelias (2011).
6. See Veblen (1899/1994, 25–26), who argued that "a life of leisure is the readiest and most conclusive evidence of pecuniary strength. . . . Conspicuous abstention from labour therefore becomes the conventional mark of superior pecuniary achievement and the conventional index of reputability; and conversely, since application to productive labour is a mark of poverty and subjection, it becomes inconsistent with a reputable standing in the community. . . . The characteristic feature of leisure-class life is a conspicuous exemption from all useful employment. . . . Abstention from labour is not only a honorific or meritorious act, but it presently comes to be requisite of decency"; see also Baltzell (1958, 6), who proposes an interesting distinction between elites and upper classes. One of my informants in Djursholm claimed the following: "Based on my background as British, I wouldn't say this is an upper-class community. In a typical upper-class community people don't need to work. They may hold positions that give them an income, but it is not necessary for their living. Here most people must work. Yes, they earn a lot, but this is necessary."
7. Barnard (1938, 279); see also Jackall (1988) for a similar argument.
8. Lamont (1992, xxiii).
9. Mills (1956/2000).
10. See Alvesson (2011) and Peters and Waterman (1982).
11. Much of the scholarly literature on leaders consists of descriptions and insightful analyses on how they make decisions, plan and organize their daily occupational lives, and what kind of ethics they follow in order to succeed and survive in their world. A number of prominent contributions in management literature can be mentioned, such as Carl-

son (1951); Dalton (1959); Jackall (1988); Kanter (1977); Mintzberg (1973); and Stewart (1967). Jackall's (1988, 11) study is a particularly good example of the dominating locus of attention: he analyses how the formal organization and bureaucracy shapes "the daily experiences, the social, cognitive, and evaluative frameworks, the self-images and worldviews, and, of course, the occupational morality of corporate managers." Overall, while the importance of the broader context in which leaders act have been pointed to in some studies and publications, there are still no thorough, systematic descriptions or reports that can be used to explain or analyze the influence of the living environment on the behavior and attitudes of leaders. Relying mostly on journalistic accounts or leaders' own personal descriptions, most analyses of leader communities are anecdotal and sporadic. Even available statistical information does not reveal a great deal about them, apart from data on, for instance, the educational level of the inhabitants, their finances, their state of health, and so on. On the other hand, there is a fairly comprehensive literature on how both young and old people are "made subordinates," powerless and incapacitated as a result of their membership in "nonelite" settings. Several of these studies are "community studies," i.e., they try to understand human behavior by paying attention to the social norms and values that make up a certain environment: e.g., Holmqvist (2008); Jahoda, Lazarsfeld, and Zeisel (1971/2002); Kusserow (2004); Lareau (2003); Scott (1969); Whyte (1943); and Willis (1997).

12. Khan (2011, 161–162) suggests the importance of this concept for understanding the reproduction of elites; see also Bourdieu (1996).

13. Max Weber argued that the possibility of exerting influence and thereby in practice functioning as a leader was not only based on the social and economic standing that a person might have, for instance, in the sense of being a manager, politician, journalist, or scientist. Such positions have to be transformed from objective and formal aspects of power into rights that are "sanctified," and only then can they become socially legitimate and influential (see Gerth and Mills 1946, 262). Bourdieu (1996) has claimed that the system of higher education has a consecrating role in our era, but in other studies he has also demonstrated how various social institutions can "give value to people," especially in relation to his ideas on cultural capital. The consecration of leaders is not so much about making it possible for certain people to gain access to, and remain in control of, formal positions of power through academic titles, or by the acquisition of particular kinds of knowledge by educational advancement. Far from it. The most important role of the education system, according to Bourdieu, is to elevate individuals by fundamentally modifying their behavior, for instance, their manner of moving, talking, dressing, and interacting with others—in other words, by giving them aesthetic training and education. Elias (2006) has emphasized that while one has to be noble in order to act nobly, it also remains true that one ceases to be noble the moment one no longer acts nobly. Durkheim (1973, 175) argued that the phenomenon of consecration is widespread in society through the sanctification of everyday things and people; nonetheless there is a particular concentration in certain institutions, where it is especially intense and significant: "In the present day just as much as in the past, we see society constantly creating sacred things out of ordinary ones. If it happens to fall in love with a man and if it thinks it has found in him

the principal aspirations that move it, as well as the means of satisfying them, this man will be raised above the others and, as it were, deified. Opinion will invest him with a majesty exactly analogous to that protecting the gods. This is what has happened to so many sovereigns in whom their age had faith; if they were not made gods, they were at least regarded as direct representatives of the deity. And the fact that it is society alone which is the author of these varieties of apotheosis, is evident since it frequently chances to consecrate men this who have no right to it from their own merit."

14. Fitzgerald (1981).

15. Economically wealthy suburbs that are the home to influential and powerful leaders exist all around the world. Here are some examples: Atherton, Menlo Park, and Palo Alto in California; Greenwich and Darien in Connecticut; Saddle River and Harding in New Jersey; Berlin's Dahlem; Paris's Neuilly; Helsinki's Grankulla; London's Oxshott; and Sydney's Point Piper. A number of recent studies in cultural geography have stressed the phenomenon of a transnational economic elite in terms of lifestyle and habits; see, e.g., Andreotti, Galès, and Moreno-Fuentes (2015); Beaverstock, Hubbard, and Short (2004); Hay (2016); and Pow (2011).

16. See Martin (2015) and Stensgaard and Bernsen (2011).

17. See http://www.theatlantic.com/magazine/archive/2015/12/the-silicon-valley-suicides /413140/. See also Pincon and Pincon-Charlot (2007a).

18. For an overview of the research on "the high price of affluence," see Luthar (2003) and Luthar and Sexton (2004). See also Chase (2008).

19. See, e.g., Baltzell (1958) and Pincon and Pincon-Charlot (2007a). Weber (1978, 44) named this "appropriation," meaning "ways in which it is possible for a closed social relationship to guarantee its monopolised advantages to the parties." Lamont and Molnár (2002) propose an illuminating examination on the role of boundaries in creating and maintaining social differences and categories; of particular interest is their discussion on symbolic versus social boundaries.

20. Pincon and Pincon-Charlot (2007b, 63, my translation).

CHAPTER 1. A SHINING CITY: THE EMPHASIS ON AESTHETICS

1. A year after my study of Djursholm was published in Sweden (see Holmqvist 2015), a recycling station was, however, built in a peripheral part of the area.

CHAPTER 3. SIGNIFICANT PEOPLE AND WINNERS

1. According to the government agency Statistics Sweden, there are significant differences between Djursholm and the rest of Sweden in terms of educational attainments, which is a traditional indicator for the influence and position of groups in society: 6.1 percent of the inhabitants of Djursholm as compared with 21.1 percent for the rest of the coun-

try, only completed nine years or less of their secondary education; 32.8 percent of residents in Djursholm completed only an upper-secondary education, as opposed to 44.5 percent for the rest of the country. In Djursholm, 61.2 percent of the residents have studied at a higher educational level. The corresponding figure for the rest of the country is 31.4 percent. Less than 4.3 percent of the men (21.6 percent in the country as a whole) and 7.6 percent of women (20.6 percent in the country as a whole) have only secondary educational qualifications or less; 22.5 percent of men in Djursholm (46.6 percent in the country as a whole) and 25.7 percent of women (42.5 percent in the country as a whole) have only upper-secondary qualifications. As for higher education, the relevant figure for men is 62.9 percent (28.5 percent in the country as a whole) and 59.5 percent for women (34.4 percent in the country as a whole). In postgraduate education the men dominate with 7.2 percent (1.3 percent in the country as a whole), while the figure for women is 5.4 percent (0.7 percent in the country as a whole). Another sign of Djursholm being populated by people in demand in the workplace is the relatively low level of unemployment. Comparatively few people are openly unemployed or taking part in government-run back-to-work schemes: 2.3 percent of the men are unemployed, and 2.8 percent of the women. The unemployment rate for men in the country as a whole is 9.2 percent, and for women, 7.8 percent. The average salary in Djursholm (2010) is US$85,500 while in the rest of the country it stands at US$37,000. The earnings differential between Djursholm and the country as a whole is therefore significant, and this is another important indicator of the residents' social and financial potency. As far as employment goes among residents aged between sixteen and sixty-four, some 67 percent are employed, as compared with 71.1 percent of the population in the rest of the country. In other words, the level of employment in Djursholm is lower than in the country as a whole, with comparatively more people of working age not in employment. This is not reflected by higher levels of unemployment in Djursholm or larger payouts of unemployment benefits in the municipality. Quite the opposite: unemployment in Djursholm is lower than the national average—1.6 percent compared with 3.4 percent (0.9 percent receiving social benefits compared with 5.1 percent in the country as a whole). In Djursholm, not only are fewer people unemployed, in fact to a large degree more people choose not to work. As far as social benefits go, only 0.7 percent of residents in Djursholm are claimants, compared with 4.7 percent in the country as a whole. In other words, despite a higher proportion of people in Djursholm not having any kind of work, a considerably lower amount of social security is claimed in the area. On the basis of this, one can infer that a relatively higher proportion of people receives income from other sources than salaries, unemployment benefits, and social security than in the rest of the country. That Djursholm is populated by people with academic qualifications and important positions in society can also be illustrated by the incidence of ill health, which is generally lower among people in the professional classes. The figure for ill health is 10.7 percent in Djursholm and 27.1 percent in the rest of the country. The clearly dominant professions among the residents are high-level jobs: (a) "work requiring theoretical, specialized skills" (36.7 percent in total; of which men, 35 percent, and women 38.3 percent); (b) "managerial positions" (20.8 percent in total; men 27.9 percent, women 13.8 percent); and (c) "work requiring upper-secondary educational qualifications or similar" (20.5 percent in total; men 18.5 percent, women 20.5 percent). This confers well with the educational qualifications of the residents, in which social science, law, business, and administration are dominant (36.2 percent in total; men 37.5 percent, women 34.9 percent), all of which are educational attainments that can lead to positions with opportunities to exert influence and make decisions. This can be contrasted with the rest of the country, where only 15 percent of the population have the same educational qualifications. The fact that the residents work within financially lucrative sectors is also illustrated by almost half of them being engaged in "the financial sector and business services," as compared with 16 percent of the national population. Djursholm also has a predominantly service-focused employment profile, with 90.2 percent engaged in services as compared with 75.1 percent in the rest of the country. This professional angle is also reflected in the types of professions with which the residents are engaged.

CHAPTER 7. FAMILY LIFE

1. Earlier I described the educational level of the local inhabitants, as well as their incomes, and so on. The statistics demonstrate that more women than men in Djursholm have only basic educational attainments (that is, nine years or less of secondary education, or only upper-secondary qualifications). The percentage of men in Sweden with only basic educational qualifications stands at 68.2 percent, while in Djursholm the figure is 26.8 percent. For women, the relevant figures are 63.1 percent for the country as a whole, and 33.3 percent in Djursholm. In other words, in the country as a whole more men than women have only basic educational qualifications, and the difference between men and women stands at 5.1 percentage units. In Djursholm more women than men have a basic educational background, and the difference between men and women is 6.5 percentage units. The conclusion one could draw from this statistical background is that the residents are comparatively well educated compared with the general population in Sweden, but that the difference between the sexes is greater in Djursholm than the rest of the country. From an educational perspective, people are considerably less educated in the country as a whole than in Djursholm, yet the difference between the sexes is less pronounced. More men than women as a national average have basic educational qualifications, but in Djursholm the opposite applies. As far as unemployment goes, there are also differences in Djursholm between the sexes. A greater proportion of women than men are unemployed in Djursholm than in the rest of the country: 1.9 percent compared with 1.3 percent. In the country as a whole, 3.2 percent of women are unemployed, and 3.7 percent of men (not counting participation in back-to-work schemes). In Djursholm 68.9 percent of men compared with 72.2 percent in the country are gainfully employed; 65.2 percent of women in Djursholm compared with 69.9 percent of women in the country are gainfully employed. More men than women

are gainfully employed in the country as well as in Djursholm. In the country as a whole there is a difference of 2.3 percentage units between the sexes, while in Djursholm the difference stands at 3.7 percentage units. As far as social benefits go, the statistics are equal for both sexes in Djursholm, when compared with the rest of the country: 0.7 percent for both men and women in Djursholm and 4.8 percent for men and 4.7 percent for women in the country as a whole. Income earned from gainful employment in Djursholm (2010) is US$118,000 (country: US$42,000) and for women US$53,000 (country: US$32,000). In Djursholm, women's income amounts to 44 percent of men's income, while in the rest of the country that figure amounts to 77 percent. In other words, Djursholm does not only indicate considerably higher average income than the rest of the country; there are also much larger economic differences between the sexes in Djursholm than in the rest of the country. Of the men in Djursholm, as earlier described, 90.6 percent work in the corporate sector and other organizations (country: 85.9 percent); for women the corresponding figure is 82.2 percent (country: 55.8 percent). Compared with the rest of the country, then, the residents are relatively equal in terms of the sectors in which they work: the difference between men and women concerning private or public employment are 8.4 percentage units; whereas in the country the difference is 30.1 percentage units. In the country 29.5 percent of employable women work in the typical "women's sector" of Swedish public administration. For the women in Djursholm this figure stands at only 8.1 percent, a difference of 21.4 percentage units between women in the country as a whole and the women in Djursholm. County councils do not greatly appeal to women in Djursholm to the same extent as in the rest of the country. In the country as a whole some 9.1 percent of women work in county council administration, whereas in Djursholm the corresponding figure is 4 percent, in other words, a difference of 5.1 percentage units.

CHAPTER 12. TACTICS FOR SUCCESS

1. See, for instance, the website "The Power of Dyslexia" for an interview with Ingvar Kamprad, founder and owner of Swedish retail giant *IKEA*; see also "Dyslexic Entrepreneurs—Why They Have a Competitive Edge" in *The Guardian*, January 15, 2015.

CHAPTER 13. LEADER COMMUNITIES: THE RISE OF THE "CONSECRACY"

1. See Mills (2000, 353–354).
2. This classical distinction, which has been described by Lampou (2002), is central to, e.g., Burns (1979) and Jackall (1988).
3. See Weber (1978, 926–939); see also Bendix (1960, 85–87); Rodenstedt (2014, 40–43); and Swedberg (2005, 269).

4. See Gaztambide-Fernández (2009, 11).
5. Cf. Courtois (2015).
6. From a linguistic point of view, it should rather be "consecratocracy," but for reasons of convenience, I have not chosen this label.
7. See Tocqueville (1998).
8. See Khan (2011, 157); see also Cookson and Persell (1985, 16). For an interesting account on "saying meritocracy and doing privilege," see also Khan and Jerolmack (2012) and Khan (2012, 480–481), where he argues that "elites consider themselves as constituted by individual talents"; however, "if we look at who makes up the 'most talented' members of society, we see that they are very likely to be the children of the already advantaged." For further discussions on this theme, see Kennedy and Power (2008); Khan (2015); and Koh (2014).
9. Jackall (1988, 45).
10. Pincon and Pincon-Charlot (1999, 125–126).
11. See Pincon and Pincon-Charlot (2007a).
12. For interesting analyses of manners, see Lamont (1992) and Le Wita (1994).
13. Bourdieu (1984).
14. See Pincon and Pincon (1999).
15. Warhol (1975, 77).
16. See Elias (1994).
17. See Goffman (1959); see also Holmqvist and Maravelias (2011); and Holmqvist and Spicer (2013).
18. See Garsten and Jacobsson (2003).
19. See Young (2008).

ACKNOWLEDGMENTS

1. This work is based on my book *Djursholm—Sveriges ledarsamhälle* (Djursholm—Sweden's leader community), which was published in Sweden in 2015. A few of the original quotes in Swedish (both from interviews and written sources) are slightly modified in order to make them intelligible to a non-Swedish readership. For instance, the names of certain well-known persons in the local context have been changed to "a senior executive" or "a high-ranking officer."

APPENDIX A: THE ETHNOGRAPHIC STUDY

1. See Swedberg (2009, 108–110).
2. Brooks (2000, 11).

INDEX